MARTHA STEWART'S
VEGETABLES

MARTHA STEWART'S
VEGETABLES

Inspired Recipes and Tips for Choosing, Cooking, and Enjoying the Freshest Seasonal Flavors

From the Editors of Martha Stewart Living

Photographs by Ngoc Minh Ngo and others

CLARKSON POTTER/PUBLISHERS
NEW YORK

CLARKSON POTTER is a trademark and POTTER with colophon is a registered trademark of Penguin Random House LLC.

ISBN 978-0-307-95444-2 eBook ISBN 978-0-307-95445-9

Printed in China

Book and cover design by Michele Outland Cover photograph by Ngoc Minh Ngo Photo credits appear on page 322

10 9 8 7 6 5 4 3 2 1

First Edition

Library of Congress Cataloging-in-Publication Data

Names: Stewart, Martha. | Martha Stewart Living Omnimedia.
Title: Martha Stewart's vegetables / the editors of Martha Stewart living.
Other titles: Vegetables
Description: First edition. | New York : Clarkson Potter/ Publishers [2016] |
Identifiers: LCCN 2016000894 (print) | LCCN 2015045146 (ebook) | ISBN 9780307954459 (ebook) | ISBN 9780307954442 (hardcover) | ISBN 9780307954459 (eBook)
Subjects: LCSH: Cooking (Vegetables). | LOGFT: Cookbooks.
Classification: LCC TX801 (print) | LCC TX801 .M294 2016 (ebook) | DDC—dc23
LC record available at http:// lccn.loc.gov/2016000894

To the numerous excellent professional
seed companies, whose catalogs
and seeds permit us to learn about and
to grow extraordinary vegetables.

And to seed-saving individuals
and organizations, who are maintaining
essential biodiversity—so important
to keeping the "business" of
vegetables and vegetable-growing
interesting and inspiring.

CONTENTS

FOREWORD
11

BULBS
13
GARLIC
LEEKS
ONIONS
RAMPS
SCALLIONS
SHALLOTS
SPRING ONIONS

ROOTS
47
BEETS
CARROTS
CELERY ROOT
JICAMA
PARSNIPS
RADISHES
RUTABAGA
SALSIFY
TURNIPS

TUBERS
81
JERUSALEM
ARTICHOKES
POTATOES
SWEET POTATOES

GREENS
109
BEET GREENS
BOK CHOY
BROCCOLI RABE
CHARD
COLLARDS
KALE
MUSTARD GREENS
TURNIP GREENS

STALKS & STEMS
139
ASPARAGUS
CELERY
FENNEL
KOHLRABI
RHUBARB

PODS
161
EDAMAME
ENGLISH PEAS
FAVA BEANS
GREEN BEANS
OKRA
SHELL BEANS
SNAP PEAS
SNOW PEAS

SHOOTS
189
FIDDLEHEAD FERNS
MICROGREENS
PEA SHOOTS
SPROUTS

LEAVES
203
CABBAGES
CHICORIES
ENDIVES
LETTUCES
SPINACH
SPRING AND WILD
GREENS

FLOWERS & BUDS
237
ARTICHOKES
BROCCOLI
BRUSSELS SPROUTS
CAULIFLOWER
CHIVE BLOSSOMS
EDIBLE FLOWERS
SQUASH BLOSSOMS

FRUITS
263
AVOCADOS
CUCUMBERS
EGGPLANTS
PEPPERS AND CHILES
SUMMER SQUASHES
TOMATILLOS
TOMATOES
WINTER SQUASHES

KERNELS
311
CORN

PHOTO CREDITS
322
ACKNOWLEDGMENTS
323
INDEX
324

RECIPES BY CHAPTER

BULBS   13

Four-Onion Soup with Ginger

Spaghetti with Mussels, Lemon, and Shallots

Roast Chicken with Onions, Shallots, Garlic, and Scapes

Israeli Couscous with Parsley and Shallots

Beer-Battered Onion Rings

Normandy-Style Chicken and Leeks with Crème Fraîche

Pasta Carbonara with Leeks and Lemon

Roasted Salmon and Spring Onions

Pickled Ramps

Grilled Ramps with Romesco

Steamed Black Bass with Ginger and Scallions

Rice Noodles with Scallions and Herbs

Garlic-Scape Toasts

Green-Garlic Butter

Herb-and-Scallion Bread Pudding

Gazpacho Ajo Blanco

Creamy Garlic, Parsley, and Feta Dressing

ROOTS   47

Roasted Beet and Potato Borscht

Sesame Carrot Slaw

Beet Salad with Ginger Dressing

Beet Risotto with Beet Greens

Spicy Carrot Soup

Celery Root and Potato Rösti

Roasted Carrots and Quinoa with Miso Dressing

Jicama-Citrus Salad

Rainbow Carrots and Chard

Lacquered Short Ribs with Celery Root Purée

Leek and Parsnip Soup

Salsify Gratin

Radish Tartine

Roasted Radishes with Capers and Anchovies

Moroccan Vegetable Soup

Rutabaga-Apple Mash

Turnip Salad with Bacon Vinaigrette

Brisket with Parsnips and Carrots

Roasted Rutabaga and Brussels Sprouts

Carrot Fries

Spiced Parsnip Cupcakes with Cream Cheese Frosting

TUBERS   81

Potato Salad, Three Ways

Potato Gnocchi

Mrs. Kostyra's Mashed Potatoes

Salt-Baked Potatoes, Shallots, and Chestnuts

Lamb Stew with Jerusalem Artichokes

Tartiflette

Twice-Cooked Potato and Leek Casserole

Yukon Gold and Sweet Potatoes Anna

Salmon Chowder

Roasted Pork Chops with Sweet Potatoes and Apples

Potato Yeasted Rolls, Two Ways

GREENS   109

Sesame Greens

Swiss Chard, Cabbage, and Brussels Sprouts Salad

Fried Rice with Collard Greens

Stuffed Collard Greens

Mustard-Greens Pesto

Mustard-Greens Caesar Salad

Skillet Pizza with Greens and Eggplant

Caldo Verde

Kale Chips with Balsamic Glaze

Kale-Ricotta Dip

Swiss Chard Lasagna

Bok Choy Salad with Cashews

Baby Bok Choy with Chile, Garlic, and Ginger

Broccoli Rabe and Ham Croque Monsieurs

Kale and Avocado Salad with Dates

Chard-Tomato Sauté

Orecchiette with Broccoli Rabe and Tomatoes

STALKS & STEMS   139

Steamed Asparagus, Three Ways

Egg, Asparagus, and Mushroom Stir-Fry

Asparagus and Potato Flatbread

Rhubarb Chutney with Pork Roast

Asparagus, Artichoke, and Farro Salad

Fennel and Smoked Salmon Salad

Clam Pan Roast with Fennel and Sausage

Celery, Cilantro, and Almond Salad

Braised Celery

PODS   161

Blanched Sugar Snap Peas, Three Ways

Risi e Bisi

Green-Pea Burgers with Harissa Mayo

Cranberry Bean Salad with Delicata Squash and Broccoli Rabe

Skillet Edamame, Corn, and Tomatoes with Basil Oil

Roasted Wax Beans with Peanuts and Cilantro

Green Bean, Shell Bean, and Sweet Onion Fattoush

White Beans with Dandelion Greens and Crostini

Grilled Fava Beans

Creamy Fava Beans

Beef and Snap-Pea Stir-Fry

Green Bean and
Watercress Salad

Tempura Green Beans

Quick-Pickled Pods

SHOOTS   189

Sesame Salmon with
Shiitake Mushrooms and
Shoots

Fiddlehead and Potato Hash
with Eggs

Kale and Lentil Bowl with
Sprouts

Sautéed Snow Peas and
Pea Shoots

Avocado-and-Sprout
Club Sandwiches

Pad Thai

LEAVES   203

Watercress and Asparagus
Pizza

Endive and Fennel Salad

Shredded Napa Cabbage
Salad

Pork Scaloppine with
Radicchio

Spinach and Fontina Strata

Garden Greens with
Chopped Eggs

Spinach and Garlic Soup

Escarole and Bean Soup

Frisée and Roasted
Pear Salad

Baby Greens with Pine Nuts
and Pancetta

Arugula and Stone Fruit
Salad with Balsamic Lamb
Chops

Fig and Arugula Crostini

Charred Romaine Salad

Free-Form Lasagna with
Edible Weeds

Braised Red Cabbage

Creamed Green Cabbage

Fried Chicken with
Puntarelle Salad

Mini Asian Meatballs
in Lettuce Cups

FLOWERS &
BUDS   237

Nasturtium Salad with
Artichokes and Asparagus

Bucatini with Cauliflower,
Capers, and Lemon

Oven-Fried Baby Artichokes

Smoky Brussels Sprouts
Gratin

Broiled Striped Bass with
Cauliflower and Capers

Roasted Cauliflower with
Herb Sauce

Crisped Brussels Sprout
Leaves

Squash-Blossom Frittata

Goat Cheese with Edible
Flowers and Arugula

Broccoli, Shrimp, and
Shiitake Stir-Fry

Braised Chicken and
Brussels Sprouts

Capellini with Chive
Blossoms

Roasted Broccoli with
Grated Manchego

FRUITS   263

Pasta with Marinated
Heirloom Tomatoes

Blistered Eggplant with
Tomatoes, Olives, and Feta

Miso Eggplant

Breaded Eggplant with
Arugula and Parmesan

Tomato and Mango Salad

Zucchini-Scallion Fritters

Pasta with Zucchini, Mint,
and Pecorino

Zucchini Quick Bread

Skillet Steak Peperonata

Pickled Jalapeños and
Cucumbers

Blistered Padrón Peppers
with Sea Salt

Whole Baked Trout with
Cherry Tomatoes and
Potatoes

Zucchini "Pasta" Primavera

Roasted Bell Peppers

Tomatillo and Chipotle Salsa

Chiles Rellenos

Cucumber, Mango, and
Shrimp Escabèche

Chilled Melon, Cucumber,
and Mint Soup

Stuffed Tomatoes with
Mozzarella

Salmon and Avocado
Tartines

Pistachio Guacamole

Roasted-Tomato Hand Pies

Butternut Squash and
Taleggio Pizza

Roasted Acorn Squash,
Three Ways

Butternut Squash and
Kale Hash

KERNELS   311

Grilled Corn,
with Three Toppings

Corn and Scallion
Chilaquiles

Corn Soup

Hatch Chile Corn Pudding

Cornmeal Shortcakes
with Corn Ice Cream and
Blueberry Compote

FOREWORD

When I think about vegetables, in the context of a "subject matter," say for a book such as this, I think of the provocative book by Lynne Truss: *Eats, Shoots & Leaves.* That book, on the subject of punctuation and grammar, has the effect of making one want to rearrange the title to *Eats Shoots & Leaves,* which of course has an entirely different meaning. It also brings to mind a few categories of vegetables. *Roots, Shoots & Leaves,* in fact, could have been the title of this book.

This book is about all kinds of vegetables, and it is full of all kinds of recipes we've developed to prepare those vegetables in the most savory and delightful ways. Everyone in the kitchens of Martha Stewart Living contributed to the content, and the expertise of our editors is evident on page after page—in the choosing of the types of vegetables, in determining the appropriate freshness of those delicious gifts from garden and farm, and in the serving and enjoying of even some very usual varieties.

There are almost infinite ways to enjoy vegetables, and we have divided the edible plant world into big chapters to lure you into trying and experimenting in many different ways with bulbs, roots, tubers, leaves, shoots, kernels, pods, stalks and stems, greens, flowers and buds, and even fruits. Why fruits? Tomatoes, eggplants, peppers, cucumbers, avocados, zucchini, and other squashes are all, botanically, fruits. The scientific reason for dividing in this way is not very complicated, and it is fascinating to think about each "vegetable" and learn the correct taxonomy.

Children, as much as adults, are fascinated with such distinctions, and it is true that cooks and our culinary traditions have clouded the categories. In any event, the recipes in this book treat both vegetables and fruits in delicious, savory, memorable ways. Enjoy as many of these recipes as you can.

Martha Stewart

BULBS

As Julia Child wrote, "It's hard to imagine a civilization without onions." Open any cookbook and you'll see she's right. *Alliums* (the botanical genus includes edible bulbs such as shallots, garlic, onions, and ramps, plus those with edible leaves like leeks, scallions, and chives) season many favorite dishes. And thanks to the proliferation of farmers' markets, we now have access to a wider range of these aromatic gems. What's more, in many places, early varieties start appearing weeks after the thaw. Clearly, these bulbs are worth celebrating. But, because they are ubiquitous, long lasting, and fairly cheap, we have the luxury of taking them for granted.

Like other underground vegetables, including roots and tubers, bulbs of the allium family stockpile the energy and nutrients absorbed from the sun and earth. But bulbs store them primarily as sugars, not carbohydrates, which may explain why they go to such lengths to defend their treasures. Inside each cell, thanks to one of nature's most brilliant defense systems, sulfur compounds are kept segregated from the enzymes that trigger them, divided by thin membranes; when the cells are broken—when you slice or bite into an onion, for example—the chemicals combine, creating the volatile gases that can make you cry.

Sulfur and sugar: the harsh married to the sweet. It is precisely this intriguing balance that makes bulbs so delicious—and essential. These alliums lend a framework to other flavors, bringing structure and flavor to dishes—and perhaps even civilizations—the world over.

GARLIC
—
LEEKS
—
ONIONS
—
RAMPS
—
SCALLIONS
—
SHALLOTS
—
SPRING ONIONS

THE BASICS

SEASONALITY

Because onions and garlic are available year-round, it's easy to think they don't have a season. But spring is when they push their tender green shoots up from the earth and begin forming a new generation of bulbs below. From March through May, seek out tender young onions, garlic, and their kin at farmers' markets—all are mild and excellent eaten raw.

Sweet onions, such as Walla Walla, and storage onions are left to continue growing underground through the summer and into fall; you can also find excellent examples of these at farmers' markets. For garlic to produce the cloves we all know and love, the flower buds, or scapes, must be harvested in spring. Green garlic, which could be mistaken for an overgrown scallion, has a mild flavor that's brighter and fresher tasting than regular cloves. And lucky for us, these springtime delicacies are readily available at farmers' markets and specialty grocers during the spring and early summer.

Ramps, also known as wild leeks, are foraged from shaded, woody areas up and down the East Coast, from Georgia to Canada, and are heralded for their garlicky flavor. Their many fans eagerly await their first appearance at farmers' markets, where you can find them from March through early June (though you can also cultivate your own).

BUYING

Common onions and garlic are "cured"—harvested when fully mature, then dried for storage. Hardiness is key when selecting these vegetables, so at the market, give them a (very gentle) squeeze. Also, avoid bruises and mold, and shun dampness—the skins should be papery and dry. Select yellow onions for long braises and high-heat cooking; they have the strongest, richest flavor, and will hold up no matter what they're paired with. White onions are slightly milder, and common in Mexican and South American dishes. Tamer still are red onions, with a touch of sweetness, making them the best choice for salads, sandwiches, and other dishes where they'll be eaten raw. Among the first vegetables to appear at farmers' markets after the snow melts, young, green-leafed bulbs—including scallions and ramps, as well as spring onions and garlic scapes—are a welcome sight; look for bunches whose greens are firm and stiff, their bulbs bright and glossy.

NOTABLE VARIETIES

Onions: White, yellow, and red are grocery-store staples, but it's worth seeking out Vidalia and Walla Walla onions, the sweetest ones of all (especially when grown in sulfur-free soil, where they absorb none of the sharpness common to other varieties). Spring onions, planted in the fall and harvested before the bulbs have had a chance to grow (in early spring, hence their name), can be found at farm stands starting in March; they are milder and sweeter than storage onions when cooked, with a notable spiciness that makes them wonderful for grilling and pickling. They resemble scallions but have a larger bulb.

Scallions: Look for purple-bulb varieties in the spring; they have the same flavor as white ones, but make a pretty garnish.

Garlic: The garlic sold in grocery stores is intended for long storage rather than flavor, making it worth the trip to the farmers' market to find other varieties that are usually only available from small growers. These local heads should have larger cloves and a more pronounced flavor. They are sometimes sold still on the stalks, and some have purple stripes or a reddish hue.

STORING

Dark, cool, and dry is how cured bulbs like it, so store onions, shallots, and garlic on an out-of-the-way shelf or in a cabinet. Light causes them to sprout, generating green tendrils within that draw nutrients and flavor from the bulb; moisture can cause mold to form beneath the skin (which can be wiped off) or between the layers of the bulb (where it can't be). Leeks, spring onions, ramps, and scallions, meanwhile, should be refrigerated, loosely wrapped in a plastic bag, and used within a few days.

PREPPING

Learning to cut onions quickly and skillfully is one of the smartest things novice cooks can do to make kitchen life more agreeable. Remove the papery skin (it's called the *tunic!*), and unless you want rings, slice the onion in half from top to root. Lay each half flat on the board and slice into the bulb first lengthwise (leaving root intact), then crosswise. If you plan to serve onions raw—in a salad, say, or on a sandwich—you may want to first soak the pieces for five to ten minutes in an ice-water bath to remove the sulfur compounds generated on cut surfaces, or give them a brief soak in vinegar. For garlic, remove the paper sheath by gently crushing each clove with the side of a knife blade, then pull off the paper; remove any green "germ" from the cloves, as these are very bitter.

Leeks, ramps, scallions, and green garlic often need to have their tunics peeled away, too—and as these are fragile and clingy, they may require scraping with the edge of a paring knife. Then cut away the scruffy roots and slice if needed, separating the stronger-flavored white parts from the green, if the recipe requires (most do). Leeks hold onto a lot of grit in their many thick layers; cut them as directed in a recipe, then submerge in a bowl of cold water and swish thoroughly. Lift out the leeks, and repeat until you don't see any more grit in the water. Drain and dry if sautéing or roasting.

COOKING

With a high proportion of sugars, onions take well to being caramelized. Indeed, you can grill or roast them until nearly black before their flavor is ruined. But they are equally happy cooked low and slow—gently sautéed in butter or olive oil, or oven-braised in a skillet. These are also the best methods for cooking delicate-flavored leeks, ramps, and scallions, which all take well to a quick pass through a hot flame, giving them a dramatic charred flavor that pairs well with meat. Ramps are excellent mixed into pestos and compound butters; sautéed and tossed with spaghetti or served over soft polenta; or treated like herbs and tucked under the skin of chicken before roasting.

As with onions, garlic's multiple personalities are highlighted by different cooking techniques: Mince or smash raw cloves to add an assertive bite to salad dressings, pestos, salsas and relishes, and no-cook pasta sauces; sauté them until pale golden in butter or oil for a flavor that's mild and mellow; roast a whole head in the oven until it turns mahogany brown for cloves that are buttery soft, rich, sweet, and earthy—and then spread the paste on bread, toss it with pasta, or incorporate it into dips and sauces.

HOW TO ROAST
(For all bulbs)

Peel onions and shallots; quarter onions, leaving wedges intact, and separate shallots (halve larger ones, if desired). Trim scallions, leeks, spring onions, green garlic, and ramps; leave whole or cut crosswise into 2-inch pieces (wash leeks well). Place on a rimmed baking sheet, drizzle with olive oil, and season with salt and pepper. Strew onions and shallots with fresh thyme or rosemary, if desired. Spread in an even layer and roast at 400°F, tossing once or twice, until tender and browned in spots, 15 to 20 minutes. Drizzle with vinegar (balsamic, cider, sherry, or white wine), and sprinkle with herbs.

(For garlic cloves)

Separate garlic cloves, and place on a rimmed baking sheet. Drizzle with olive oil, season with salt and pepper, and toss to coat. Roast at 400°F until skins are deep golden brown and flesh is very tender, 20 to 30 minutes. When cool enough to handle, slip out of skins, and use in dressings or sauces, or spread on crostini.

(For whole garlic)

Slice off top quarter of garlic head, exposing as many cloves as possible, with a serrated knife. Drizzle with olive oil and season with salt and pepper; top with fresh thyme, if desired. Wrap in parchment, then foil, sealing to form a packet. Roast at 400°F until cloves are golden and very soft, 50 to 60 minutes. When cool enough to handle, squeeze head from bottom to push out cloves. Stir into mashed potatoes, whisk into vinaigrettes, or spread on sandwiches.

HOW TO GRILL
(For onions, scallions, leeks, spring onions, green garlic, ramps)

Peel onion, cut all the way through root end into 8 wedges (keep wedges intact), or slice into ½-inch-thick rounds. Trim scallions, spring onions, green garlic, and ramps. Trim leeks, halve lengthwise, and wash well. Toss with olive oil, and season with salt and pepper. Cook on a medium-hot grill, turning as needed, until tender and lightly charred in spots, 10 to 20 minutes. Sprinkle with fresh lemon juice or red-wine or sherry vinegar, drizzle with more oil, and top with chopped fresh herbs (parsley, mint, or basil).

(For shallots)

Peel and halve or quarter shallots, leaving wedges intact. Thread onto skewers; drizzle with olive oil, and season with salt and pepper. Cook over a medium-hot grill, turning as needed, until tender and lightly charred in spots, 45 to 50 minutes. Drizzle with red-wine or sherry vinegar while still warm.

HOW TO BRAISE
(For all bulbs)

Peel onions and shallots and trim roots, leaving bulbs intact. Halve or quarter onions, leaving wedges intact; halve shallots. Trim scallions, spring onions, green garlic, and ramps; leave whole or cut to fit into skillet. Trim leeks, halve lengthwise, and wash well. Heat butter or olive oil in a large cast-iron (or other ovenproof) skillet over medium. Add bulbs, season with salt and pepper, and sauté until golden brown, 2 to 5 minutes on each side. Add enough braising liquid (chicken or vegetable broth or water, or a combination) to cover and a few sprigs of thyme, if desired. Cover and cook in a 350°F oven until tender, 30 to 50 minutes. To glaze the bulbs, remove foil, raise oven heat to 450°F, and continue cooking until liquid reduces, thickens, and coats vegetables, 10 to 15 minutes more.

FLAVOR PAIRINGS

Onions are used in such a wide variety of dishes, it would be almost quicker to list the things they *don't* go with than those they do. Garlic, too, lends character to an astonishing range of preparations. Shallots can be substituted for either in a pinch; their mild, sweet flavor makes them a classic in salad dressings. Scallions and especially ramps introduce spicy, fresh, green, almost herbal notes.

GARLIC: chicken, lamb, rosemary, tomato, lemon, feta, ginger, soy sauce, mushrooms

ONIONS: chicken, meat, cheese, beer, wine, mustard, vinegar, ginger, thyme, nuts, greens

RAMPS: asparagus, eggs, mint, morels, vinegar, lentils, potatoes, fish, Parmesan

SCALLIONS: ginger, garlic, rice, eggs, bitter greens, butter, parsley, rice, tomatoes

SHALLOTS: butter, tarragon, mustard, garlic, salad greens, vinegar, fish, dried fruit

SWEET ONIONS: goat cheese, blue cheese, basil, cayenne, nutmeg, ham

Four-Onion Soup with Ginger

Caramelized onions are a remarkable flavor booster. Sliced thin to expose all their starches, onions slowly soften, turn a deep golden brown, and become wonderfully sweet. They are, of course, at the heart of French onion soup. In this update on the traditional recipe, we round out the flavors with three types of onion—red, white, and yellow—and combine them with an equal amount of shallots and a nice amount of fresh ginger.

SERVES 6

2 tablespoons extra-virgin olive oil, plus more

1½ pounds each white, yellow, and red onions, thinly sliced lengthwise

1 piece (3 inches) fresh ginger, peeled and finely julienned

1½ pounds shallots, thinly sliced

2 tablespoons very thinly sliced fresh sage leaves, plus whole leaves for garnish

2 quarts low-sodium chicken broth

Coarse salt and freshly ground pepper

½ baguette, halved lengthwise and sliced

½ cup finely grated Gruyère cheese

1. In a large high-sided skillet, heat oil over medium. Add onions and ginger; cook, stirring occasionally, until soft and translucent, 45 minutes. Add shallots and sage. Continue cooking, stirring occasionally as onions reduce, until they are very soft and caramelized, about 1 hour. (Add a few tablespoons broth or water to skillet if onions start to stick.)

2. Preheat oven to 350°F. Pour broth into skillet, and bring to a boil. Reduce heat to a simmer, and cook 15 minutes more, stirring occasionally. Season with salt and pepper.

3. Meanwhile, arrange bread on a baking sheet; brush with oil, season with salt and pepper, and sprinkle with cheese. Toast in oven until cheese is melted and golden, about 8 minutes.

4. While toast is in oven, heat 2 inches oil in a medium saucepan until shimmering. Fry sage leaves until just crisp, 15 to 20 seconds; use a slotted spoon or wire skimmer to transfer to paper towels to drain.

5. Divide soup among six bowls; garnish with sage leaves, and serve with cheese toasts.

TIP
Make a big batch of caramelized onions, and store them in an airtight container in the refrigerator up to five days. Use as a filling for omelets, a topping for burgers or steaks, or a sandwich spread. They are also delicious tossed with pasta.

Spaghetti with Mussels, Lemon, and Shallots

Shallots lack the bite of onions, and offer a milder, sweeter flavor that's just right for steaming mussels—at least according to classic French preparations. In that spirit, we created a broth of shallots, red-pepper flakes, parsley stems, and white wine. You could serve the mussels with rustic bread, but we use them to make a "sauce" for spaghetti.

SERVES 6

1 pound spaghetti

Coarse salt

¼ cup plus 2 tablespoons extra-virgin olive oil

4 large shallots, diced

1 teaspoon red-pepper flakes

¼ cup finely chopped fresh flat-leaf parsley stems, plus 1 cup coarsely chopped leaves

¾ cup dry white wine, such as Sauvignon Blanc

2 pounds mussels, scrubbed and beards removed

½ lemon, zested and juiced

1. Cook spaghetti in a pot of salted boiling water until al dente, according to package instructions. Reserve 1½ cups cooking water; drain pasta.

2. Meanwhile, in another pot, heat ¼ cup oil over medium high. Sauté shallots, red-pepper flakes, and parsley stems until tender, stirring occasionally, about 5 minutes. Add wine; cook until liquid is reduced by one-third, stirring frequently, about 2 minutes. Add mussels, cover with a tight-fitting lid, and steam until they open, 5 to 6 minutes (discard any unopened mussels).

3. Add pasta to pot, tossing until well combined. Add reserved pasta water, and continue to toss and cook over medium-high heat until sauce has reduced and coats pasta. Remove from heat. Stir in parsley leaves and lemon zest and juice, then remaining oil, and serve immediately.

TIP
To clean mussels, rinse them under cold running water and scrub the shells with a stiff sponge or vegetable brush. Discard any that are chipped or open. Next, grip the tough fibers (or beard) extending from the shell and tug to remove. Rinse again in cold water, drain, and chill until ready to use.

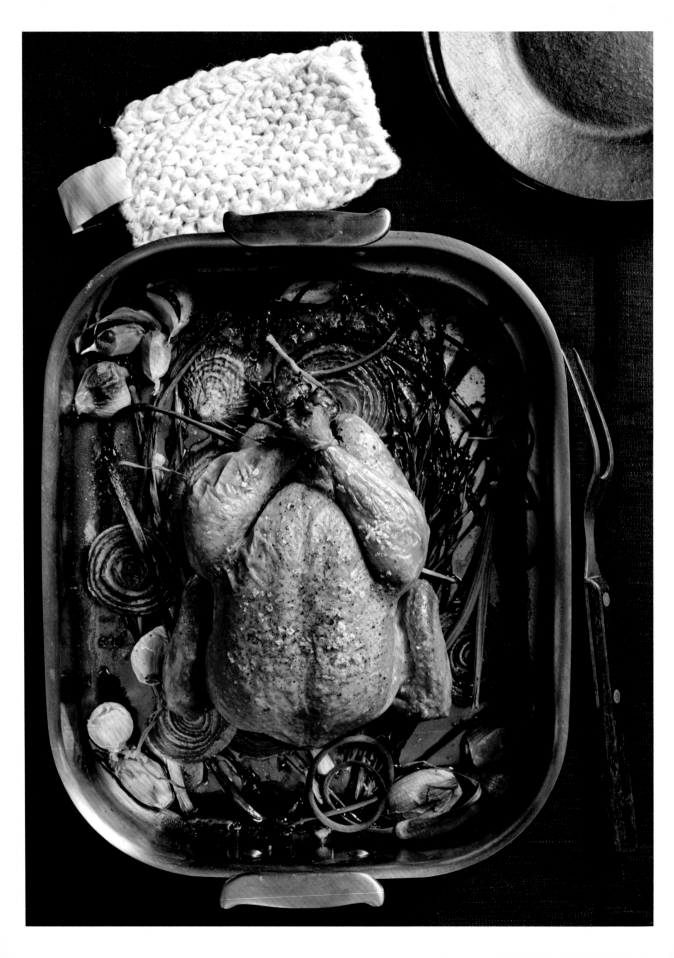

Roast Chicken with
Onions, Shallots, Garlic, and Scapes

Roasting chicken on a bed of onions achieves two things: the onions impart flavor to the chicken, and they become wonderfully darkened. We've included a bunch of different alliums in this otherwise straightforward recipe, for a host of flavors: sliced red onion, whole shallots, fresh chives, and garlic in two forms (cloves and scapes). All can be enjoyed alongside the chicken, with crusty bread.

SERVES 4 TO 6

1 whole chicken
(4 to 4½ pounds)

Coarse salt and freshly
ground pepper

1 bunch fresh oregano

1 red onion, thinly sliced

10 garlic cloves, unpeeled

6 shallots, peeled

2 bunches fresh chives

2 bunches garlic scapes

1. Preheat oven to 425°F. Season chicken all over with salt and pepper. Tuck oregano into cavity. Scatter onion, garlic, shallots, chives, and scapes around a roasting pan. Place chicken, breast side up, in pan, and tuck wings under. Tie legs together with kitchen twine.

2. Roast chicken until juices run clear and an instant-read thermometer inserted into the thickest part of a thigh (do not touch bone) reaches 165°F, about 1 hour 15 minutes. Let rest for 10 minutes before carving and serving.

TIP
Trussing a chicken encourages even cooking. To truss a chicken, place it with tail end closest to you and tuck the wing tips under. Center a long piece of twine, and run it around the neck; then pass it over the drumsticks, and tuck it under their joints. Crossing it over their joints, tighten to bring legs together and plump up the breast. Wrap one end all the way around the tail end, and tie into a knot.

Israeli Couscous with Parsley and Shallots

When you want a more subtle (less sweet) flavor than caramelized onions, try sautéing thinly sliced shallots over medium-high heat; they'll soften and brown after just a few minutes. Here, the shallots are tossed with couscous, lemon juice, and parsley to make a bright side dish for chicken, pork, or fish, or a nice packable salad for lunch.

SERVES 4

1 cup Israeli (pearl) couscous

Coarse salt and freshly ground pepper

1 tablespoon extra-virgin olive oil

8 shallots, halved and thinly sliced

½ cup packed fresh flat-leaf parsley leaves, coarsely chopped

1 tablespoon fresh lemon juice

1. Cook couscous in a pot of boiling salted water until al dente, according to package instructions. Drain and transfer to a bowl.

2. Meanwhile, heat oil in a medium skillet over medium high. Add shallots; season with salt and pepper. Cook, stirring frequently, until browned, 7 to 8 minutes. Add to bowl with couscous. Add parsley and lemon juice, and toss to combine. Season with salt and pepper, and serve.

Beer-Battered Onion Rings

Thinly layered, slightly spicy yellow onions are used to make the light, crisp rings at Balthazar in New York City. (This recipe is adapted from the restaurant's cookbook, and it is Martha's hands-down favorite.) Beer flavors the batter and adds body, thanks to the bubbles. Baking powder, a leavening agent, helps to enlarge these bubbles as the batter fries.

SERVES 6

2 cups all-purpose flour

1 teaspoon coarse salt, plus more for sprinkling

¼ teaspoon freshly ground white pepper

½ teaspoon baking powder

1 cup beer, preferably lager or pilsner

2 tablespoons ice water

Peanut oil, for frying

2 medium yellow onions, cut crosswise into ½-inch-thick slices, separated into rings

1. Whisk together 1 cup flour, the salt, white pepper, and baking powder in a bowl. Whisk in beer and ice water until combined. Place remaining cup flour in a shallow dish.

2. Preheat oven to 200°F, with a baking sheet on middle rack. Heat 3 inches of oil to 375°F in a medium pot over medium high. Dredge onions in flour, turning to coat; tap off excess. Working in batches (about 8 at a time), dip onions in batter, shaking off excess. Carefully add to hot oil. Cook until golden brown, 2 to 3 minutes. Transfer to paper towels to drain. Sprinkle with salt. Transfer to baking sheet to keep warm while cooking remaining onions. Adjust heat as necessary to keep oil at a steady temperature. Serve hot.

Normandy-Style Chicken and Leeks with Crème Fraîche

Leeks grow in abundance in Normandy, in northern France, where the alliums are celebrated for their ability to transform even the simplest dish into something spectacular. Take chicken Normande, a multi-layered main course of braised chicken, hard apple cider (another local specialty), and of course, leeks. Serve this with crusty bread.

SERVES 4

1 whole chicken (about 4 pounds), cut into 10 pieces (each breast cut in half crosswise)

Coarse salt and freshly ground pepper

1 tablespoon unsalted butter

2 teaspoons olive oil

4 small leeks (white and pale-green parts only), cut crosswise into 3-inch pieces, rinsed well (about 1 pound)

1 cup good-quality hard apple cider

1 tablespoon coarsely chopped fresh thyme leaves

½ cup crème fraîche

1 tablespoon finely chopped fresh flat-leaf parsley

1. Season chicken all over with salt and pepper. Melt the butter with the oil in a large enameled cast-iron Dutch oven over medium-high heat until just bubbling. Add half the chicken pieces, skin side down; cook, turning once, until golden, 2 to 3 minutes per side. Transfer chicken pieces to a plate. Repeat with remaining chicken pieces; add to plate. Remove pot from heat; let cool slightly.

2. Return pot to medium-low heat, and add leeks. Cook, stirring frequently, until leeks begin to soften and are pale golden, about 3 minutes. Add hard cider and thyme. Move leeks to edges of pot, and add all the chicken pieces to center, skin side down. Arrange leeks over chicken. Cover and cook 15 minutes (if liquid is bubbling rapidly, reduce heat to low). Turn chicken pieces, and cook until breasts are cooked through, about 5 minutes more. Use a slotted spoon to transfer chicken breasts to a plate, and cover to keep warm. Adjust leeks so they are submerged in liquid. Cook, uncovered, until the remaining chicken pieces are tender and cooked through, about 10 minutes.

3. Transfer all the chicken to a warm serving platter. Remove leeks from pot, and arrange them around the chicken. Cover to keep warm. Return pot to medium heat. Cook, uncovered, until liquid has reduced by about half (to a scant ⅔ cup), 8 to 10 minutes.

4. Reduce heat to medium low. Whisk in the crème fraîche and parsley. Ladle pan sauce over chicken and leeks. Serve immediately.

TIP
Regular apple cider or a dry white wine, such as Sauvignon Blanc, can be used in place of the hard cider.

Pasta Carbonara
with Leeks and Lemon

*When it comes to carbonara, there are those who adhere to the original combination
of egg, guanciale (or bacon or pancetta in its place), and grated cheese, and
those who favor adding heavy cream to the mix. We say there's room for both in your
repertoire, including this version that's enhanced with the flavor of sautéed leeks.
Fresh parsley and lemon zest and juice add brightness.*

SERVES 4

6 slices bacon, cut crosswise into 1-inch pieces

4 leeks (white and pale-green parts only), halved lengthwise, thinly sliced, rinsed well

Coarse salt and ground pepper

12 ounces short pasta, such as gemelli or campanelle

2 large eggs

¼ cup grated Parmigiano-Reggiano cheese, plus more for serving

1 tablespoon finely grated lemon zest, plus 1 tablespoon lemon juice

½ cup fresh flat-leaf parsley leaves, coarsely chopped

1. In a large skillet, cook bacon over medium, stirring occasionally, until crisp, 8 to 10 minutes. With a slotted spoon, transfer bacon to paper towels to drain. Pour off all but 2 tablespoons fat from skillet. Add leeks, season with salt and pepper, and cook, stirring often, until leeks are golden brown, about 10 minutes.

2. Meanwhile, cook pasta in a pot of salted boiling water until al dente, according to package instructions. In a large bowl, whisk together eggs, cheese, and lemon zest and juice.

3. Measure out ¼ cup pasta water and whisk into egg mixture. Drain pasta and immediately add to egg mixture, along with bacon, leeks, and parsley. Season with salt and pepper, and stir to combine. Sprinkle with more cheese, and serve immediately.

Roasted Salmon and Spring Onions

Because of when they arrive in the market, spring onions are often paired with other seasonal produce, including asparagus and peas, and as here, with wild salmon, whose season kicks off in April. The spring onions are roasted until golden brown; unlike storage onions and shallots, they don't soften so much as become tender and chewy, a nice textural contrast to the salmon. A mint-almond-caper pesto is served alongside.

SERVES 8 TO 10

1 cup extra-virgin olive oil

1½ pounds spring onions, trimmed and halved lengthwise

Coarse salt and freshly ground pepper

1 piece (3 pounds) skinless salmon fillet, preferably wild Pacific

2 cups lightly packed fresh mint leaves

2 tablespoons slivered blanched almonds, toasted

¼ cup plus 2 tablespoons capers, rinsed and drained

Flaky sea salt, such as Maldon, for sprinkling

2 lemons, cut into wedges, for serving

1. Preheat oven to 400°F, with racks in upper and lower thirds. Coat two rimmed baking sheets with 1 tablespoon oil each. Divide onions between baking sheets and drizzle each with 2 tablespoons oil; season generously with coarse salt and pepper. Roast until bottoms of onions are golden brown, 25 to 30 minutes, rotating sheets from top to bottom halfway through. Remove from oven; reduce temperature to 325°F. Let onions cool, then combine on one sheet.

2. Place salmon on top of onions. Brush with 2 tablespoons oil and season with coarse salt and pepper. Roast on lower rack of oven until partially opaque in center, about 20 minutes.

3. Meanwhile, combine remaining ½ cup oil, the mint, almonds, capers, ¾ teaspoon coarse salt, and ½ teaspoon pepper in a mini food processor or blender, and purée mixture until smooth.

4. Remove salmon and onions from oven; carefully transfer to a serving platter. Sprinkle with sea salt; serve with lemon wedges and mint-caper pesto.

Pickled Ramps

One of the most popular ways to preserve the flavor of ramps is pickling. The brine for these is infused with coriander and fennel seeds and thyme. Serve the ramps as an accompaniment to roasted meats, on a cheese board, or to garnish a cocktail.

MAKES ABOUT 2 CUPS

1 cup white-wine vinegar

½ cup sugar

1¼ teaspoons coarse salt

1 teaspoon coriander seeds

½ teaspoon fennel seeds

¼ teaspoon whole black peppercorns

Pinch of red-pepper flakes

3 sprigs thyme

2 cups water

1 bunch ramps, trimmed and rinsed well

1. Stir together the vinegar, sugar, salt, coriander seeds, fennel seeds, peppercorns, red-pepper flakes, thyme, and the water in a medium saucepan. Bring to a boil. Add ramps; return to a boil. Reduce heat and simmer until tender, 5 to 7 minutes.

2. Remove from heat, and let ramps cool completely in the liquid, about 1½ hours, before storing or serving. (Pickled ramps can be refrigerated in their liquid in an airtight container up to 1 month.)

Grilled Ramps with Romesco

The intense wild flavor of ramps makes them excellent candidates for grilling. Plus, the bulbs hold their shape beautifully, while the greens wilt just enough to be tender. We especially love grilled ramps served with a smear of Spanish romesco sauce, rich with the smoky flavor of roasted piquillo peppers.

SERVES 4 TO 6

¼ cup blanched almonds, toasted

1 garlic clove

1 jar (10 ounces) roasted piquillo chiles, drained

¼ cup plus 3 tablespoons extra-virgin olive oil, plus more for grill

2 teaspoons sherry vinegar

2 bunches ramps

Coarse salt and freshly ground pepper

1. Pulse almonds and garlic in a food processor until coarsely ground. Add chiles, ¼ cup oil, and the vinegar; purée until smooth. Store romesco sauce in refrigerator, covered, up to 1 day; bring to room temperature before serving.

2. Heat grill to medium high. Trim and discard the tiny roots from the ramps.

3. Place ramps on a rimmed baking sheet. Drizzle with remaining 3 tablespoons oil, and toss to coat. Season with salt and pepper, and toss to combine. Brush hot grates with oil. Arrange ramps on grill in a single layer. Grill until hot and charred in spots, about 1 minute per side. Transfer to a platter. Serve warm or at room temperature, with romesco.

Steamed Black Bass with Ginger and Scallions

Here, a mixture of aromatic scallions and fresh ginger is stuffed into the cavity of a whole fish as it steams, and the rest is spread on top, for unbeatable flavor all around (red onion is also used to line the steamer basket). Red snapper or trout is a good alternative to black bass. Serve with cooked rice or rice noodles.

SERVES 2

½ cup low-sodium soy sauce

1 tablespoon plus 1½ teaspoons toasted sesame oil

2 whole black bass (each 1½ to 2 pounds and 1½ inches thick), scaled and gutted, gills removed

1 piece (2 inches) peeled fresh ginger, cut into matchsticks

5 scallions, halved lengthwise, and cut into 2- to 4-inch pieces; plus more, chopped, for sauce

1 large red onion, sliced ½ inch thick

1. Whisk together soy sauce and sesame oil in a 9-by-13-inch baking dish. Cut a few slits into the fish on both sides using a sharp paring knife. Transfer evenly to dish; turn to coat fish.

2. Toss ginger with scallions; stuff some into each fish cavity. Spread remaining mixture on top of fish. Let stand, covered, spooning marinade over fish often, for 30 minutes.

3. Bring about 2 cups water to a boil in a large skillet or wok. Arrange red onion on bottom layer of a 12-inch bamboo steamer. Remove fish from marinade with ginger-scallion mixture still on top, and arrange side by side on onion; reserve marinade. Set steamer in skillet. Steam, covered, until fish is cooked through and vegetables are tender, about 15 minutes.

4. Meanwhile, bring marinade to a boil in a small saucepan. Cook until reduced by half. Strain through a fine sieve; add chopped scallions. Serve fish and vegetables with sauce.

TIP
If you don't have a bamboo steamer, you can arrange the fish side by side in a steamer basket set in a pot filled with one inch of water.

Rice Noodles
with Scallions and Herbs

This recipe demonstrates how the often-discarded dark green parts of the scallion can add great taste and color to a dish. This is true of lots of Asian recipes, where scallions are used along with garlic and fresh ginger, and which often involve brief cooking at most (think stir-fries). Here, scallion greens are cooked for a mere ten seconds, just long enough to release their flavor and make them a bit more tender.

SERVES 4

8 ounces rice vermicelli

½ cup water

¼ cup fish sauce, such as *nam pla* or *nuoc nam*

3 tablespoons fresh lime juice (from 2 to 3 limes)

2 tablespoons packed light-brown sugar

1 teaspoon sliced fresh red chile, preferably Thai bird chile

¼ cup safflower oil

1 garlic clove, minced

4 scallions (dark-green parts only), thinly sliced

3 large leaves Boston or Bibb lettuce, very thinly sliced

1 medium carrot, peeled and julienned

¼ cup each lightly packed fresh mint and basil leaves, torn into small pieces

1. Bring a pot of water to a boil. Cook vermicelli, stirring occasionally, just until tender, about 4 minutes. Drain, then rinse with cold water. Let vermicelli drain in colander for 30 minutes, tossing occasionally.

2. Meanwhile, combine the water, fish sauce, lime juice, brown sugar, and chile in a small bowl.

3. Heat oil in a skillet over medium. Add garlic and scallions, and cook, stirring, for 10 seconds. Remove from heat.

4. Toss scallion mixture and sauce with noodles in a serving bowl. Add lettuce, carrot, and herbs, and toss to combine.

Garlic-Scape Toasts

Scapes are slightly spicy and, along with fresh chives, make a lovely topping for toasts spread with butter. They can also be used as a substitute for ramps—in other words, pickled, grilled, and used in pestos and pasta dishes.

SERVES 6 TO 8

1 baguette, sliced ½ inch thick

3 tablespoons unsalted butter, room temperature

2 garlic scapes, cut on the bias

2 tablespoons coarsely snipped fresh chives

Coarse salt and freshly ground pepper

Heat grill to medium high. Toast baguette halves, cut side down, on grill until golden brown. Dividing evenly, spread butter on toasts, then top with scapes and chives, season with salt and pepper, and serve.

Green-Garlic Butter

Green garlic mixed with softened butter, Parmesan, and chives makes a compound butter that is as versatile as can be. Here, it's melted atop steak, with hearts of romaine alongside; try it over scrambled eggs, steamed asparagus, or boiled new potatoes.

SERVES 4

½ cup (1 stick) unsalted butter, room temperature

½ cup grated Parmigiano-Reggiano cheese

3 tablespoons chopped young green garlic stalks (white and green parts)

1 garlic clove, halved

1 tablespoon snipped fresh chives

Fine sea salt and freshly ground black pepper

Pinch of red-pepper flakes

In a bowl, mix together butter, Parmesan, both garlics, chives, ¼ teaspoon each salt and black pepper, and the red-pepper flakes until combined. Green-garlic butter can be refrigerated, covered, up to 1 week or frozen up to 3 months. Serve at room temperature.

Herb-and-Scallion Bread Pudding

*A full two bunches of scallions—white bulbs, pale-green parts, and dark-green tops—
go into this savory side dish. We use a combination of parsley, sage, and thyme,
but other herbs (chervil, oregano, and marjoram) would also work. Consider adding
this to your Thanksgiving menu, or to accompany crown roast or beef tenderloin
at Christmas—or with roast chicken, for no occasion at all.*

SERVES 8

10 cups cubed day-old challah
or brioche, in 1-inch cubes
(from 1 or 2 loaves)

½ cup packed fresh flat-leaf
parsley leaves, coarsely
chopped

¼ cup packed fresh sage
leaves, coarsely chopped

2 tablespoons fresh thyme
leaves, coarsely chopped

5 tablespoons unsalted butter,
plus more for baking dish

4 celery stalks,
coarsely chopped

3 garlic cloves, minced

Coarse salt and freshly
ground pepper

2 bunches scallions,
thinly sliced

8 large eggs, lightly beaten

2 cups low-sodium
chicken broth

2 cups heavy cream

1. Combine bread cubes, parsley, sage, and thyme in a
large bowl. Melt 4 tablespoons butter in a large skillet over
medium-high heat. Reduce heat to medium. Cook celery
and garlic with a pinch of salt until celery is tender, 10 to 12
minutes. Add scallions and cook until tender but still bright
green, about 4 minutes. Pour mixture into bowl with bread,
and stir. Let cool.

2. Preheat oven to 325°F. Butter a 3-quart round baking
dish (2 to 3 inches deep) or a 9-by-13-inch baking dish.
Whisk together eggs, broth, and heavy cream, and season
with salt and pepper. Pour over bread mixture, tossing until
bread is evenly soaked. Transfer to baking dish, pressing
into corners, and dot top with remaining tablespoon butter.

3. Bake until top puffs and center is set, about 1 hour.
Let cool slightly before serving.

Gazpacho Ajo Blanco

Ajo blanco ("white garlic") is a tomato-free gazpacho from Málaga, on Spain's southern coast. Garlic cloves are briefly boiled to soften and mellow before being puréed with the other ingredients, including almonds. Grapes and Marcona almonds garnish each serving.

SERVES 6

3 cups cubed crustless day-old rustic bread

5 garlic cloves

2 cups blanched almonds

2½ teaspoons sherry vinegar

Coarse salt and freshly ground pepper

½ cup extra-virgin olive oil, plus more for drizzling

Sliced red seedless grapes and chopped Marcona almonds, for serving

1. Soak bread in water for 15 minutes. Cover garlic with water in a saucepan, and bring to a boil. Cook for 3 minutes; drain.

2. Pulse blanched almonds in a food processor until finely ground. Squeeze excess liquid from bread, discarding liquid, and transfer bread to processor. Add garlic, vinegar, and 1½ teaspoons salt; purée mixture until smooth. With machine running, add oil in a slow, steady stream, alternating with ¼ cup cold water, blending until emulsified. Blend in another 2¼ cups cold water. Strain through a fine sieve into a bowl, pressing on solids to extract liquid; discard solids. Season with salt.

3. Chill gazpacho, at least 1 hour or up to 1 day. Season with salt and pepper. Divide gazpacho among bowls. Drizzle with oil and top with grapes and almonds, just before serving.

Creamy Garlic, Parsley, and Feta Dressing

A tablespoon of chopped raw garlic may seem like an overabundance (unless you are fending off vampires), but it's the starting point for a creamy dressing that's kept in check with bright parsley and lemon juice, fruity olive oil, sharp feta, and tangy yogurt. Toss it with mild, tender lettuces, such as Boston or Bibb, or drizzle over grilled chicken.

MAKES ABOUT 1½ CUPS

⅓ cup chopped fresh flat-leaf parsley leaves

¼ cup water

1 tablespoon minced garlic

⅔ cup plain Greek yogurt

⅔ cup extra-virgin olive oil

¼ cup fresh lemon juice (from 2 lemons)

1 ounce feta cheese, crumbled (3 tablespoons)

1 teaspoon coarse salt

Purée parsley, the water, and garlic in a blender until smooth, 1 to 2 minutes. Add remaining ingredients, and blend until just combined. Refrigerate, covered, at least 30 minutes and up to 1 week; stir to combine again before serving.

ROOTS

We used to act like root vegetables. Back in the days before refrigeration, we humans would gather nourishment during the warm, bright seasons and store it underground in our cellars for lean times. This is essentially what carrots, beets, celery root (or celeriac), parsnips, and their earth-dwelling kin do: stockpile a plant's energy and stow it safely in the dark, protective earth. No wonder these vegetables are sweet and dense-fleshed (at least compared with, say, more tender, water-packed vegetables like cucumbers, green beans, and celery); roots are warehouses of natural sugars and carbohydrates. No wonder, too, they keep so well. Holding steady is written into their genes. Which is not to suggest that root vegetables are nothing more than long-lived energy sources. Most also contain concentrated doses of the distinctive vitamins, minerals, and phytochemicals created or gathered by the plant.

In the kitchen, home cooks used to divide roots into those we eat raw (such as radishes) and those we eat cooked (including beets, turnips, and parsnips). The exception to this is carrots, which can go either way, and whose versatility has long been appreciated by chefs and bakers, as well as anyone looking for a quick, crunchy, wholesome snack. But the truth is that young beets, celery root, and spring turnips are wonderful raw, and radishes are delectable roasted. Jicama, meanwhile, is enjoyable whether you eat it cooked or raw. Indeed, the moment you start to explore the versatility of familiar roots, you're in for revelations—kind of like finding precious treasures tucked away in your basement.

BEETS
—
CARROTS
—
CELERY ROOT
—
JICAMA
—
PARSNIPS
—
RADISHES
—
RUTABAGA
—
SALSIFY
—
TURNIPS

THE BASICS

SEASONALITY

Roots are so hardy and reliable, most are available year-round—at least in some form—but their character varies from season to season. For tender, just-picked young carrots, turnips, beets, and radishes (including strikingly beautiful watermelon radishes and French Breakfast varieties), visit a greenmarket in late spring and early summer. During the hotter months, radishes and turnips turn pithy, hollow, and dry; carrots and beets simply grow bigger and more flavorful. Watch for celeriac from midsummer well into fall. Autumn brings a new crop of turnips—the purple tops, which are better for cooking than tossing into salads, as well as the all-white Japanese varieties—and radishes, including daikon and Black Spanish, which are wonderful raw or pickled. Rutabaga, parsnips, and salsify are best after a frost—or even in early spring, having wintered over in the dirt. Only a few patient farmers take the trouble to nurture them through the snow, however, so count yourself lucky if you find one!

BUYING

Many root vegetables are sold with their greens attached, which are a useful indicator of freshness: The greens should be tender, young, and firm, not wilted. Celeriac, rutabaga, parsnips, and other cool-season roots (including wintertime carrots and beets) are typically without greens; they've been cured for storage. With those vegetables, avoid ones that are split or cracked, have soft spots, or appear slimy or brown at either end. As for whether to buy "baby" or mature roots, true babies will be mild and tender (so-called baby carrots sold in bags are really just older carrots that have been cut and polished). Many roots, including parsnips and carrots, sweeten as they mature—so as long as they aren't woody or dry, older can be better. With jicama, look for smooth-skinned, firm roots without any bruises or spots. If a few spiky greens are growing from the top, they should be tender and bright-hued, not wilted.

NOTABLE VARIETIES

Beets: Besides the wine-red beets you find in supermarkets, there are a rainbow of colors to choose from: Golden Globe is slightly sweeter and milder than red ones and starts out orange but turns yellow when cooked; Albina Verduna is pure white and very sweet, with bright, curly tops; Chioggia, an Italian heirloom, is a great slicer, revealing pink and white concentric rings; and Cylindra is dark red and cylindrical. Kleine Bol ("Little Ball"), a true baby beet variety, is tender and perfectly shaped. Most beets can be used interchangeably in recipes, though their cooking times will vary.

Carrots: In addition to the familiar, tapering Imperator varieties, keep an eye out for blunt-tipped Nantes, which taste especially sweet; short, stout Chantenays; and small round Romeos. Other heirloom varieties may be purple, red, yellow, even white. These, too, can be swapped one for another.

Radishes: Cherry Belle radishes are the most common variety, with their lipstick-red skins and snow-white flesh. Try also sweeter, milder Pink Beauties and slender, ultra-crunchy French Breakfast radishes; mildly pungent and slightly peppery White Icicle varieties; watermelon radishes with green skins and striped pink interiors; golfball-shaped white Snow Belles; long, mild daikon varieties; and even spicy black-skinned Black Spanish Rounds.

Salsify: Also called "oyster plant," salsify comes in two types: white (called salsify) and black (known as scorzonera), the latter of which is harder to find but more highly regarded by cooks for its distinctive color and flavor.

Turnips: Like their cousins the radishes, turnips come in various shapes and sizes. Purple Topped White Globe is the most common and has a clean, peppery bite; Japanese white turnips (Hakurei) are mild and sweet even when raw; Golden Ball turnips have sweet, golden flesh and skin; Scarlet Queen has reddish skin but the typical white flesh; Gilfeather has greenish-white skin and creamy skin. If you spot something labeled a black turnip, it's actually a black radish.

STORING

Because nature designed roots to be supply tanks for the stems and greens—and eventually the seeds that sprout from their tops—you should cut off the greens as soon as you get them home, or they'll draw moisture from the root (for information on how to cook such greens, see pages 110–112). Store roots (except jicama) loosely wrapped in a plastic bag in the vegetable bin of the refrigerator. Winter roots can keep up to three weeks, but the young ones of spring and early summer should be eaten within three days for the best flavor and texture. Jicama is best stored in a cool, dark, dry place, similar to potatoes, and not in the refrigerator.

PREPPING

Much of the characteristic flavor of a beet, carrot, or radish resides in its skin, as does a concentration of nutrients. But so do pesticides, so buy organic and scrub the vegetables with a soft-bristled brush, rather than peeling, before serving. Other roots, such as celeriac, parsnips, salsify, and rutabaga, must be peeled before cooking—not only are the peels bitter, but they tend to be knobby and gnarly, and to hold dirt and grit. Celeriac in particular has a gnarled surface, and requires a generous hand with the peeler or paring knife. Beets, too, need peeling; but if you do so prior to cooking, much of the vegetable's flavor and color will leach out, so hold off until after, when the skins will slip off with a gentle rub (wear gloves to prevent your hands from staining). Jicama should also be peeled; its tough skin undermines the refreshing texture of its crisp white flesh.

COOKING

Cooking a root not only softens its dense, firm flesh but also enhances its inherent sweetness by breaking down cell walls and releasing stored sugars so they become available to our taste buds. Most roots benefit from roasting, which caramelizes these natural sugars, adding depth to the flavor. Sautéing, which browns the surface, can do the same. Steaming, meanwhile, imparts a cleaner essence than boiling, which can wash away the roots' subtler aromas and earthy notes. Like carrots, radishes, and celery root, young beets and turnips can be served raw—grate on the large holes of a box grater (or with the grating disc of your food processor), slice translucent-thin with a sharp knife or mandoline, or cut into matchsticks, and add to salads or slaws. Jicama is typically served raw—in fruit or vegetable salads—though it can also be roasted. In Mexico, it is sometimes also added to soups, where it has the character of a mild turnip.

HOW TO ROAST
(For all roots except beets)
Trim and peel vegetables; leave whole or cut into uniform pieces. On a rimmed baking sheet, drizzle with olive oil, season with salt and pepper, and sprinkle with chopped fresh herbs such as thyme or rosemary. Spread evenly and roast at 450°F, tossing, until tender and caramelized, 20 to 30 minutes depending on size of pieces. Drizzle with oil, and top with herbs and/or grated sharp cheese.

(For whole beets)
Place whole, unpeeled beets on a piece of foil lined with parchment. Drizzle with olive oil, and season with salt and pepper. Wrap to enclose beets, and place on a rimmed baking sheet. Roast at 450°F until knife-tender, 45 to 60 minutes. Remove from oven; let cool, then rub off skins with paper towels. Leave whole or cut into wedges, drizzle with oil and lemon juice, and sprinkle with goat cheese and/or herbs.

HOW TO STEAM
(For all roots except jicama)
Trim and peel vegetables; leave whole or cut into uniform pieces. Place in a steamer basket (or colander) set in a pot with 1 inch water; bring to a boil. Cover and steam until tender, 10 to 20 minutes depending on size of pieces. Toss with olive oil, apple cider vinegar, salt, and pepper.

HOW TO GLAZE
(For all roots except jicama)
Trim and peel vegetables; leave whole or cut into 1-inch pieces. Heat safflower oil in a large skillet over medium-high until shimmering. Add vegetables; cook, stirring occasionally, until golden brown, 5 to 8 minutes for pieces; 10 to 12 minutes for whole. Add enough broth to cover, season with salt, and cover. Simmer until vegetables are knife-tender, 8 to 10 minutes for pieces; 15 minutes or more for whole vegetables, depending on size. Remove lid and boil until liquid has reduced to a syrupy glaze, stirring occasionally, 8 to 10 minutes more. Season with salt and pepper. Remove from heat, and toss with butter or olive oil to coat.

HOW TO MASH OR PUREE
(For all roots except jicama)
Trim, peel, and chop vegetables evenly. Bring a pot of water to a boil, then add salt and veg-

etables. Return to a boil, then reduce heat and simmer until very soft, 10 to 15 minutes. Drain and return vegetables to pot, and cook over low heat, stirring, to dry, 1 to 2 minutes. For coarse mashes, mash with a potato masher or wooden spoon with enough warm milk, cream, or broth (or a combination) to achieve desired consistency, along with butter and salt and pepper to taste; or pass through a food mill (for a slightly smoother mash). For velvety purees, puree in a blender with liquid and seasonings.

HOW TO USE RAW
(For all roots except rutabaga and salsify)
Trim and peel vegetables. Shave as thin as possible on a mandoline, grate on the large holes of a box grater, or cut into matchsticks with a sharp knife. Carrots and parsnips can also be peeled into strips using a vegetable peeler. Toss with olive oil, vinegar or citrus juice, and salt and pepper, and top with chopped fresh herbs such as basil, mint, or parsley. Add chopped toasted nuts, such as almonds or walnuts, or crumble in a fresh cheese, such as feta or goat.

FLAVOR PAIRINGS

Go with it or against it? That's the cook's dilemma. You can play up a root's inherent sweetness with sugary ingredients like maple syrup, honey, and brown sugar, or counteract it with acidic vinegar and lemon juice, sharp mustard, tart goat cheese and tangy yogurt, or bitter arugula or watercress. Most roots pair nicely with nuts and nut oils, which bring out their earthy flavors. Herbs add wonderful notes

of freshness. Mild-flavored turnips taste similar to potatoes, especially when cooked; pair them with bacon, garlic, thyme, or vinegar. Celeriac's flavor is likened to a cross between celery and parsley, making it well suited to sweeter companions like maple syrup and pears. Salsify is slightly sweet and is often described as tasting similar to asparagus or artichokes. Jicama is juicy and crunchy and tastes like a cross between an apple and a potato (hence its nickname, "Mexican potato"). And keep in mind: the flavors of roots generally complement one another, so don't be afraid to combine at a whim (cook beets separately and add them at last minute to prevent an entire dish from coloring). Potatoes, too, combine beautifully with roots, whether roasted, mashed, or fried.

BEETS: orange, rosemary, tarragon, mint, basil, yogurt, goat cheese

CARROTS: parsley, cilantro, dill, honey, garlic

CELERY ROOT: Dijon mustard, apples, allspice, cream, parsley

JICAMA: lime, orange, grapefruit, mango, avocado, cucumbers, chiles, cilantro

PARSNIPS: nutmeg, maple syrup, sage, pancetta

RADISHES: butter, chives, rye bread, parsley, feta, vinegar

RUTABAGA: apples, pears, honey, cream, ginger, nutmeg, cardamom

SALSIFY: butter, cream, wine, honey, shallots, prosciutto, Parmesan

TURNIPS: bacon, garlic, duck, maple syrup, vinegar, thyme

Roasted Beet and Potato Borscht

You can find dozens of variations on borscht, the Russian beet soup. Some (like this one) are served hot, others chilled, some pureed until smooth, others not—but all showcase the beauty of beets. This version calls for roasting peeled and chopped beets, rather than boiling, for a deeper, richer flavor; potatoes are added for more heft. Sour cream is the traditional topping, and helps to balance the sweetness of the beets.

SERVES 4

2 pounds red beets, scrubbed, peeled, and cut into medium dice

1 pound russet potatoes, peeled and cut into medium dice

2 shallots, coarsely chopped

3 to 5 sprigs thyme

2 tablespoons extra-virgin olive oil

Coarse salt and freshly ground pepper

5 cups low-sodium chicken broth or water

1 tablespoon red-wine vinegar

Sour cream, thinly sliced scallion greens, and chopped fresh flat-leaf parsley, for serving

1. Preheat oven to 400°F. In a roasting pan or on a rimmed baking sheet, toss together beets, potatoes, shallots, thyme, and oil; season with salt and pepper. Arrange in a single layer and roast until beets and potatoes are tender, about 45 minutes.

2. Discard thyme. Transfer vegetables to a pot, along with broth. Bring to a simmer over medium high and cook to heat through. With a potato masher or the back of a wooden spoon, mash some vegetables until soup is thick and chunky. Stir in vinegar and season with salt and pepper. Divide among bowls, top with sour cream, scallion greens, and parsley, and serve.

TIP
You can make the soup with water in place of chicken broth for a vegetarian option.

Sesame Carrot Slaw

Besides more classic versions, such as all-American carrot-and-raisin salad, carrot slaws are endlessly adaptable. You can toss in other shaved vegetables, including cabbage, fennel, beets, jicama, or asparagus. Rice vinegar, lime zest and juice, scallions, and toasted sesame seeds give this slaw Asian flavors.

SERVES 4

1 tablespoon sesame seeds

¾ pound carrots, peeled and shaved with a vegetable peeler

4 scallions, thinly sliced lengthwise

1 tablespoon rice vinegar

1 tablespoon safflower oil

½ teaspoon finely grated lime zest, plus 1 tablespoon fresh lime juice

Coarse salt and freshly ground pepper

1. Heat a small skillet over medium. Toast sesame seeds, shaking pan frequently, until golden and fragrant, 2 to 3 minutes. Transfer to a plate to cool.

2. Combine carrots, scallions, vinegar, oil, sesame seeds, and lime zest and juice in a bowl. Season with salt and pepper, and toss to combine.

Beet Salad with Ginger Dressing

Roasting really brings out the beet's sweeter side, mellows its flavor, and breaks down all those pent-up starches to create a silken texture. We love them as a versatile base for many different salads and sides. Here, beets and fresh ginger make a wonderful pairing, with balsamic vinegar adding sharp-sweet notes and pistachios lending crunch.

SERVES 4

6 small beets (about 2 pounds), scrubbed

2 tablespoons extra-virgin olive oil

1 tablespoon balsamic vinegar, preferably white

1 tablespoon finely grated peeled fresh ginger

   Coarse salt and freshly ground pepper

½ cup shelled pistachios, toasted and chopped

1. Preheat oven to 425°F. Wrap beets in parchment, then foil, and place on a rimmed baking sheet. Roast until knife-tender, about 45 minutes. When cool enough to handle, rub with a paper towel to remove skins. Cut into ¾-inch wedges.

2. In a large bowl, whisk together oil, vinegar, and ginger; season with salt and pepper. Toss beets in dressing, sprinkle with pistachios, and serve.

TIP Remember that beets of different sizes and colors will roast at different rates, but all are done when they are knife-tender and their skins rub off with relative ease. Cooked beets are best seasoned while they are still warm and better able to absorb flavors.

Beet Risotto with Beet Greens

Here's a risotto that makes excellent use of beet roots and their green tops. When it comes to cooking, beet greens, kale, collards, and other sturdy greens are basically interchangeable—they can all be sautéed, simmered in stews, or braised. (In fact, you could substitute beet greens in many of the recipes beginning on page 109.)

SERVES 6

1 pound small beets with greens attached, roots and greens separated, roots scrubbed, greens chopped and washed with water left clinging to leaves

2 tablespoons extra-virgin olive oil

1 garlic clove, minced

1 small onion, finely chopped

3 cups low-sodium chicken broth

1 cup Arborio rice

½ cup dry white wine

2 tablespoons unsalted butter

½ cup finely grated Parmigiano-Reggiano cheese

Coarse salt and freshly ground pepper

1. Preheat oven to 425°F. Wrap beets in parchment, then foil, and place on a rimmed baking sheet. Roast until knife-tender, about 45 minutes. When cool enough to handle, rub with a paper towel to remove skins. Cut into ½-inch dice.

2. Heat 1 tablespoon oil in a large skillet. Cook garlic, stirring frequently, until softened, about 1 minute. Add greens and cook, stirring occasionally, until just tender and wilted, 3 to 4 minutes. Remove from heat.

3. Meanwhile, heat remaining tablespoon oil in a pot over medium. Cook onion, stirring frequently, until golden brown and soft, about 10 minutes. Bring broth to a simmer in a saucepan; reduce heat and keep warm.

4. Stir rice into the pot with onion, and cook, stirring, 2 minutes. Stir in wine; cook, stirring, until reduced by half, about 3 minutes. Ladle ½ cup broth into pot; simmer, stirring, until almost all liquid is absorbed (the rice should be thinly veiled in liquid at all times during cooking). Add remaining broth, ½ cup at a time, stirring until almost all liquid is absorbed before adding more, until rice is still opaque in the center and suspended in liquid the consistency of heavy cream (you may not need to use all broth), about 25 minutes total.

5. Stir in beets, greens, butter, and cheese; season with salt and pepper. Serve immediately.

TIP
The key to a foolproof risotto is in the stirring: too fast and the risotto will be slightly gluey; too slow and it will be watery. Risotto will continue to thicken off the heat, so don't overcook it—take it off the stove while the rice is still opaque.

Spicy Carrot Soup

*Carrots take well to simmering in broth, along with basic aromatics,
to make a puréed soup that tastes, purely and simply, of the root itself.
Harissa paste gives this soup some nice heat.*

SERVES 4

1 tablespoon extra-virgin
olive oil

1 medium leek (white and
pale-green parts only),
halved lengthwise and sliced
crosswise ¼ inch thick,
rinsed well

1 bunch carrots (about 6),
peeled and sliced crosswise
¼ inch thick

2 teaspoons harissa

Coarse salt

3 cups low-sodium chicken
broth

Fresh flat-leaf parsley,
for serving

1. Heat oil in a large saucepan over medium. Cook leek until just soft, stirring occasionally, 4 to 5 minutes. Stir in carrots and harissa, and season with salt. Cook until carrots are just soft, stirring occasionally, 8 to 10 minutes. Add chicken broth, and bring to a simmer. Cook until vegetables are tender, 10 to 12 minutes more.

2. Purée half the soup in a blender until smooth (be careful not to fill the jar of the blender more than halfway). Stir into remaining soup. Serve immediately, topped with parsley.

Celery Root and Potato Rösti

With its mild flavor—somewhere between celery and parsley—celeriac is often used to round out the flavor of potato dishes, like rösti, a savory Swiss pancake.

SERVES 8

4 pounds Yukon Gold potatoes, peeled and shredded on the large holes of a box grater

1 medium celery root (about 1 pound), trimmed, peeled, and shredded

2 tablespoons salt

Freshly ground pepper

½ cup extra-virgin olive oil

Chives, snipped, for serving

Sour cream, for serving

1. Working in batches, wrap shredded vegetables in cheesecloth and squeeze out liquid. Transfer to a bowl, add salt, and season with pepper; toss to combine.

2. Preheat oven to 400°F. Heat 3 tablespoons oil in a 12-inch ovenproof nonstick skillet over medium low. Spread potato mixture evenly in skillet; press gently to flatten with a spatula. Cook for 10 minutes. Run spatula around edge to loosen; spoon 2 tablespoons oil around edge. Cook until underside is golden and begins to crisp, 10 to 15 minutes more. Run spatula around edge to loosen; invert onto a plate.

3. Add remaining 3 tablespoons oil to skillet. Return rösti to skillet, golden side up; press gently. Cook, shaking occasionally, until underside is golden, about 20 minutes. Transfer skillet to oven. Bake until cooked through, 10 to 15 minutes. Serve with chives and sour cream.

Roasted Carrots and Quinoa with Miso Dressing

This vegetarian main course is an excellent study in building a salad with substance. Roasted carrots and onion provide sink-your-teeth-into-something satisfaction along with caramelized flavor, wilted spinach offers color contrast, and nutty, chewy quinoa adds protein.

SERVES 4

1 pound carrots, peeled and cut into 1-inch pieces

1 small red onion, cut into ½-inch wedges

1 tablespoon fresh thyme leaves

3 tablespoons extra-virgin olive oil

Coarse salt and freshly ground pepper

1 cup quinoa, preferably red, rinsed

1¼ cups water

3 cups baby spinach

1 tablespoon white (shiro) miso

1 tablespoon fresh lemon juice

1. Preheat oven to 400°F. Toss together carrots, onion, thyme, and 2 tablespoons oil on a rimmed baking sheet. Season with salt and pepper, and spread in a single layer. Roast until tender, tossing halfway through, about 40 minutes.

2. Bring quinoa and the water to a boil in a small saucepan. Cover; reduce heat and simmer until tender, about 15 minutes. Remove from heat. Add spinach, cover, and let stand 5 minutes.

3. Transfer to a large bowl; top with carrot mixture. In a small bowl, whisk together miso, lemon juice, and remaining tablespoon oil. Drizzle over salad, toss to combine, and serve.

TIP
Be sure to use white (shiro) miso in the dressing; it's sweeter, milder tasting, and less salty than other types.

Jicama-Citrus Salad

*Sliced paper thin, jicama retains its crisp quality as ribbons that mingle
with the other elements of this fruit-filled salad. Its mellow flavor is also an excellent
match for tart-sweet citrus, as well as Granny Smith apples.*

SERVES 4

1 red grapefruit

1 navel orange

3 tablespoons fresh lime juice, plus wedges for serving

1½ tablespoons finely chopped fresh cilantro leaves, plus sprigs for garnish

¼ teaspoon red-pepper flakes

¼ teaspoon coarse salt

1 small jicama, peeled and thinly sliced into half-moons

1 Granny Smith apple, cored and thinly sliced into half-moons

1. Remove peel and pith from grapefruit and oranges. Working over a large bowl, carefully carve out sections of grapefruit and orange from membranes using a paring knife, letting sections fall into bowl and reserving membranes. Transfer juices to a small nonreactive bowl; squeeze juice from membranes into bowl. Discard membranes.

2. Add lime juice, chopped cilantro, red-pepper flakes, and salt to the small bowl with the juices; stir to combine. Add jicama and apple to the large bowl with the fruit. Pour juice mixture over fruit mixture. Gently toss to coat. Let salad stand for 10 minutes before serving with lime wedges and garnished with cilantro sprigs.

Rainbow Carrots and Chard

Taste the rainbow: Carrots come in an array of beautiful colors. For this striking side dish, we blanched carrots in a variety of hues just until tender and bright, then tossed them with a lemon vinaigrette and the color-coordinated stems of rainbow chard.

SERVES 4

1 pound small carrots, trimmed and scrubbed

Coarse salt and freshly ground pepper

1 bunch rainbow Swiss chard, stems trimmed (leaves reserved for another use)

2 tablespoons fresh lemon juice, plus ½ lemon, thinly sliced into rounds

1 teaspoon sugar

¼ cup extra-virgin olive oil

Fresh mint leaves, for serving

1. Prepare a large ice-water bath. Cook carrots in a pot of generously salted boiling water until crisp-tender, about 7 minutes. Transfer to ice bath until cool, then remove with a spider and pat dry.

2. Cook chard stems in boiling water until crisp-tender, about 4 minutes. Transfer to ice bath, drain, and pat dry.

3. Whisk together lemon juice and sugar in a small bowl; season with salt and pepper. Add oil in a slow, steady stream, whisking until combined.

4. Combine carrots, chard, and lemon rounds in a large bowl. Toss with some dressing (refrigerate the rest in an airtight container), then transfer to a platter. Top with mint and serve.

Lacquered Short Ribs with Celery Root Purée

Creamy, ultra-rich celery root purée makes a fine partner for Asian-style braised short ribs. (For the best flavor, braise the ribs a day before serving.) We topped the duo with a tart salad of thinly sliced Asian pear, celery, scallions, and jalapeño, all tossed with equal parts olive oil and lime juice and seasoned with salt and pepper.

SERVES 8

FOR THE RIBS

- 3 tablespoons safflower oil
- 5 pounds short ribs
- Coarse salt and freshly ground pepper
- 9 garlic cloves, chopped
- 4 shallots, chopped
- 1 large onion, chopped
- 2 dried red chiles, seeded and chopped
- 2 scallions, chopped
- 1 Asian pear, chopped
- 5 whole star anise
- 1 cup low-sodium soy sauce
- 2 cups Gewürztraminer or Riesling wine
- 1⅓ cups champagne vinegar
- ½ cup honey
- 3 ounces fresh ginger, sliced

FOR THE PURÉE

- 2 medium celery roots, peeled and cut into 1-inch cubes
- 6 cups heavy cream
- Coarse salt and freshly ground pepper

1. Make ribs: Preheat oven to 325°F. Heat oil in a large Dutch oven over medium high. Season ribs with salt and pepper, and cook in batches until golden brown, 3 to 4 minutes per side. Transfer to a plate (leave drippings in pot).

2. Reduce heat to medium. Add garlic, shallots, onion, and chiles, and cook, stirring frequently, until golden, about 10 minutes. Return meat to pot and add scallions, pear, star anise, soy sauce, wine, vinegar, honey, and ginger. Add enough water to cover by 1 inch (about 5 cups), and bring to a simmer. Cover and transfer to oven. Cook until ribs are fork-tender, about 3 hours. (Ribs in liquid can be cooled, covered, and refrigerated up to 2 days. Bring to room temperature, then proceed with step 4.)

3. Make purée: Bring celery root and cream to a boil in a saucepan. Reduce heat and simmer until celery root is tender, about 30 minutes. Drain celery root, reserving cream. Purée celery root with 2 cups of reserved cream in a blender until smooth. Season with salt and pepper.

4. Transfer ribs to a plate and strain sauce through a fine sieve. Skim fat from top, and discard. Return sauce to pot, and cook over medium until sauce just coats the back of a spoon, about 10 minutes. Add ribs to sauce, and cook, basting often, until ribs are hot and sauce coats meat, about 5 minutes. Serve ribs on top of celery root purée, and drizzle with sauce. Top with pear salad (see note, above).

Leek and Parsnip Soup

This elegant version of vichyssoise replaces half of the potatoes with parsnips.

SERVES 8

2 tablespoons unsalted butter

2¾ pounds leeks (white and pale-green parts only), rinsed well and cut into ¼-inch-thick half-moons

Coarse salt and freshly ground pepper

1 pound parsnips

1 pound Yukon Gold potatoes

3 cups chicken broth

2½ cups water

2 dried bay leaves

½ cup whole milk

½ cup crème fraîche

1 jar (2 ounces) whitefish caviar (optional)

1. Cut a round of parchment to fit inside a large pot. Melt butter in pot over medium. Add leeks and a pinch of salt; cover with parchment. Cook, lifting parchment to stir occasionally, until leeks are tender, 10 to 15 minutes.

2. Peel parsnips and potatoes; cut into ¼-inch-thick pieces. Add to pot with broth, the water, and bay leaves. Season with salt. Bring to a boil; reduce heat to medium low. Simmer gently, partly covered with lid, until parsnips are soft, about 20 minutes. Discard bay leaves. Let cool slightly. Working in batches, purée mixture in a blender (do not fill jar of blender more than halfway). Return to pot, and stir in milk. Reheat over medium (do not let boil).

3. Stir ¼ teaspoon pepper into crème fraîche. Divide soup among bowls, and top each with a dollop of peppered cream and ½ teaspoon caviar, if desired.

Salsify Gratin

When peeled or sliced, salsify will begin to turn brown, so you need to keep it in a bowl of acidulated (lemon) water until ready to cook. The root becomes wonderfully tender when boiled, then baked with golden breadcrumbs and Parmigiano-Reggiano on top.

SERVES 4 TO 6

¼ cup plus 1 teaspoon fresh lemon juice (from 2 lemons)

2 pounds salsify

Coarse salt and freshly ground pepper

1½ tablespoons unsalted butter

½ cup heavy cream

Pinch of freshly grated nutmeg

¼ cup fresh breadcrumbs, lightly toasted

¼ cup finely grated Parmigiano-Reggiano cheese

1. Preheat oven to 425°F, with rack in highest position. Fill a large bowl with cold water; add ¼ cup lemon juice. Trim salsify and peel, transferring to bowl as you work. Cut salsify into 2-inch lengths, and return to bowl. Drain.

2. Cover salsify with cold water by 2 inches in a saucepan; add ½ teaspoon salt. Bring to a boil. Reduce heat to medium high. Simmer just until tender, 10 to 15 minutes; drain.

3. Melt butter in a saucepan over medium. Stir in salsify; stir in cream and remaining teaspoon lemon juice. Bring to a bare simmer; remove from heat. Add nutmeg and season with salt and pepper. Pour mixture into an 8-inch square baking dish or 8-cup gratin dish. Sprinkle with breadcrumbs and cheese. Bake until golden brown, about 20 minutes.

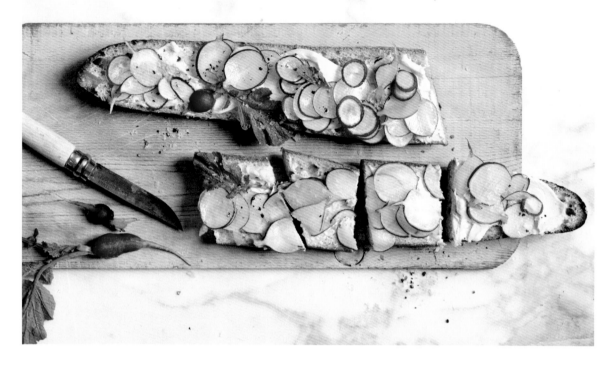

Radish Tartine

*With names like Pink Beauty, Cherry Belle, and Purple Plum, radishes are
the diminutive darlings of the root world. French Breakfast radishes,
in particular, are mild, sweet, and crunchy—just right for slicing paper-thin
and enjoying on a buttered baguette, as they do in France.*

SERVES 6

1 baguette

Unsalted butter, room
temperature

1 pound radishes, preferably
French Breakfast, thinly
sliced into rounds

Flaky sea salt,
such as Maldon

Preheat oven to 350°F. Split baguette horizontally and toast
on a baking sheet until lightly crisp, 8 to 10 minutes. Let
cool, then spread butter generously over each half. Top with
radishes, dividing evenly. Sprinkle with sea salt, and cut into
pieces to serve.

Roasted Radishes
with Capers and Anchovies

Radishes, members of the mustard family, have a spiciness that stands up to other assertive flavors, like the salty anchovies and briny capers paired with them here. Roasting tames all three, and a squeeze of lemon brightens the whole lot. This dish makes a nice appetizer to enjoy with drinks, or great accompaniment to chicken or pork.

SERVES 4

12 ounces radishes, halved or quartered if large

2 teaspoons capers, rinsed and chopped

6 anchovy fillets, finely chopped

1 garlic clove, minced

2 tablespoons extra-virgin olive oil

Coarse salt and freshly ground pepper

½ lemon, for serving

Preheat oven to 375°F, with rack in upper third. Toss together radishes, capers, anchovies, garlic, and oil on a rimmed baking sheet; season with salt and pepper. Spread in a single layer, and roast, stirring once, until radishes are shriveled and fragrant, 30 to 35 minutes. Serve warm, with lemon.

Moroccan Vegetable Soup

Unlike many soups and stews, where everything is simmered slowly over low heat until tender, this one takes just under a half hour to cook, start to finish. The result? Root vegetables that retain some texture. Carrots and rutabaga are shown here, but you can swap one or both for parsnips, turnips, or celery root.

SERVES 6

1 pound carrots, peeled and cut on the bias into 3-inch-long pieces

½ large rutabaga (about 1 pound), peeled and cut on the bias into 2-inch-long pieces

3 tablespoons extra-virgin olive oil

½ cup thinly sliced shallots (2 to 3 small)

Coarse salt

1 teaspoon ground cumin

2 tablespoons harissa

⅓ cup dry white wine

1 can (15.5 ounces) chickpeas, drained and rinsed

Pinch of saffron threads

1½ cups Israeli (pearl) couscous

Coarsely chopped fresh cilantro, for garnish (optional)

1. Bring a large pot of water to a boil. Add carrots and rutabaga, and simmer 2 minutes. Reserve 6 cups cooking water, then drain vegetables.

2. Heat oil in a large, wide, deep pot over medium high. Add shallots and 1 teaspoon salt, and cook, stirring occasionally, until shallots are softened and golden brown in places, about 5 minutes. Add cumin and harissa, and cook, stirring constantly, 1 minute. Add wine and simmer 30 seconds.

3. Add reserved vegetables, the chickpeas, reserved cooking water, and saffron to pot. Bring to a boil. Reduce heat and cover. Simmer until vegetables are crisp-tender, 8 to 10 minutes. Season with 2 teaspoons salt.

4. Meanwhile, bring a large pot of salted water to a boil, and cook couscous until al dente, about 7 minutes. Drain.

5. Divide couscous among six bowls. Ladle soup over couscous, and garnish with cilantro. (Soup and couscous can be refrigerated in separate containers up to two days; let cool completely before refrigerating. Gently reheat together in a covered pot over medium, stirring occasionally, and garnish with cilantro before serving.)

TIP
Harissa is a fiery North African paste that is used as a condiment as well as in cooking. Look for it at supermarkets, in specialty grocers, or online.

Rutabaga-Apple Mash

With its peppery taste, rutabaga pairs nicely with sweet apples or pears—either of which can be used in this recipe. And just as when roasted, the root becomes mashably tender after boiling, while the fruit softens to a sauce. Serve with lamb or crown roast.

SERVES 4

1 large rutabaga, peeled and cut into 1-inch pieces (about 5 cups)

1 sweet apple, such as Gala, or pear, such as Anjou, peeled, cored, and cut into 1-inch pieces

Coarse salt and freshly ground pepper

2 tablespoons unsalted butter, plus more for serving

1 cup heavy cream

Fresh thyme, for serving

1. Combine rutabaga and apple in a saucepan, and cover with water by 2 inches. Bring to a boil and add salt. Reduce heat and simmer until rutabaga is tender, 15 to 20 minutes. Drain; transfer to a bowl.

2. Meanwhile, heat butter and cream in another saucepan until butter is melted and mixture is hot (do not boil).

3. Add butter mixture to rutabaga mixture and mash with a potato masher or wooden spoon, just until pieces break down but mash is coarse. Season with salt and pepper, and serve topped with more butter and fresh thyme.

Turnip Salad with Bacon Vinaigrette

Baby turnips have none of the sharpness of mature ones, and their greens are also more tender—all the better for combining in a salad dressed with a warm vinaigrette.

SERVES 4

2 bunches baby turnips, trimmed, greens reserved, turnips cut into wedges

1 teaspoon extra-virgin olive oil

Coarse salt and freshly ground pepper

2 teaspoons sherry vinegar

2 teaspoons grainy mustard

4 cups baby spinach

2 slices bacon, thinly sliced crosswise

1 shallot, minced

2 tablespoons pecans, toasted and coarsely chopped

1. Preheat oven to 375°F. Toss turnip wedges with oil and ½ teaspoon salt on a rimmed baking sheet. Roast, tossing after 15 minutes, until golden brown and tender, about 35 minutes.

2. Whisk together vinegar, mustard, ¼ teaspoon salt, and ¼ teaspoon pepper in a small bowl.

3. Wash turnip greens well, and tear into 3-inch pieces. Toss greens with spinach.

4. About 5 minutes before turnips are finished roasting, heat a small high-sided skillet over medium high. Add bacon and cook, stirring, until crisp, 4 to 5 minutes. Add shallot and cook until soft, 1 to 2 minutes. Remove from heat, and stir in vinegar mixture. Fold warm bacon vinaigrette into greens. Transfer to a platter; top with roasted turnips and pecans.

Brisket with Parsnips and Carrots

Root vegetables are essential to this dish's appeal: Just think what you would be missing without all those carrots or parsnips on your plate. A few hours in a low oven not only makes inexpensive cuts like brisket falling-apart tender, it also turns dense, starchy roots into soft, deeply flavorful receptacles for the delicious pan juices.

SERVES 8

1 first-cut of beef brisket (5 pounds)

Coarse salt and freshly ground pepper

3 tablespoons extra-virgin olive oil, plus more if needed

1 large onion, halved and thinly sliced

2 garlic cloves, minced, plus 1 head, halved horizontally

2 tablespoons tomato paste

1½ cups dry red wine, such as Pinot Noir

4½ cups low-sodium chicken broth

2 fresh or dried bay leaves

1 pound parsnips, peeled and halved

20 small carrots (about 8 ounces), peeled and stem ends trimmed to ½ inch

10 ounces red pearl onions, peeled (about 2½ cups)

1 tablespoon balsamic vinegar

1. Preheat oven to 325°F. Season both sides of brisket with salt and pepper. Heat a large Dutch oven or roasting pan over medium high. Add 3 tablespoons oil to pan, swirl to coat, and heat until hot but not smoking. Add brisket; sear until browned on all sides, 4 to 5 minutes per side. Transfer to a platter.

2. Reduce heat to medium. Add onion and minced garlic to pan; cook, stirring frequently, until soft, about 4 minutes. (Add more oil to pan if needed.) Stir in tomato paste, and cook, stirring, 1 minute. Stir in wine, and cook, scraping any browned bits from bottom of pan, until almost evaporated.

3. Add chicken broth and bay leaves, and bring to a boil. Add brisket, then cover and roast 2 hours. Flip meat over. Add halved head of garlic. Cover and roast 30 minutes more.

4. Arrange parsnips, carrots, and pearl onions around brisket; cover and roast until beef and vegetables are tender, about 1 hour. Transfer vegetables and garlic to a platter and meat to a cutting board, reserving pan sauce. Tent meat with foil, and let rest.

5. Let sauce stand in pan for 15 minutes, then skim fat from top. Cook over medium heat until sauce is reduced by slightly more than half, about 20 minutes. (You should have about 2 cups.) Remove bay leaves, and stir in vinegar.

6. Thinly slice brisket against the grain. Arrange slices on a platter with the vegetables. Season with pepper, and drizzle with some sauce. Serve immediately with remaining sauce.

TIP
A whole brisket typically weights 8 to 12 pounds and is sold cut into two pieces—the first, or flat, cut; and the second, or point, cut. Select a first cut that's evenly thick with a cap of fat on one side. For an extra-moist brisket, don't trim the fat.

Roasted Rutabaga and Brussels Sprouts

As with most root vegetables, roasting highlights rutabaga's richness and turns it wonderfully sweet. Here, the root is roasted alongside nutty brussels sprouts with maple syrup and lemon juice, which combine to form a delectable glaze.

SERVES 4 TO 6

½ cup pure maple syrup

2½ tablespoons extra-virgin olive oil

1 tablespoon fresh lemon juice

Coarse salt and freshly ground pepper

2 pounds rutabaga, peeled and cut into 1½-inch pieces

¾ pound brussels sprouts, trimmed and halved lengthwise

¼ cup hazelnuts, toasted and chopped

1. Preheat oven to 400°F. Whisk together maple syrup, oil, lemon juice, and ¼ teaspoon salt. Add rutabaga and toss.

2. Transfer rutabaga and all but 2 tablespoons glaze to a rimmed baking sheet (leave remaining glaze in bowl). Spread rutabaga in a single layer, sprinkle with ¼ teaspoon salt, and roast for 35 minutes, tossing halfway through.

3. Raise oven temperature to 450°F. Add brussels sprouts and ¼ teaspoon salt to remaining glaze in bowl and toss. Toss sprouts with rutabaga on sheet, and spread in a single layer. Roast vegetables, tossing every 5 minutes, until glaze is very thick and vegetables are deep golden brown, about 20 minutes. Season with pepper, and sprinkle with hazelnuts.

Carrot Fries

For the same reason sweet potatoes make such good fries, so do carrots: They're naturally sweet, and the sugars help the fries turn golden brown in the oven. First cut the carrots into sticks (producing maximum surface area for crisping); then toss them with grated Parmesan cheese before baking, or with ground cayenne pepper or cumin.

SERVES 4

1 pound carrots, peeled and cut into ¼-inch-thick sticks

2 tablespoons extra-virgin olive oil

½ cup finely grated Parmigiano-Reggiano cheese

Coarse salt and freshly ground pepper

Preheat oven to 425°F. Toss together carrots, oil, and cheese in a large bowl until evenly coated; season with salt and pepper. Arrange in a single layer on two rimmed baking sheets. Bake, rotating sheets and tossing carrots halfway through, until golden brown and crisp, 20 to 25 minutes. Serve immediately.

Spiced Parsnip Cupcakes with Cream Cheese Frosting

Carrots aren't the only root vegetable for baking into desserts. Naturally sweet parsnips work exceptionally well in cakes, too—and, along with brown sugar and safflower oil, help keep them moist. Warm, fragrant cardamom flavors these cupcakes, which are finished with swirls of cream cheese frosting, carrot cake's familiar counterpart.

MAKES 12

1 cup all-purpose flour

1 teaspoon ground cardamom

1½ teaspoons baking powder

¼ teaspoon fine salt

¾ cup packed light-brown sugar

2 large eggs

⅔ cup safflower oil

1 tablespoon pure vanilla extract

2 cups coarsely grated parsnip

8 ounces cream cheese, room temperature

4 tablespoons unsalted butter, room temperature

½ cup confectioners' sugar

1. Preheat oven to 350°F. Line 12 standard muffin cups with paper liners. In a large bowl, whisk together flour, cardamom, baking powder, and salt. In another bowl, whisk together brown sugar, eggs, oil, 2 teaspoons vanilla, and the grated parsnip. Stir in flour mixture until combined.

2. Divide batter evenly among lined cups. Bake until a toothpick inserted in center of a cupcake comes out with only a few moist crumbs attached, 18 to 20 minutes. Let cool completely in pan on a wire rack.

3. In a large bowl, beat cream cheese, butter, confectioners' sugar, and remaining teaspoon vanilla until combined. Spread frosting onto cooled cupcakes. (Frosted cupcakes can be refrigerated in an airtight container up to 2 days.)

TUBERS

Potatoes are the most popular vegetable in America—we eat, on average, more than 50 pounds per person each year. But they have a secret: Potatoes are clones. So, for that matter, are sweet potatoes and yams (not to mention Jerusalem artichokes, ginger, and manioc)—each is capable of sprouting its own roots, stems, and leaves, and becoming a fully formed plant, genetically identical to its parent. Of course, cloning isn't controversial if you're a tuber or rhizome, the name for such plant parts. Nor is it of much concern to the cook, who cares more about what a vegetable can do in the kitchen than what it gets up to underground.

And in the kitchen, tubers are stars. Mild in flavor, they are versatile players that can round out any meal, from everyday scrambled eggs, to healthful vegetable soups, to the finest filet mignons. Their high proportion of natural starches means these vegetables are capable of remarkable textural feats, becoming crisp or buttery, creamy, fluffy, crunchy, even sticky, depending on how they're cooked. And cooked they should be, for unlike other roots, which consist of simpler carbohydrates, tubers require heat for their nutrients to be digestible.

Perhaps the best thing about tubers is that they're so easygoing. Because, as popular as they are, they're more than happy to share the limelight—and make anything they're served with a little (even a lot) easier to love.

JERUSALEM
ARTICHOKES
—
POTATOES
—
SWEET
POTATOES

THE BASICS

SEASONALITY

Stored properly, most tubers keep so well that grocery stores and even greenmarkets happily stock them year-round. In truth, however, these vegetables have definite seasons—and unless you can replicate ideal storage conditions at home, old potatoes will soon turn spongy and sprout eyes in your kitchen. Sweet potatoes and yams, which come from warm, humid climates, ripen in fall and winter (thus their annual appearance on Thanksgiving tables). Look for them throughout the colder months. Fresh new potatoes are available only in early summer, and they are most delicious eaten within days of harvesting. Mature boiling and russet potatoes are best in late summer and throughout the fall and early winter. Jerusalem artichokes—which are neither artichokes nor from Jerusalem—are available in early fall. (These flowering plants are in the sunflower family and are indigenous to North America, where they are also known as sunchokes. Turns out they were popular in Italy, where the word for "sunflower," *girasole,* morphed over time into *Jerusalem,* and they were thought to taste like artichokes—hence their more common name.)

BUYING

When shopping, look for firm, hard tubers and rhizomes, without soft or spongy spots, or patches of dark or wrinkled skin. New potatoes should be rock-hard, and they will have translucent, "feathered" skin that looks as if it is peeling off. Whatever their age, potatoes must be free of green patches, which indicate the presence of a potentially toxic substance generated by exposure to light. And avoid any potatoes starting to sprout eyes.

With sweet potatoes, opt for plump ones of average size, as the spindly or oversize ones may be fibrous. And don't fret over the difference between sweet potatoes and yams. True yams are tropical tubers that may grow as big as 100 pounds; they seldom appear in American markets. But we've called certain orange-fleshed sweet potatoes "yams" since a 1930s marketing campaign kicked off the practice, and there's no harm in the misnomer.

As for which potato variety to select, it depends on how you plan to use them. So-called boiling potatoes have waxy, firm flesh that is great for potato salads and gratins. Baking or russet potatoes have skin that looks like a dusty rock and a higher starch content that makes them fluff up when cooked—ideal for baking, frying, and mashing. With sweet potatoes, let color be your guide. The orange-fleshed ones are sweetest and softest. White-fleshed ones are firmer and have a nutty flavor. Red ones fall somewhere in between.

NOTABLE VARIETIES

Potatoes: Even the most "exotic" potatoes have been around for a long, long time—thousands of years, in fact. The unusual varieties that have caught on fastest with growers and cooks are purple potatoes, because their color is so striking, and fingerlings, because they taste so good.

Purple Peruvian potatoes are medium in size and deeply purple throughout; others include Daku Round, a purple potato with slashes of red and a moist, white flesh; Scamp, with marbled purple and yellow flesh; All Blue, which is truly blue inside and out, with a dry texture; Purple Majesty, an oblong potato with very dark purple skin and purple moist, firm flesh; and Cherries Jubilee, a small potato whose sweet and crumbly flesh is a pretty, mottled magenta when cooked.

Most fingerlings, so named for their long, thin shape, have a warm yellow or ivory-colored flesh; they are firm when sliced, like waxy new potatoes, but they also have some of the dry, floury qualities of Idaho baking potatoes. The best fingerlings, such as Ruby Crescent and Russian Banana, have so much flavor—sweet, nutty, earthy, even buttery—a quality many people mistakenly ascribe to any yellow-fleshed potato. Red Mandel is a waxy fingerling with a sweet, flowery taste; Ruby Crescent (pinkest when freshly picked) has yellow flesh and a buttery flavor, both sweet and sharp; Red Thumb (a favorite among chefs) has a bright red skin and pink flesh; French Fingerling is an heirloom variety with smooth, pink skin and yellow flesh.

Other varieties worth looking for are Katahdin, another "all-purpose" potato similar to Yukon Gold; the medium-starch, pleasantly earthy-tasting Early Ohio; Gloria, a Dutch variety with firm, bright-yellow flesh; Caribe, with white, creamy, delicately flavored flesh; Rosa Lund, a medium-starch potato that's ivory inside, with a hearty flavor; Kennebec, a large potato with tan skin and white flesh that holds together when boiled; Red Gold, a medium-size, red-skinned potato with golden, sweet, nutty flesh; and Peanut, an old Scandinavian variety with a russet skin and a taste reminiscent of chestnuts.

Sweet potatoes: With more than four hundred varieties grown around the world, it's worth going beyond the familiar Jewels, with their copper skin and deep-orange flesh, and Garnets, named for the color of their skin, with their moist, pumpkin-like flesh. Another common variety, Beauregard, has dusky golden skin and paler flesh that's firmer than the others. Look for these heirloom and hybrids: Hannahs have tan skin and a creamy interior that is lightly sweet and dry when cooked; Creamsicle has cream-colored skin and a bright orange flesh; Covington is a pinkish-skinned sweet potato with moist, orange flesh; Nuggets have reddish skin and a pale orange flesh that's dense and holds its shape when cooked; O'Henry, whose pale copper skin and white flesh can be mistaken for a regular potato, is sweet and creamy when cooked; Japanese sweet potatoes have a distinctive ruby-red skin with flesh that is creamy white and slightly dry; Murasakis, related to the Japanese variety, have reddish-purple skin and dry, creamy white flesh; Purple Sweet Potatoes have firm, lightly sweet flesh that's also slightly tart; and Stokes, purple inside and out, are an earthy-tasting favorite among chefs.

STORING

New potatoes and Jerusalem artichokes should be refrigerated, but all other tubers are best stored elsewhere, as the refrigerator is too damp and cold an environment for them. Instead, keep them in a dark, cool place (their ideal temperature is 45°F) that is free of moisture. Kitchen wisdom has it that leaving dirt on their skin makes potatoes last longer, perhaps because it both shades and dries the vegetables—though doing so makes for more prep work when it comes time to cook them.

PREPPING

The skins of potatoes, sweet potatoes, and Jerusalem artichokes contain flavor and nutrients, so if your recipe doesn't call for peeling, a quick scrub may be all the prep work these ingredients need. If you do plan to peel or cut them first, keep a bowl of water handy and drop the pieces in as you work, since they'll turn gray if their cut surfaces are exposed to air. Don't worry too much about gray spots in the flesh; they're merely bruises caused by handling, and don't indicate spoilage. But be sure to cut away eyes and any hint of green.

COOKING

Baking and roasting are great options for most potatoes, as the oven's dry heat plays up the vegetables' firm, chalky consistency. And potatoes like it hot in there: 400°F or higher will crisp the outside while the insides soften.

Sweet potatoes also take well to these cooking methods, as they convert their natural starches to sugars. The longer the process, the more sweetness will result: Whole sweet potatoes can spend an hour or more in the oven. And a slow roast makes Jerusalem artichokes soft and almost translucent, with a flavor like their namesake artichokes, but they can also be prepared like potatoes and even enjoyed raw.

HOW TO ROAST
Scrub potatoes and sweet potatoes (or peel, if desired); peel Jerusalem artichokes. Cut into wedges or 1-inch pieces (or leave small potatoes whole or cut into halves). Place on a rimmed baking sheet, drizzle with olive oil, season with salt and pepper and chopped fresh herbs; toss to combine. Spread evenly and roast at 425°F (375°F for Jerusalem artichokes), tossing, until tender, 45 minutes, depending on size.

Note: Parboiling potatoes before roasting creates a light and fluffy inside, with a golden exterior (much like a french fry). Scrub potatoes and peel, if desired; cut into uniform pieces (¾ to 2 inches), or leave small ones whole or halve them. Place in a pot with enough water to cover. Bring to a boil, then season with salt. Reduce heat and simmer just until potatoes are tender, 10 to 15 minutes. Drain thoroughly and immediately toss with olive oil, salt, and pepper. Roast at 450°F, flipping once, until golden and crisp, about 35 minutes, depending on size.

HOW TO BAKE
Scrub vegetables and prick all over with a fork. Bake on a baking sheet at 400°F (350°F for

Jerusalem artichokes) until tender, 45 to 60 minutes. Split open and top with butter, sour cream or yogurt, chopped bacon, sautéed greens, sliced avocado, caramelized onions, kimchi, maple syrup (you name it!). Or, set out a variety of toppings for a potato "bar."

HOW TO STEAM

Peel vegetables and cut into 2-inch pieces (halve or quarter smaller potatoes). Place in a steamer basket set in a pot filled with 1 inch of water. Bring to a boil, cover, and steam until tender, 10 to 20 minutes, depending on size. Toss with butter or olive oil, salt and pepper, and chopped fresh parsley or thyme.

HOW TO BOIL

Peel vegetables and cut into 2-inch pieces (leave smaller potatoes whole, or cut into halves or quarters). Bring to a boil in a pot with 2 inches water to cover, then add salt. Boil vegetables until knife-tender, 10 to 20 minutes, depending on size. Drain; while still warm, toss with butter or olive oil and chopped fresh herbs; or mash and season as desired.

HOW TO DEEP-FRY

(For potatoes, sweet potatoes)
Peel vegetables and cut lengthwise into matchsticks, placing in a bowl of cold water to cover as you work. Drain and pat dry thoroughly. Heat 3 to 4 inches safflower oil in a heavy-bottomed pot over medium until it reaches 375°F on a deep-fry thermometer. Working in batches, carefully add potatoes and cook, turning occasionally, just until tender, 5 to 6 minutes. (They will not take on color at this point.) Transfer to paper towels to drain. Return oil to 375°F, and

fry again until golden, 1 to 2 minutes. Drain again, sprinkle with salt, and serve.

HOW TO GRILL

(For potatoes, sweet potatoes)
Scrub small potatoes, or peel larger ones and cut into quarters. Place in a pot with enough water to cover. Bring to a boil, then season with salt. Reduce heat and simmer just until potatoes are tender, 10 to 15 minutes. Drain; let cool slightly. Toss with olive oil. Grill potatoes directly on grates, turning once, until lightly charred and crisp, 1 to 2 minutes per side. Toss with more olive oil and chopped fresh herbs, such as thyme, rosemary, or parsley. Season with salt.

FLAVOR PAIRINGS

Versatile potatoes adore every kind of dairy; they've never met a piece of meat, poultry, or fish they didn't like; and they get along with all kinds of herbs and other vegetables. And sweet potatoes are right at home in creamy custards, cheesecakes, and pies. Both potatoes and sweet potatoes have made their way into most of the world's cuisines—you'll find them in curries, tagines, and tacos, not to mention on tables across Europe.

JERUSALEM ARTICHOKES: butter, cream, cheese, bacon, thyme, parsley, sage

POTATOES: butter, cream, cheese, bacon, eggs, chicken, beef, pork, lamb, leeks, onions, rosemary, thyme, parsley

SWEET POTATOES: bacon, lime, orange, apples, ginger, pecans, thyme, parsley, sage, cilantro

Potato Salad, Three Ways

If anything demonstrates the versatility of potatoes, it's potato salad, which starts by boiling the tubers. From there, the formula is endlessly adaptable. Vary the theme with different spuds—we chose russets in the classic all-American salad with mayonnaise and hard-cooked eggs; small red ("new") potatoes in a warm vinegar-and-mustard French version; and fingerlings for a salad with bacon, watercress, and celery leaves.

SERVES 4

2 **pounds russet, small red, or fingerling potatoes**

1 **tablespoon coarse salt**

In a large saucepan, cover potatoes with cold water by 2 inches. Bring to a boil over high; add salt. Reduce heat and simmer until potatoes are knife-tender, about 25 minutes for russets, 15 for small reds or fingerlings; drain. When cool enough to handle, rub off skins, if desired. Halve or cut as instructed, then transfer to a bowl. Toss with remaining ingredients while still warm, unless otherwise directed (see below).

1
CLASSIC

Peel and chop boiled russet potatoes into 1-inch pieces. Drizzle with 1 to 2 tablespoons apple cider vinegar; let cool. Combine 1 peeled and diced large hard-cooked egg, ½ cup mayonnaise, ½ teaspoon dry mustard, and ¼ teaspoon celery seeds in a large bowl; season with salt and pepper, and whisk to combine. Stir in potatoes, 1 diced celery stalk, ½ small diced onion, 5 diced cornichons, 1 chopped scallion, and 1 tablespoon chopped fresh flat-leaf parsley. Refrigerate at least 30 minutes or up to 1 day before serving, topped with sliced hard-cooked eggs and sprinkled with sweet paprika.

2
FRENCH

Whisk together ¼ cup extra-virgin olive oil, 3 tablespoons Dijon mustard, 2 tablespoons sherry vinegar, 1 minced small shallot, 3 tablespoons chopped fresh flat-leaf parsley, and 1 teaspoon chopped fresh thyme leaves; season with salt and pepper. Add halved (quartered if large) boiled new potatoes and ¼ small thinly sliced red onion, and toss to combine. Serve warm. (Salad can be refrigerated, covered, up to 1 day; serve at room temperature.)

3
WITH CELERY, CRESS, AND BACON

While potatoes are cooking, cook 4 strips thick-cut bacon over medium heat until fat is rendered and bacon is crisp, 10 to 12 minutes. Transfer to a paper-towel-lined plate to drain. Break into bite-size pieces. Transfer halved boiled fingerling potatoes to a large bowl; gently toss with ¼ cup plus 1 tablespoon extra-virgin olive oil and 2 tablespoons white-wine vinegar. Season with salt and pepper; fold in 1 cup inner celery leaves, 2 cups trimmed watercress, and the bacon. Serve warm or at room temperature.

Potato Gnocchi

The petite, feather-light, airy Italian dumplings known as gnocchi are made from mashed potatoes, with flour added to balance the moisture content and just enough egg to bind the mixture. We like to top gnocchi with a simple tomato sauce, but tossing them with browned butter and sage is also traditional, as is pairing them with a meaty ragù.

SERVES 4 TO 6

2 pounds Yukon Gold or russet potatoes

2 tablespoons coarse salt

2 cups all-purpose flour, plus more for dusting

2 large eggs

¼ teaspoon freshly ground pepper

Tomato Sauce (recipe follows)

Finely grated Parmigiano-Reggiano cheese, for serving

Fresh basil, for serving

1. In a large saucepan, cover potatoes with cold water by 2 inches. Bring to a boil over high; add 1 tablespoon salt. Reduce heat and simmer until potatoes are knife-tender, about 25 minutes; drain. When cool enough to handle, rub off skins, then pass flesh through a potato ricer or food mill. Sprinkle with flour; then add eggs, 1 tablespoon salt, and the pepper. Stir mixture with a fork to combine well.

2. Turn out dough onto a lightly floured surface; very gently knead until soft and smooth, about 3 minutes. Using a bench scraper or a sharp knife, divide dough into four to six pieces. Roll each piece into a long rope about ¾ inch thick. Cut ropes crosswise into 1-inch pieces.

3. Roll a cut side of each dumpling against the tines of a fork with your thumb (each piece will have ridges on one side and an indentation on the other). Place on a lightly floured baking sheet as you work. (At this point, gnocchi can be refrigerated on baking sheet up to several hours.)

4. Working in batches, cook gnocchi in a large pot of salted boiling water until they float to the top, 2 to 3 minutes. Use a slotted spoon to transfer to a colander to drain. To serve, toss gnocchi with tomato sauce, and top with cheese and basil.

Tomato Sauce

MAKES 4 CUPS

1 tablespoon extra-virgin olive oil

1 large garlic clove, finely chopped

Pinch of red-pepper flakes

1 can (28 ounces) whole peeled tomatoes, chopped

Coarse salt and freshly ground black pepper

Heat oil, garlic, and red-pepper flakes in a pot over medium, stirring frequently, just until fragrant and sizzling, about 2 minutes. Add tomatoes and season with salt and black pepper. Bring to a boil over high heat, then reduce to a rapid simmer and cook, stirring occasionally and mashing tomatoes, until thickened, about 15 minutes. Sauce can be cooled and refrigerated in an airtight container up to 1 week; reheat over low before serving.

Mrs. Kostyra's Mashed Potatoes

Thanks to all the different varieties of the humble tuber, you can have mashed potatoes any way you like—fluffy but grainy (russets), smooth and creamier (Yukon Gold and long white), chunky with skins for added texture (new potatoes). This creamy, smooth, ultra-rich recipe came from Martha's mother, Mrs. Kostyra.

SERVES 8

3½ pounds white or Yukon Gold potatoes

Coarse salt and freshly ground pepper

8 ounces cream cheese, room temperature

½ cup (1 stick) unsalted butter, room temperature

¼ cup whole milk, warmed

½ cup heavy cream, warmed

1. In a large saucepan, cover potatoes with cold water by 2 inches. Bring to a boil over high; add 1 tablespoon salt. Reduce heat and simmer until potatoes are knife-tender, about 25 minutes; drain. When cool enough to handle, rub off skins and cut potatoes into large pieces.

2. With an electric mixer on medium speed, beat potatoes, cream cheese, butter, milk, and ¼ cup cream until smooth. Season with salt and pepper and beat to combine.

3. Return potato mixture to pan and heat over medium. Stir in remaining ¼ cup cream and cook, stirring, until heated through. Serve immediately, or keep warm in a covered bowl over a pan of simmering water up to 2 hours.

Salt-Baked Potatoes, Shallots, and Chestnuts

Fingerlings have a meaty flavor that mates well with the chestnuts in this holiday (or any cool-weather day) side dish. Baking the potatoes, chestnuts, and shallots buried in salt traps their moisture as it seals in their flavors, without leaving them overly salty.

SERVES 8 TO 10

3 cups coarse salt, plus more for serving

3 pounds small fingerling potatoes, preferably red

1 cup peeled roasted chestnuts

1 pound shallots, peeled

5 large sprigs rosemary, cut into twenty 2-inch pieces, plus more for serving

⅓ cup extra-virgin olive oil, for drizzling

Freshly ground pepper

1. Preheat oven to 350°F. Pour 1 cup salt into a 2-quart baking dish. Nestle potatoes, chestnuts, and shallots upright in salt, with rosemary in between. Pour remaining 2 cups salt over top; shake dish gently to distribute evenly. Cover with foil, and bake until potatoes can be easily pierced with a knife, about 2 hours. Keep covered at room temperature until ready to serve.

2. Remove potatoes, chestnuts, and shallots from dish, rubbing off any large bits of salt. Discard salt and rosemary. Slice potatoes and shallots in half lengthwise, and arrange on a serving platter with chestnuts. Drizzle with oil; season with salt and pepper. Top with rosemary sprigs and serve.

Lamb Stew
with Jerusalem Artichokes

*The texture of Jerusalem artichokes is similar to potatoes when cooked,
but without potatoes' starchiness, so they hold their shape when
added to stews. This recipe pairs the tubers with lamb and tomatoes, and
is flavored with cardamom, saffron, caperberries, and cilantro.*

SERVES 6

3 tablespoons extra-virgin olive oil

1½ pounds boneless lamb shoulder, cut into 1½-inch cubes

Coarse salt and freshly ground black pepper

1½ pounds Jerusalem artichokes (about 15 small), peeled, cut into ¾-inch cubes, and placed in cold water (drain and pat dry before using)

2 cups coarsely chopped onion (about 1 large)

2 garlic cloves, minced

1 tablespoon freshly grated peeled ginger (1-inch piece)

1 cinnamon stick

2 whole cloves

2 green cardamom pods, lightly crushed

½ teaspoon red-pepper flakes

1 can (35 ounces) whole peeled plum tomatoes with juice

1 cup low-sodium chicken broth

⅛ teaspoon crumbled saffron threads

1 jar (10 ounces) small caperberries, drained

¼ cup finely chopped fresh cilantro

1. Heat 2 tablespoons oil in a large, heavy pot over medium high. Season the lamb with salt and black pepper; brown the meat (in batches, if necessary) on all sides, about 8 minutes. Transfer to a bowl.

2. Cook the artichokes in remaining tablespoon oil in same pot over medium-high heat, stirring occasionally, until well browned on all sides, about 7 minutes. Using a slotted spoon, transfer artichokes to a separate bowl.

3. Add onion, garlic, and ginger to remaining oil in pot; sauté over medium-high heat, stirring occasionally, until onion is translucent, about 4 minutes. Add cinnamon, cloves, cardamom, and red-pepper flakes; cook, stirring constantly, 2 minutes.

4. Stir in tomatoes and juice, broth, saffron, and 1 teaspoon salt. Using the side of a wooden spoon, break up tomatoes. Add reserved lamb and accumulated juices; bring mixture to a boil. Reduce heat to low; cover, and simmer until meat is tender, about 1 hour.

5. Return reserved artichokes to pot. Continue to simmer until artichokes are tender, about 25 minutes; add caperberries during final 5 minutes of cooking. Season with salt and black pepper. Discard cinnamon, cloves, and cardamom before serving, topped with cilantro.

Tartiflette

This traditional Alpine dish (which, like the Alps, straddles France and Switzerland; tartiflies is Swiss dialect for "potatoes") is the best example of scalloped potatoes, with melted cheese binding the potatoes in place of heavy cream. Lardons of crisp, smoky bacon are layered throughout and scattered over the top.

SERVES 4 TO 6

Unsalted butter,
for baking dish

2½ pounds fingerling potatoes,
scrubbed and cut lengthwise
into ½-inch-thick slices

Coarse salt and freshly
ground pepper

8 ounces sliced thick-cut
bacon, cut into 1-inch pieces

1 medium onion, thinly sliced

½ cup dry white wine,
such as Sauvignon Blanc

14 ounces Reblochon-style
cheese, cut into
¼-inch-thick slices

1. Preheat oven to 375°F. Butter a shallow 2-quart baking dish. In a saucepan, cover potatoes with cold water by 2 inches. Bring to a boil over high heat; add 1 tablespoon salt. Reduce heat and simmer until potatoes are knife-tender, about 10 minutes; drain.

2. Meanwhile, cook bacon in a large skillet over medium heat, turning, until crisp and golden, about 12 minutes. Transfer to a paper-towel-lined plate; pour off all but 1 tablespoon fat from skillet. Add onion; cook over medium heat, stirring occasionally, until lightly caramelized, about 15 minutes. Add wine and cook until reduced, about 2 minutes. Stir in bacon.

3. Arrange half the potatoes in prepared dish. Season with salt and pepper. Top with half the bacon mixture and half the cheese. Repeat with remaining ingredients. Bake until cheese is bubbling, about 25 minutes. Serve immediately.

TIP
Although Reblochon is a must in France, other cheese created in its spirit, such as Preferes des Montagnes, will work just fine; Italian Robiolo Bosino and Brie are also excellent (but milder) substitutes.

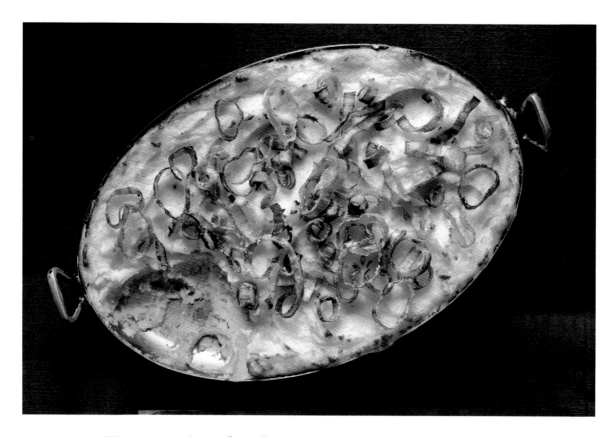

Twice-Cooked Potato and Leek Casserole

SERVES 6 TO 8

2 pounds sweet potatoes (about 5 small), peeled and cut into ½-inch pieces

2 pounds russet potatoes (about 7 small), peeled and cut into ½-inch pieces

Coarse salt and freshly ground black pepper

¾ cup whole milk, warmed

¾ cup heavy cream, warmed

¾ cup (1½ sticks) unsalted butter, melted

2 tablespoons all-purpose flour

Pinch of cayenne pepper

1 leek (white and pale-green parts only), cut into ¼-inch rings, rinsed well

Safflower oil, for frying

1. Preheat oven to 425°F. Cover sweet potatoes and russet potatoes each with 1 inch water in two separate saucepans. Bring to a boil, salt generously, and boil until fork-tender, about 8 minutes; drain. Return potatoes to respective pans.

2. In a bowl, combine milk, cream, and butter. Divide milk mixture between saucepans. Mash both potatoes until smooth; season with salt and black pepper. Spread mashed sweet potatoes evenly in the bottom of a shallow 2-quart baking dish. Top with mashed russet potatoes; spread evenly to edges. Bake until golden, about 25 minutes.

3. Meanwhile, in a bowl, combine flour and cayenne. Add leek; toss to coat. In a medium saucepan, heat 2 inches oil over medium high until a thermometer registers 350°F. Working in batches, add leek rings and cook, turning, until crisp and light golden around edges, about 1 minute. With a slotted spoon, transfer to paper towels to drain. Season with salt. Sprinkle fried leeks over potatoes and serve.

Yukon Gold and Sweet Potatoes Anna

SERVES 6 TO 8

1¼ pounds Yukon Gold potatoes
(3 to 4 medium), peeled

1¼ pounds sweet potatoes
(2 medium), peeled

6 tablespoons unsalted butter,
melted

Coarse salt and freshly
ground pepper

1. Preheat oven to 425°F. Cut potatoes into ⅛-inch-thick slices, keeping potato varieties separate.

2. Brush an ovenproof 9-inch nonstick skillet with some butter. Starting in center of pan, arrange about 20 Yukon Gold slices, slightly overlapping, in a circular pattern, covering surface. Brush with some butter, and generously season with salt and pepper. Make next layer with sweet potato slices; brush with butter and season. Repeat, alternating colors. Drizzle remaining butter on top of potatoes.

3. Cook potatoes over medium-high heat until butter vigorously bubbles in pan, about 4 minutes. Transfer to oven, and bake 30 minutes. Tent loosely with foil; continue to bake until potatoes are easily pierced with a knife, about 20 minutes more. Remove from oven, and run a heatproof flexible spatula around edges of potatoes to loosen. Let cool; carefully invert onto a plate, cut into wedges, and serve.

Salmon Chowder

Frugal cooks have long relied on cold-storage crops like potatoes to make meals with substance during long winters. Chowders are among the easiest and most delicious of those. No thickeners are needed since the potatoes contribute their own starches. In fact, potato starch is a thickener in its own right, similar to cornstarch; it's used in sauces, soups, and pie fillings, while potato flour is used for yeasted rolls and other baked goods.

SERVES 6

2 tablespoons unsalted butter

1 leek (white and pale-green parts only), halved lengthwise, thinly sliced, and rinsed well

1 red onion, quartered and thinly sliced

Coarse salt and freshly ground white pepper

3 small Yukon Gold potatoes, peeled and cut into ¾-inch cubes

2 carrots, halved lengthwise and thinly sliced

6 cups homemade or store-bought low-sodium fish stock

12 ounces skinless salmon fillet (or cod or halibut), cut into ¾-inch cubes

½ cup heavy cream

1 tablespoon chopped fresh dill

1. Heat butter in a medium stockpot over medium low. Cook leek and red onion until soft, 6 to 8 minutes. Season with 1 teaspoon salt. Stir in potatoes and carrots. Add stock and bring to a boil. Reduce heat to low, and simmer until potatoes are almost tender, 6 to 8 minutes.

2. Add salmon and simmer until opaque, about 3 minutes. Stir in cream and heat through. Stir in dill, season with salt and pepper, and serve.

Roasted Pork Chops
with Sweet Potatoes and Apples

Kitchen wisdom holds that produce that's in season at the same time will taste great on the same plate (what grows together, goes together, as the saying goes). Here, sweet potatoes, apples, and Vidalia onion are roasted along with pork chops for an autumnal one-pan supper. The tubers soak up the pan juices—flavored with apple cider vinegar, apple cider, and caraway seeds—that are also drizzled over each serving.

SERVES 4

4 bone-in pork chops (each about 10 ounces and 1 inch thick)

Coarse salt and freshly ground pepper

1 tablespoon extra-virgin olive oil

2 medium sweet potatoes, scrubbed and cut into ¼-inch-thick rounds

1 large sweet onion, such as Vidalia, cut into ¼-inch-thick rounds

⅓ cup apple cider vinegar, preferably unfiltered

½ cup unsweetened apple cider, preferably unfiltered

1 teaspoon caraway seeds

2 apples, preferably Honeycrisp, thinly sliced, seeds removed

1. Preheat oven to 375°F. Season pork with salt and pepper. Heat a large ovenproof skillet over medium high; swirl in oil. Cook chops until golden brown, turning once, about 8 minutes total. Transfer to a plate. Remove all but 2 tablespoons fat from skillet.

2. Reduce heat to medium. Add potatoes and onion; season with salt. Cook until golden in spots, about 10 minutes. Add vinegar and cider. Cover and simmer, stirring a few times, until potatoes are tender, about 5 minutes. Sprinkle with caraway seeds.

3. Return pork and juices to skillet; tuck apple slices between chops. Roast until a thermometer inserted into thickest part of chops (without touching bone) registers 138°F, about 10 minutes. Serve pork, vegetables, and apples with pan juices.

Potato Yeasted Rolls, Two Ways

When making yeasted rolls, try adding mashed potatoes to the dough. Not only do they act as an agent for fermentation, ensuring a nice rise, but they also help keep the rolls moist and light. Bonus: Both doughs (this one and the potato dough on the following page) can be made with leftovers, or an equal amount of mashed pumpkin or winter squash.

Sweet Potato Yeasted Rolls

MAKES 20

¼ cup warm water (110°F)

1 envelope (¼ ounce) active dry yeast

1 cup milk

6 tablespoons unsalted butter, plus more, melted, for brushing

½ cup sugar

1 tablespoon plus 1 teaspoon coarse salt

1 teaspoon ground cardamom

2 cups mashed cooked peeled sweet potatoes (from about 2 medium)

1 teaspoon fresh lemon juice

1 large egg, lightly beaten

7 cups sifted all-purpose flour

1. Place the warm water in a small bowl, and sprinkle with yeast. Let stand until yeast is dissolved and mixture is foamy, about 7 minutes.

2. In a small saucepan, heat milk over medium just until it begins to steam and bubble around the sides. Remove from heat; add butter, and stir until melted and combined. Stir in sugar, salt, and cardamom. Let cool slightly.

3. With an electric mixer on medium speed, beat sweet potatoes and lemon juice until smooth, 2 to 3 minutes. Beat in egg and milk and yeast mixtures until smooth.

4. Switch to the dough hook. Add flour, 1 cup at a time, beating until a stiff dough forms. Continue kneading dough on medium speed until smooth, about 8 minutes more; the dough will still be slightly sticky. Transfer to a buttered bowl; cover with a clean kitchen towel. Let rise in a warm spot until doubled in bulk, about 1 hour.

5. Punch down dough, and knead with your hands, just until smooth. Using a bench scraper or sharp knife, cut dough into 20 equal pieces, and shape into rolls. Place rolls on parchment-lined baking sheets about 2 inches apart; cover with a kitchen towel, and let rise again in a warm spot until doubled in bulk, about 40 minutes.

6. Preheat oven to 400°F. Using kitchen scissors or a sharp paring knife, snip an X in the top of each roll. Brush rolls with melted butter. Bake until tops of rolls are golden, rotating sheet halfway through, about 20 minutes. Serve warm or at room temperature.

continued >

Potato Dinner Rolls

MAKES 30 TO 35

2 small russet potatoes, peeled and cut into 2-inch pieces

2 envelopes (¼ ounce each) active dry yeast

2 tablespoons sugar, plus a pinch

1 cup buttermilk, room temperature

4 tablespoons butter, melted and cooled, plus more for bowl, plastic wrap, and brushing

1 tablespoon plus 1 teaspoon coarse salt

5½ to 6½ cups bread flour, plus more for dusting

1. Place potatoes in a medium saucepan with enough cold water to cover. Bring to a boil; reduce heat and simmer until tender, about 15 minutes. Drain, reserving ½ cup liquid. Let reserved liquid cool to 110°F. Meanwhile, mash potatoes with a potato masher or pass through a potato ricer.

2. In the bowl of an electric mixer, whisk together reserved liquid, yeast, and pinch of sugar. Let stand until mixture is foamy, about 5 minutes.

3. Attach bowl to electric mixer fitted with the dough hook. With mixer on low speed, add remaining sugar, the potatoes, buttermilk, butter, and salt. Add enough flour, 1 cup at a time, to make a dough that's slightly tacky. Continue kneading dough until smooth, about 2 minutes more. Transfer to a buttered bowl; cover with buttered plastic wrap. Let rise in a warm spot until doubled in bulk, 1 to 1½ hours.

4. Preheat oven to 375°F. Turn out dough onto a lightly floured work surface. Using a floured rolling pin, roll out dough ¾ inch thick. Cut into 2-inch-wide strips. Cut strips into triangles or squares; place at least 1¼ inches apart on parchment-lined baking sheets. Brush tops generously with melted butter; cover with buttered plastic wrap. Let rise until dough is no longer springy to the touch, about 15 minutes.

5. Bake until tops of rolls are golden, rotating sheets halfway through, about 20 minutes. Serve warm or at room temperature.

GREENS

Literature is full of tales of the humble outcast who proves himself to be a true hero. The story of collards, kale, and mustard, beet, and turnip greens is a bit like that. For centuries, they were the rejected siblings of leafy greens. Deemed unworthy of fine tables, they were the food of the poor and downtrodden. Fortunately, those who embraced them were anything but deprived when it came to culinary ingenuity, and they transformed these greens into dishes as life sustaining as they were delicious.

It helped that the coarse and often bitter greens were endowed with considerable gifts. They are among the most nutrient-dense vegetables available, according to the Centers for Disease Control and Prevention—as are broccoli rabe, a member of the turnip family (its name means "turnip broccoli" in Italian), and bok choy, an Asian cousin. After all, like lettuce and endive, these hardy greens are factories of photosynthesis, transforming sunlight into edible energy. And despite their occasional rough-around-the-edges character, they are delicious, with flavors that range from sweet and mineral-like, to bracingly bitter, to spicy hot—though all are tamed by a long, slow simmer, especially if a salty, smoky bit of ham hock or a pig's ear is added to the pot.

Luckily, deliciousness ignores classifications. Some of these greens, like kale, have not merely shaken off their earlier stigma but have also become downright popular. And that means a happy ending for all: the underdog greens, and those of us who get to eat them.

BEET GREENS

—

BOK CHOY

—

BROCCOLI RABE

—

CHARD

—

COLLARDS

—

KALE

—

MUSTARD GREENS

—

TURNIP GREENS

THE BASICS

SEASONALITY

Greens prefer cooler temperatures, and although popular ones like kale and broccoli rabe are now available year-round, they are sweetest in fall and winter, with collards and mustard greens continuing right through to spring. At farmers' markets, you can also find these greens at the baby stage in early and mid-summer. Baby mustard and turnip greens may be included in Asian braising or salad mixes; baby chard and kale in mesclun salad mixes.

BUYING

Chard, collards, kale, broccoli rabe, mustard greens, and turnip greens should be vivid green, their edges crisp. Avoid limp, flaccid bunches and any that are turning yellow. Examine the stems as well: they should be taut and compact. Pass by stems that are oversize—they are likely to be coarse and fibrous—and shun any that are brown or slimy. Also, examine the cut ends for dryness or cracking. Beet greens will be sold attached to the roots they sprouted from; both they and the beets should look fresh and firm. With bok choy, look for thick, crisp, bright-white stems without brown spots, and bright green leaves.

NOTABLE VARIETIES

Chard: You'll typically find three types of chard in stores and at farmers' markets: Fordhook Giant is identifiable by crinkly leaves and thick, white, tender stalks; Rainbow chard has colorful red, pink, yellow, or white stalks; and Ruby Red (or Rhubarb) chard has thin red stalks and a slightly stronger flavor than the others.

Kale: Curly kale—the most recognizable variety—has tight ruffled leaves and fibrous stalks, and the flavor is quite pungent. You can find it in bright green or reddish-purple hues. Lacinato kale (also known by many other names: Tuscan, Cavolo Nero, Black, or Dinosaur) has tall, broad, wrinkly blue-green leaves that are hearty enough to retain their firmness even after cooking. The flavor is sweeter and more delicate than curly kale. Red Russian kale boasts a bittersweet taste that's slightly peppery; its bright green leaves are flat and fringed, with reddish stems running through them and tough, woody stalks. You can also find purple and white varieties that are edible but more often used for ornamental plantings.

Mustard Greens: Southern Giant Curled is the most traditional mustard green you can find, but this pungent leafy green ranges in color from light to dark green, purple, red, or variegated, and in texture—smooth, frilly, or serrated. There are many Asian varieties (such as those found in salad mixes) that are harvested younger and are therefore more tender (perfect for eating raw); these mustard greens can also pack a hot, spicy, mustardy flavor.

Bok Choy: Also known by its Chinese name, pak choi, this Asian green is most commonly the larger, more mature variety with white stems and dark green leaves. Baby bok choy is also easy to find in supermarkets. But there are other varieties available at farmers' markets, with stems ranging in thickness and shape and even color (green pak choi is prized for being more tender and flavorful). The leaves also vary; some have frilly shapes, others are lighter green, verging on yellow, and one variety has leaves in a tight head with hardly any stems at all. They all share a mustardy flavor; the older leaves are good for pickling (as in kimchi).

STORING

Remove any twist ties or rubber bands constricting the stems. Loosely wrapped in a plastic bag, hearty greens will keep in the fridge for several days, though they lose sweetness and nutrients over time, so don't wait too long. Kale and collards have a naturally occurring wax on their leaves (you can see it when you dunk them in water) that helps them last up to a week.

PREPPING

These hearty greens come with sturdy stems, so you'll need to separate the two. To do so, grab the stem in one hand and gently encircle the base of the green in the other, then slide this hand up toward the tip, pulling the leaf off as you go. You can also fold the leaves in half lengthwise and slice out the stem. To chop greens before cooking, stack several in a pile, fold or roll the stack loosely, and cut into wide or narrow strips, as desired.

COOKING

Versatile kale can be prepared almost any way a cook can dream up: blanched, steamed, sautéed, roasted, baked into gratins or casseroles, juiced, or eaten raw in salads. (Note: To soften kale leaves, rub them together vigorously until they darken, shrink, and become tender; you can also do this in a salad bowl with olive oil or mashed avocado and salt, rubbing it into the greens.) Chard and mustard, beet, and turnip greens are good raw only when they are young, otherwise they're better cooked—and if their flavor is especially potent, blanching first can soften that bite. (You can sauté the chard stems, too; rinse, dry, and cut into small pieces first.) Tender beet greens and juicy bok choy need only a quick steam or sauté, though they can also be roasted.

HOW TO WILT

Remove stems; trim broccoli rabe and bok choy. Leave whole, chop, or slice into ½-inch strips. Heat olive oil in a skillet over medium. Add greens in batches, letting each cook down before adding the next and tossing frequently, just until wilted, 3 to 5 minutes.

HOW TO BLANCH

Remove stems; trim broccoli rabe and bok choy. Blanch greens in a pot of salted boiling water until bright green and just tender, 15 seconds (for spinach and chard) to 2 minutes (all the rest); drain. When cool enough to handle, squeeze out excess liquid. Drizzle with olive oil, season with salt and pepper, and serve with lemon. Or save for recipes: Let cool completely on a rimmed baking sheet, then store in an airtight container in the refrigerator up to 4 days.

HOW TO STEAM

Remove stems; trim broccoli rabe and bok choy. Chop greens and place in a steamer basket (or colander) set in a pot with 1 inch water. Bring to a boil, cover, and steam until bright green and tender, 5 to 10 minutes. Drizzle with olive oil and season with salt and pepper.

HOW TO SAUTÉ

Remove stems; trim broccoli rabe and bok choy. Chop greens; wash and then rain, leaving water clinging to leaves. Heat olive oil in a large skillet over medium high. Cook minced garlic (and a pinch of red-pepper flakes, if desired) until golden, stirring frequently, 2 to 3 minutes. Add greens and season with salt and pepper. Cover and cook until tender, stirring occasionally, 10 to 15 minutes. Remove cover and continue cooking until moisture evaporates, 2 to 3 minutes more.

HOW TO ROAST

Remove stems; trim broccoli rabe and bok choy. Cut greens into 2-inch strips. Toss with olive oil, and season with salt and pepper; then spread evenly on a rimmed baking sheet. Roast at 375°F until tender and crisp and brown on the edges, tossing once or twice, 15 to 20 minutes.

HOW TO BRAISE

Remove stems; trim broccoli rabe and bok choy. Halve greens lengthwise. Heat butter or olive oil in a large skillet over medium. Add diced onion and thinly sliced garlic and cook, stirring

frequently, until softened, about 5 minutes. Add greens and season with salt; cook, stirring, until wilted, 3 to 5 minutes. Add enough chicken broth to cover; reduce heat to low, cover pan, and cook until tender, 20 to 25 minutes more. Season with salt and pepper, and squeeze with lemon.

FLAVOR PAIRINGS

Hardy greens get along well with garlic, olive oil, and red-pepper flakes, and are equally contented with onions and bacon or other bits of smoked pork. A splash of vinegar or another acidic ingredient like lemon juice complements both these flavor groupings, and potatoes are seldom an unwelcome partner.

BEET GREENS: goat cheese, rosemary, mint, orange, walnuts

BOK CHOY: garlic, ginger, soy sauce, coconut milk, lime, cilantro, shiitake mushrooms, carrots, pork, chile peppers, cashews

BROCCOLI RABE: olive oil, garlic, anchovies, chickpeas, red-pepper flakes, Italian sausage, Parmesan, parsley, tomato paste, capers

CHARD: olive oil, lemon, garlic, sherry vinegar, red-pepper flakes, Pecorino Romano

COLLARD AND TURNIP GREENS: onions, bacon or salt pork, apple cider, vinegar

KALE: olive oil, citrus, hazelnuts, balsamic vinegar, Parmesan or Pecorino Romano, pancetta, roasted tomatoes, sweet peppers

MUSTARD GREENS: garlic, soy sauce, sesame, ginger, chile peppers

Sesame Greens

This recipe shows how using minimal seasonings and a simple method (blanching) can yield tasty greens. You can even blanch the greens a couple of days ahead of time, squeeze out the excess liquid, then cool completely on a rimmed baking sheet before refrigerating in an airtight container. Chop and toss with seasonings just before serving.

SERVES 4

1 pound Swiss chard, kale, mustard greens, or collard greens, stems trimmed

Coarse salt

2 tablespoons low-sodium soy sauce

1 tablespoon fresh lime juice

1 teaspoon toasted sesame oil

Sesame seeds, for sprinkling

1. Blanch greens in a pot of salted boiling water until tender, about 15 seconds for chard, 2 minutes for the other greens. Drain; when cool enough to handle, squeeze out excess liquid and coarsely chop leaves.

2. Whisk together soy sauce, lime juice, and sesame oil in a large bowl. Season with salt. Add greens and toss to coat. Sprinkle with sesame seeds and serve.

Swiss Chard, Cabbage, and Brussels Sprouts Salad

In this raw salad, tender slices of Swiss chard, cabbage, and brussels sprouts are rubbed with sugar and salt, then chilled to soften before being tossed with the dressing.

SERVES 8

12 ounces Swiss chard

8 ounces brussels sprouts

½ head Savoy cabbage

2 teaspoons sugar

2 teaspoons coarse salt

1 cup walnuts

3 tablespoons sherry vinegar

2 teaspoons Dijon mustard

1 teaspoon soy sauce

½ cup extra-virgin olive oil

1 ounce Pecorino Romano cheese, shaved

1. Trim and thinly slice chard and brussels sprouts; core and thinly slice cabbage. Combine all greens in a large bowl. Rub with sugar and 1 teaspoon salt until slightly damp. Refrigerate 30 to 60 minutes.

2. Preheat oven to 350°F. Toast walnuts on a rimmed baking sheet, tossing occasionally, until darkened, 8 to 10 minutes. Transfer to a plate; let cool and coarsely chop.

3. In a small bowl, whisk together vinegar, mustard, soy sauce, and remaining 1 teaspoon salt. Slowly whisk in oil. Toss greens with three-quarters of dressing. Add cheese and walnuts; toss to combine. Refrigerate at least 10 minutes and up to 1 hour. Serve, tossing with more dressing, if desired.

Fried Rice with Collard Greens

While collards are most often associated with Southern cooking, where they're braised for hours with ham hocks, these greens are much more versatile than that. They can also stand in for other greens (such as bok choy, kale, and mustard greens) in many dishes from across the globe. Here, collards are the highlight of a meatless Thai-style stir-fry that also demonstrates how the leaves soften even after brief cooking.

SERVES 4

1 cup jasmine rice

1 cup water

Coarse salt

1 pound collard greens, stems trimmed

3 tablespoons coconut oil

1 tablespoon minced garlic

1 tablespoon minced peeled fresh ginger

¼ cup sliced shallots

1 Thai chile, thinly sliced

1 tablespoon fresh lime juice, plus lime wedges for serving

1 teaspoon fish sauce, such as *nam pla* or *nuoc mam*

Cilantro sprigs, for serving

1. Bring rice, water, and 1 teaspoon coarse salt to a boil in a saucepan. Stir once, reduce heat, and simmer, covered, 15 minutes. Remove from heat and let steam (still covered) 5 to 10 minutes more. Fluff with a fork. Let cool completely before refrigerating in an airtight container up to 3 days.

2. Blanch collard greens in a pot of salted boiling water until bright green and just tender, about 2 minutes. Drain; when cool enough to handle, squeeze out excess liquid and coarsely chop greens.

3. Heat oil in a large skillet over medium high. Add garlic, ginger, and shallots, and cook, tossing, 1 minute. Add rice, chile, and collards; cook, stirring constantly, until heated through. Stir in lime juice and fish sauce. Top with cilantro; serve immediately, with lime wedges.

TIP
The secret to any fried rice recipe is to use day-old rice (substitute about 1½ cups for uncooked rice). It's drier than freshly steamed, so it fries easily without sticking to the wok.

Stuffed Collard Greens

The ultimate dark leafy greens, collards have the mild flavor of spinach and the robust texture of kale. Blanching renders the greens tender and pliable, but still sturdy enough for filling, rolling, and baking, as in this update on stuffed cabbage. Cooked spelt and white beans go into the stuffing; farro and rice can be substituted for the spelt.

SERVES 6

1 can (28 ounces) whole peeled tomatoes with juice

¼ cup extra-virgin olive oil

½ small onion, finely chopped

Pinch of red-pepper flakes

Coarse salt and freshly ground black pepper

1 cup spelt

1 pound collard greens

1 can (15 ounces) white beans, drained and rinsed

2 tablespoons finely grated Parmigiano-Reggiano cheese

2 teaspoons chopped fresh sage

1. Pulse tomatoes with their juices in a food processor until chopped. Heat 2 tablespoons oil in a saucepan over medium. Add onion and red-pepper flakes; cook, stirring occasionally, until onion is softened, about 6 minutes. Add tomatoes and bring to a boil. Reduce to a simmer; cook, stirring occasionally, until slightly thickened, about 20 minutes. Season with salt. Let sauce cool.

2. Stir spelt into a saucepan of salted boiling water. Reduce to a steady simmer; cook, uncovered, until tender, about 40 minutes. Drain and let cool.

3. Meanwhile, working in batches, blanch collard greens in a pot of salted boiling water until bright green and tender, about 3 minutes. Remove with tongs and drain; let cool. Trim off stems and thick leaves. Reserve 12 large leaves; chop any remaining leaves.

4. Preheat oven to 375°F. Coarsely mash beans in a bowl. Add cooked spelt, remaining 2 tablespoons oil, the cheese, sage, and any chopped collards. Stir to combine. Season with salt and pepper.

5. Working with one collard green at a time, arrange ¼ cup filling in center. Fold stem end over filling. Fold in sides. Roll collard over to form a bundle, overlapping ends to seal. Transfer, seam side down, to a 9-by-13-inch baking dish.

6. Spread sauce evenly over stuffed collards. Cover with parchment, then foil; bake until sauce is bubbling and collards are tender, about 30 minutes. Serve immediately.

TIP
For quicker assembly, prepare the tomato sauce and spelt up to two days ahead; let cool and refrigerate them separately in covered containers.

Mustard-Greens Pesto

Mustard greens pack a sharp, peppery bite that's just right for making pesto. This out-of-the-ordinary version uses very little oil and cheese, getting its rich texture from roasted garlic (two full heads) and toasted almonds (in place of pine nuts). Beyond the pasta bowl, try it on crostini or as a sauce for grilled chicken and fish.

MAKES 1 CUP

2 heads garlic

¼ cup almonds

3 tablespoons extra-virgin olive oil

⅓ cup finely grated Pecorino Romano cheese

½ large bunch mustard greens, stems trimmed and coarsely chopped (about 4 cups)

2 tablespoons water

Coarse salt and freshly ground pepper

1. Preheat oven to 425°F. Slice off top quarter of garlic heads. Wrap garlic in parchment, then foil, and roast until cloves are very soft, 50 to 60 minutes. Unwrap and let cool completely. Squeeze garlic from skins, discarding skins.

2. Meanwhile, toast almonds on a rimmed baking sheet until fragrant and darkened, tossing occasionally, about 5 minutes. Transfer to a plate; let cool, then coarsely chop.

3. Pulse together garlic, almonds, oil, cheese, mustard greens, and the water in a food processor until a thick paste forms. Season with salt and pepper. (Pesto can be refrigerated in an airtight container up to 3 days.)

Mustard-Greens Caesar Salad

*Mustard greens are a good match for anchovies and garlic—here used
in the oil that flavors the croutons in a heartier Caesar salad.
Let the salad stand for a few minutes once you've tossed everything together.*

SERVES 4

¼ cup plus 3 tablespoons
extra-virgin olive oil

3 oil-packed anchovies,
chopped

2 garlic cloves, minced

4 slices rustic bread, each
sliced into 3 or 4 strips

1 pound baby mustard greens

3 tablespoons fresh lemon
juice

Coarse salt and freshly
ground pepper

Parmigiano-Reggiano or
Pecorino Romano cheese

1. Preheat oven to 400°F. Heat ¼ cup plus 2 tablespoons oil
in a small saucepan over low. Add anchovies and garlic, and
cook, stirring frequently, until anchovies are broken up and
garlic is pale golden, 12 to 15 minutes. Pour mixture into a
large bowl.

2. Meanwhile, toast bread on a rimmed baking sheet until
golden brown, 8 to 10 minutes. Add to bowl with anchovy oil,
and toss to coat.

3. Add mustard greens, lemon juice, and remaining tablespoon oil to bowl, and toss to coat. Season with salt and
pepper. Let stand for 5 minutes before serving, topped with
shaved cheese.

Skillet Pizza with Greens and Eggplant

Leafy greens make excellent pizza toppings—they stand up to the high heat of the oven and marry so well with other Italian ingredients, including eggplant and provolone. This pie is truly unique: Unlike for most doughs, here you start by mixing the yeast and salt with the flour and water (so the dough is softer and more tender). Then it rises in the same cast-iron skillet it will be baked in, for the ultimate in ease.

MAKES TWO 10-INCH PIZZAS

FOR THE DOUGH

- 2¾ cups all-purpose flour, plus more for dusting
- 2 teaspoons coarse salt
- 1 teaspoon active dry yeast
- 1¼ cups water
- ¼ cup extra-virgin olive oil

FOR THE SAUCE

- 2 tablespoons extra-virgin olive oil
- ½ small onion, finely chopped
- Pinch of red-pepper flakes
- 1 can (28 ounces) diced tomatoes with juice
- Coarse salt and freshly ground black pepper

FOR THE TOPPINGS

- 1 eggplant (about 12 ounces), cut lengthwise into 1-inch-thick slices
- Coarse salt
- 3 tablespoons extra-virgin olive oil
- 1 garlic clove, thinly sliced
- 1 pound Swiss chard, kale, or beet greens, tough stems trimmed and leaves cut into 2-inch pieces
- 12 ounces provolone cheese, thinly sliced
- Fresh oregano leaves, for serving

1. Make the dough: Stir together flour, salt, yeast, and the water in a large bowl until dough is very sticky. Cover with plastic wrap; let stand 12 to 18 hours at room temperature.

2. Sprinkle dough with flour. Divide in half. Divide oil between two 10-inch ovenproof nonstick skillets (preferably cast iron). Swirl to coat. Add dough to each skillet; turn to coat with oil. Gently flatten dough with your hand. Cover; let rise in a warm spot until doubled in bulk, about 2 hours.

3. Make the sauce: Heat oil in a pot over medium. Cook onion and red-pepper flakes, stirring occasionally, until onion is softened, 6 to 8 minutes. Add tomatoes and juices. Bring to a boil, then reduce heat and simmer, stirring occasionally, about 20 minutes. Let cool slightly. Purée sauce in a blender, working in batches (do not fill jar more than halfway). Season with salt and black pepper.

4. Make the toppings: Preheat oven to 400°F. Place eggplant in a colander; season with salt. Let stand 30 minutes.

5. Rinse eggplant, drain, and pat dry. Arrange on a rimmed baking sheet; brush with 2 tablespoons oil. Roast, turning once, until very tender, about 25 minutes. Let cool slightly, then cut into ½-inch pieces.

6. Heat remaining tablespoon oil in a large skillet over medium. Cook garlic, stirring, until fragrant, about 30 seconds. Add chard in batches with 1 to 2 tablespoons water. Cook, stirring, until just wilted, about 5 minutes. Season with salt. Let cool.

7. Preheat oven to 475°F, with rack in lower third. For each pizza, press dough until it touches edge of skillet. Ladle ¾ cup sauce over dough, leaving a ½-inch border. Top with 3 ounces cheese. Add ½ cup each chard and eggplant. Top with another 3 ounces cheese. Bake until crust is golden brown, about 18 minutes. Serve topped with oregano.

Caldo Verde

Caldo verde, or "green broth," is a plentiful stew of kale, potatoes, and sausage; it is widely considered the national dish of Portugal. The soup base is traditionally puréed, as here, to a wonderfully thick consistency (thanks to the potatoes), then kale is stirred in and simmered just until tender.

SERVES 8 TO 10

¼ cup extra-virgin olive oil, plus more for drizzling

1 large onion, finely chopped

4 garlic cloves, minced

2½ pounds russet potatoes (about 5 medium), peeled and cut into 1-inch cubes

8 cups low-sodium chicken broth

8 ounces firm chorizo or linguiça, halved lengthwise

12 ounces kale, tough stems trimmed and leaves thinly sliced

Coarse salt and freshly ground pepper

1. Heat oil in a large pot over medium high. Add onion and garlic, and cook, stirring occasionally, until softened, about 4 minutes. Add potatoes and chicken broth. Bring to a boil, then reduce heat and simmer until potatoes are soft, about 15 minutes.

2. Meanwhile, heat a medium skillet over medium. Add chorizo and cook until golden brown, 3 to 4 minutes per side. Transfer to a cutting board. When cool enough to handle, thinly slice crosswise.

3. Purée soup with an immersion blender or in a regular blender (work in batches; do not fill jar more than halfway). Return to pot and stir in kale; simmer 5 minutes. Season with salt and pepper to taste. Serve soup drizzled with oil and topped with chorizo.

TIP
You want a hardy green that can hold its own in this type of soup; try collards in place of kale. Chorizo is a traditional choice, though linguiça is used as well.

Kale Chips with Balsamic Glaze

Kale turns crisp in the oven, and when stored airtight, stays that way for days. Tuscan (or Lacinato) kale is the best option for making chips; the leaves are flatter and heartier than curly kale. The simply seasoned leaves are just fine as snacks on their own, but even better served with a balsamic dipping glaze.

SERVES 8

2¼ cups balsamic vinegar

¼ teaspoon honey (optional)

Pinch of coarse salt

2 pounds Tuscan kale, tough stems trimmed

2 tablespoons extra-virgin olive oil

Flaky sea salt, such as Maldon, for sprinkling

1. Bring vinegar to a boil in a small heavy saucepan; reduce to a simmer, and cook until thickened and syrupy, about 15 minutes. Remove from heat; stir in honey, if desired, and coarse salt. Let cool completely; glaze will thicken slightly as it cools. (Glaze can be refrigerated in an airtight container up to 1 week; bring to room temperature before serving.)

2. Meanwhile, preheat oven to 375°F. Toss kale with oil, and divide between two large rimmed baking sheets. Spread in a single layer and bake, tossing kale and rotating sheets halfway through, until crisp, 15 to 20 minutes. Let cool completely on sheets. Sprinkle with sea salt, toss to coat, and serve with balsamic glaze.

Kale-Ricotta Dip

Here's a healthier update on creamy spinach dip: Sauté the kale until wilted,
then mix with ricotta and bake until golden brown. Ricotta has all the deliciousness
of the sour cream used in original versions, and is a better flavor partner for kale.

SERVES 4 TO 6

2 tablespoons extra-virgin
   olive oil

1 small bunch kale, tough
   stems trimmed and leaves
   coarsely chopped (about
   1 cup)

1 cup fresh ricotta cheese

   Coarse salt and freshly
   ground pepper

   Crackers or crostini,
   for serving

1. Preheat oven to 425°F. Heat oil in a large skillet over medium high. Add kale and cook, tossing frequently, until wilted, about 5 minutes. Transfer to a plate and let cool.

2. Mix ricotta with kale in a shallow baking dish, and season with salt and pepper. Bake until golden brown on top and bubbling, about 12 minutes. Let cool slightly before serving, with crackers.

TIP Other greens work well here, too: spinach, mustard greens, Swiss chard, collards, beet greens, and turnip greens each contribute their distinctive flavor, all with slightly different results.

Swiss Chard Lasagna

It used to be that spinach was the green of choice when making a meat-free lasagna. But Swiss chard (or kale) actually makes more sense; it doesn't lose nearly as much volume as spinach does during cooking, and you get the crunch of the stems along with the tenderness of the leaves. Other than that, this recipe is pretty traditional, with its simple tomato sauce and layers of mozzarella and noodles.

SERVES 4

- 3 tablespoons extra-virgin olive oil
- 1 medium onion, coarsely chopped
- 1 pound Swiss chard, stems and leaves separated, both thinly sliced
- Coarse salt
- 4 garlic cloves, minced
- ½ teaspoon red-pepper flakes
- 1 can (28 ounces) whole peeled plum tomatoes with juices
- 8 no-boil lasagna noodles (9 ounces)
- 1 pound whole-milk mozzarella, shredded (about 4 cups)

1. Preheat oven to 375°F. Heat a large skillet over medium high. Add 2 tablespoons oil, the onion, and chard stems. Cook, stirring occasionally, until onion is softened, about 4 minutes. Stir in chard leaves, season with salt, and cook until tender, about 2 minutes. Transfer to a plate.

2. Wipe skillet; return to medium-high heat. Add remaining tablespoon oil, the garlic, and red-pepper flakes. Cook, stirring, until fragrant, about 30 seconds. Add tomatoes with their juices and simmer, breaking them into pieces, until liquid is thickened, about 3 minutes. Season with salt.

3. Spread ½ cup tomato sauce in bottom of an 8-inch square baking dish. Top with two lasagna noodles, ¾ cup sauce, one-third of chard mixture, and 1 cup cheese. Repeat layering twice more. Top with remaining noodles, sauce, and cheese. Loosely cover with parchment, then foil. Bake 30 minutes. Uncover and bake until bubbly, about 15 minutes more. Let cool 20 minutes, then slice and serve.

Bok Choy Salad with Cashews

Bok choy delivers crunch and sweetness in this vibrant slaw, and makes an excellent stand-in for cabbage. Try it with grilled pork chops, chicken, or steak.

SERVES 4

1 tablespoon plus 1 teaspoon rice vinegar (unseasoned)

1 tablespoon low-sodium soy sauce

1 teaspoon toasted sesame oil

¾ teaspoon sugar

1½ pounds bok choy, thinly sliced (about 5 cups)

2 tablespoons chopped raw cashews

Whisk together vinegar, soy sauce, sesame oil, and sugar in a large bowl. Add bok choy and toss to coat. Top with cashews and serve.

Baby Bok Choy with Chile, Garlic, and Ginger

Baby bok choy is prized for its small size (meaning heads can be cooked whole or halved, as here) and tender leaves. This recipe can also be made with full-size bok choy sliced lengthwise into bite-size pieces, which will steam in the same amount of time.

SERVES 4

2 teaspoons safflower oil

1 red or green jalapeño chile, thinly sliced (remove ribs and seeds for less heat)

1 garlic clove, thinly sliced

1 piece (1 inch) fresh ginger, peeled and thinly sliced

1 pound baby bok choy, halved lengthwise

3 tablespoons water

Coarse salt

Heat oil in a large skillet over medium high. Cook jalapeño, garlic, and ginger, stirring frequently, until softened, about 1 minute. Add bok choy and the water; cover and cook until tender, 7 to 8 minutes. Uncover and cook until any remaining liquid evaporates. Season with salt and serve.

Broccoli Rabe and Ham Croque Monsieurs

Here's a wonderful way to perk up a ho-hum grilled ham and cheese: Layer on broccoli rabe. After all, the vegetable pairs well with pork. It also makes a simple sandwich more of a satisfying meal-in-one when topped with béchamel, as a croque monsieur. Start by blanching the broccoli rabe, then sauté it with garlic for flavor and to wilt the greens.

SERVES 4

FOR THE BÉCHAMEL

- 2 tablespoons unsalted butter
- ½ shallot, finely diced
- 2 tablespoons all-purpose flour
- ¾ cup whole milk
- ¼ cup finely grated Parmigiano-Reggiano cheese
- Coarse salt and freshly ground pepper

FOR THE SANDWICHES

- 1 pound broccoli rabe, trimmed
- Coarse salt
- 1 tablespoon extra-virgin olive oil
- 1 garlic clove, thinly sliced
- 2 tablespoons plus 2 teaspoons fig jam
- 8 slices best-quality white bread
- 1 tablespoon plus 1 teaspoon Dijon mustard
- 8 ounces fontina cheese, thinly sliced
- 8 ounces sliced ham
- ¼ cup grated Gruyère cheese

1. Make the béchamel: Melt butter in a saucepan over medium heat. Add shallot; cook, stirring occasionally, until tender, about 2 minutes. Add flour, and whisk until mixture bubbles slightly, about 1 minute. Gradually add in milk, and cook, stirring occasionally, until thickened, 5 minutes. Remove from heat, add Parmesan, and season with salt and pepper.

2. Meanwhile, make the sandwiches: Preheat oven to 450°F. Working in batches, blanch broccoli rabe in a pot of salted boiling water until just tender, about 2 minutes. Drain.

3. Heat oil in a large skillet over medium. Add garlic; cook, stirring, 30 seconds. Add broccoli rabe; cook, stirring, 2 minutes. Season with salt. Let cool slightly, then finely chop garlic and broccoli rabe.

4. For each sandwich, spread 2 teaspoons jam on one bread slice and 1 teaspoon mustard on another. Layer one slice with fontina cheese, broccoli rabe, and ham, dividing evenly. Close sandwich and place on a rimmed baking sheet; top with 2 tablespoons béchamel. Sprinkle Gruyère evenly over tops.

5. Bake until browned and bubbling, about 10 minutes. Serve immediately.

TIP Fig jam adds sweetness, but you could forgo that and just use Dijon mustard. You can also skip the béchamel: Assemble the sandwiches, brush both sides with softened butter, then cook in a hot cast-iron skillet over medium heat until golden brown, about 3 minutes per side.

Kale and Avocado Salad with Dates

This salad has it all: The winning buttery-meets-crisp combination of avocado and kale, with pine nuts, Parmesan, and dates all adding their own notes to the dish. Make the salad up to an hour before serving; the texture of the kale actually improves with time.

SERVES 8

¼ cup pine nuts

1 bunch baby Tuscan kale

⅓ cup extra-virgin olive oil

3 tablespoons fresh lemon juice

2 avocados, halved, pitted, peeled, and cut into ¼-inch slices

2 ounces Parmigiano-Reggiano cheese, shaved

8 large or 10 medium dried dates, pitted and sliced

Coarse salt and freshly ground pepper

1. Toast pine nuts in a small dry skillet over medium heat until golden, tossing frequently, about 3 minutes.

2. In a large bowl, toss together kale, pine nuts, oil, and lemon juice. Add avocados, cheese, and dates, and toss gently to combine. Season with salt and pepper, and serve.

Chard-Tomato Sauté

*In France and Italy, you'll often find chard sautéed with extra-virgin olive oil
and garlic; we've built on that tradition by adding tomato, capers, and fresh basil,
along with Parmesan grated over the top.*

SERVES 4

1 pound Swiss chard,
preferably Ruby Red, stems
trimmed and leaves chopped

Coarse salt and freshly
ground pepper

3 tablespoons extra-virgin
olive oil, plus more

2 garlic cloves, thinly sliced

1 large tomato, chopped

2 tablespoons capers, drained
and rinsed

¼ cup sliced fresh basil,
plus small leaves for serving

Parmigiano-Reggiano
cheese, for serving

1. Blanch chard in a pot of salted boiling water until bright
green and just tender, about 15 seconds. Drain; when cool
enough to handle, squeeze out excess liquid and coarsely
chop greens.

2. Heat oil in a large skillet over medium high. Add garlic,
tomato, and capers; cook, stirring constantly, 2 minutes. Add
chard and sliced basil; cook, tossing, until heated through.
Season with salt and pepper. Drizzle with more oil, top with
whole basil leaves and finely grated Parmesan, and serve.

Orecchiette with Broccoli Rabe and Tomatoes

For this pasta dish, broccoli rabe and orecchiette are cooked together in one pot. You could stop there, and simply finish with a drizzle of olive oil and some finely grated Pecorino Romano, but it's exceptionally good tossed with an all-star Italian sauce of anchovies, garlic, capers, and tomatoes, and topped with golden toasted breadcrumbs.

SERVES 6

¼ cup and 3 tablespoons extra-virgin olive oil, plus more for drizzling

1½ cups plain fresh breadcrumbs

Coarse salt

4 anchovy fillets, rinsed and patted dry

6 garlic cloves, thinly sliced

2 tablespoons capers, preferably salt-packed, rinsed, drained, and chopped

1 pound cherry tomatoes, halved

¼ teaspoon red-pepper flakes

1 pound orecchiette

1 pound broccoli rabe, trimmed and cut into 2-inch pieces

1. Heat 3 tablespoons oil in a large sauté pan over medium. Add breadcrumbs and season with salt. Cook, stirring frequently, until crisp and golden, about 5 minutes. Transfer breadcrumbs to a plate.

2. Heat 2 tablespoons oil in pan over medium. Add anchovies and stir until they dissolve into oil, about 1 minute. Add garlic and capers, and cook, stirring, until garlic is golden, 2 to 3 minutes. Add tomatoes, red-pepper flakes, and remaining 2 tablespoons oil. Raise heat to medium high, and cook, stirring occasionally, until tomatoes begin to break down, about 5 minutes.

3. Meanwhile, cook pasta in a large pot of salted boiling water until pasta is al dente, according to package instructions, adding broccoli rabe 2 minutes before end of pasta cooking time. Reserve ¼ cup pasta water, and drain pasta and broccoli rabe.

4. Add pasta, broccoli rabe, and reserved pasta water to tomato mixture in pan. Cook over medium-high heat, stirring gently, until combined and liquid thickens slightly, about 2 minutes. Transfer to a serving dish, top with breadcrumbs, and serve immediately.

STALKS & STEMS

Stalks and stems are the "interstate highways" of the vegetable world: botanical thoroughfares for the passage of water, sugars, and nutrients between the plant's roots down below and its leaves above. But the stalks and stems of asparagus, celery, rhubarb, and other such edible plant parts—including the bulb-like stems of fennel and kohlrabi—have transformed the route into a scenic byway—and one of the plants' greatest assets. Indeed, celery stalks were once considered so elegant that they were displayed, like calla lilies, in crystal vases.

For a cook, understanding the role of stalks and stems in the life of a plant can help with selecting, preparing, and cooking them. Ripeness—the age of a vegetable when harvested—matters with all fruits and vegetables. But with stalks and stems, it's of foremost importance, surpassing even freshness (in other words, how recently it was harvested). Picked young, just as they are reaching toward the sky, stalks such as asparagus, celery, and rhubarb will be crisp, lithe, and tender. But allow a few days or weeks to pass, and they begin to turn stringy, even woody, because nature has designed them to stiffen into reliable support structures for the growing plant. Techniques like paring away the celery and fennel "strings," and peeling away the outer layer of rhubarb or kohlrabi can alleviate this problem. Better yet, hit the road yourself, in search of the youngest ones your farmers' market has to offer.

ASPARAGUS
—
CELERY
—
FENNEL
—
KOHLRABI
—
RHUBARB

THE BASICS

SEASONALITY

Emerging from the just-thawed earth, asparagus is a harbinger of spring, and its season is brief. A few weeks later, rhubarb begins to reach skyward; it's best just as late spring crosses into summer. Look for kohlrabi in early summer if you like it raw; by July, its turnipy nature begins to assert itself. Fennel likes cool weather, and is available from fall into very early spring. Celery won't tolerate extremes of heat or cold, but it is available year-round thanks to cultivation in both northern and southern states.

BUYING

Does size matter? When it comes to some stalks, the answer is yes, but for others, not so much. Contrary to what many people think, thinner asparagus spears are not younger, more tender versions of thicker-speared asparagus. Instead, long, thick spears with tightly closed heads are usually the best tasting and have the best texture. In contrast, those shorter, thinner inner celery stalks are more tender than the outer ones. But the length and thickness of a rhubarb spear, or the plumpness of a fennel bulb, are no indications of quality. Instead, try inspecting the cut ends of these vegetables. With observation, you may be able to determine their maturity—those of younger plants will have a uniform, smooth, almost creamy appearance; older ones will look coarse and woody. However, the only sure way to determine the age of stalk and stem vegetables is to buy them in season at a greenmarket, from a farmer who grew them herself. Kohlrabi is one

exception: Look for bulbs no larger than a tennis ball that do not appear cracked or overgrown; the leaves should be unblemished.

NOTABLE VARIETIES

Asparagus: Green, purple, or white—they are all the same varieties but with different tastes and textures. The hue of any purple asparagus, such as Purple Passion, is only skin deep and the stalks will turn green when cooked, so enjoy it raw; it is more tender and sweeter-tasting than green. White, on the other hand, stays creamy white when cooked, thanks to being deprived of sunlight during growing to avoid its turning green; as such, it has a milder taste (and much tougher skins).

Celery: Most celery is of the familiar greenish-white type; the varieties at farmers' markets tend to have more vibrant leaves attached (and, often, stalks that are more tender), all the better for using in salads and to garnish soups. Celery also comes in red (often called "Red Giant"); the stalks are sturdier, even when cooked, and have a more robust flavor, making them ideal for simmering in soups and stews.

Fennel: The familiar type of fennel (*finocchio*) with the white bulb is called Florence (or Florentine) fennel; you can also find it labeled "sweet anise" or just "anise." Wild fennel (*finocchietto*) looks nothing like the domesticated variety; instead of a bulb it has a root, and it is harvested for the feathery fronds (which are added to soups and stews and egg dishes) and the seeds (used in pickling and making sausages). Wild fennel has a more intense licorice flavor than domesticated fennel. Fennel pollen, the golden dust extracted from flowers on bolted plants, has also become more common; it is prized for having the most intense (concentrated) licorice taste, with hints of citrus, too. It can be used in any dish where you would use the bulb or wild fennel fronds and seeds, either added while cooking or as a garnish.

Kohlrabi: This knobby vegetable may be pinkish purple (often called "violet" or "red") or greenish (called "white"); both have white flesh and are identical in taste.

Rhubarb: Its colors range from deep crimson to green; the color does not affect flavor. (Here's a tip for helping rhubarb take on a rosier hue: Add a few slices of red beet to the liquid when poaching or stewing.)

STORING

Asparagus can be stored like fresh flowers: Slice vertically into the spears' ends and stand them upright in water, with the tips lightly covered with a damp paper towel. Celery, fennel, and rhubarb like a slightly moist, chilly environment; wrap them loosely in a slightly damp paper towel and place them in a plastic bag in the refrigerator for up to three or four days. The kohlrabi stems (or bulbs) will keep for several weeks in the refrigerator. If you have an abundance of rhubarb, the easiest way to store it so you can enjoy rhubarb when it's out of season is to freeze it: Cut the stalks into 1-inch pieces,

lay them flat on a baking sheet, and freeze until firm, at least 2 hours. Then transfer to sealable plastic bags, and store in the freezer up to a year.

PREPPING

You'll know how to prep stalks the moment you start working with them; they have built-in guidelines. For example, if you cut halfway through an outer stalk of celery or fennel and pull downward, do tough strings pull away? If so, pare them off. Next, inspect the cut end: Is it hollow and fibrous? If so, discard the outer stalks. Asparagus, meanwhile, will naturally break where the tough bottom end meets the more tender upper stalk; bend gently to feel for the junction, then snap off and discard the bottom portion. You can use a paring knife to peel away the silky outer skin of kohlrabi (younger ones won't need peeling), rhubarb, and asparagus, if necessary; white asparagus always needs peeling.

COOKING

Long spears of delicate, young asparagus are succulent in springtime, and the tender inner stalks of celery and fennel are delightful to eat from tip to toe. But given the fibrous nature of these vegetables' cell structures, cutting them crosswise is often the best solution, especially for older ones. Slice firm stalks on the bias into short chunks or even paper-thin slices to eliminate stringiness. Thus prepared, fennel, celery, kohlrabi, and even asparagus are wonderful raw in salads. Fennel and asparagus also take well to grilling and roasting. Tart rhubarb, too, is lovely roasted with sugar, and when stewed for just a few minutes, it melts into a silky compote: Slice ¼ inch thick, combine in a saucepan with sugar or honey, fresh ginger, and just enough water to cover the bottom of the pan. Cover tightly, and cook 7 to 10 minutes, or until the pieces fall apart. Serve over Greek yogurt, ice cream, or waffles.

HOW TO SERVE RAW
(For asparagus, celery, fennel, kohlrabi)
Trim tough ends of asparagus and peel into ribbons with a vegetable peeler, or cut thinly on the bias; thinly slice celery, fennel, and kohlrabi (preferably on a mandoline) or cut fennel and kohlrabi into matchsticks. Toss with extra-virgin olive oil and lemon juice (orange is also nice with fennel) or red-wine vinegar, and season with salt and pepper. Add apples, carrots, radishes, scallions, or red onion, cut into similar-size pieces as the stalk, if desired. Top with shaved or grated Parmesan or Pecorino Romano.

HOW TO STEAM
(For asparagus, celery, fennel, kohlrabi)
Fill a pot with enough water to come just under a steamer insert; bring to a simmer. Snap off tough ends of asparagus; slice celery and fennel ½ inch thick; cut kohlrabi into ½-inch cubes. Place in steamer basket, cover, and cook until just tender, 5 to 10 minutes (less for very thin asparagus stalks). Toss with extra-virgin olive oil, lemon juice and/or zest, fresh herbs (parsley, mint, or basil), and season with salt and pepper.

HOW TO BRAISE
(For asparagus, celery, fennel)
Trim tough ends of asparagus and tips of celery stalks, leaving heads intact; trim stems from fennel and cut bulbs into halves or quarters lengthwise. (Make sure asparagus spears can all fit in pan.) Sauté in butter or olive oil over medium-high heat until browned in spots, turning once, 2 to 3 minutes. Season with salt and pepper, and add enough liquid (chicken or vegetable broth, or orange juice and/or water) to cover. Simmer, covered, until very tender, 10 to 12 minutes; add more water if pan becomes too dry. Top with grated lemon or orange zest (and chopped fennel fronds for fennel), fresh or dried herbs, a drizzle more olive oil, and pepper.

HOW TO ROAST

(For asparagus, fennel, kohlrabi, rhubarb)

Leave asparagus or rhubarb whole, or cut on the bias into 1-inch pieces; cut fennel into ½-inch wedges; and cut kohlrabi into ¼-inch slices. Toss with olive oil just to coat. Season with salt and pepper. (Toss rhubarb instead with a bit of sugar or honey.) Spread on a baking sheet, and roast at 425°F until browning in spots, turning vegetables halfway through, about 15 minutes.

HOW TO GRILL

(For asparagus and fennel)

Trim tough ends from asparagus; trim fennel and halve or quarter bulb. Toss with olive oil, salt, and pepper. To grill skinnier stalks, thread them on skewers. Place on a medium-hot grill, and cook until beginning to char, turning frequently, 5 to 7 minutes. Sprinkle with fresh herbs and grated sharp cheese.

HOW TO BAKE CHIPS

(For kohlrabi)

Toss very thinly sliced kohlrabi with olive oil, salt, and pepper, and spread evenly on a baking sheet lined with a nonstick mat. Bake at 250°F until crisp and golden, rotating sheet once, 35 minutes to 1 hour. Transfer to paper towels to drain, and sprinkle with salt.

FLAVOR PAIRINGS

What to pair with stalks and stems? It all depends. Celery, part of the essential flavor bases of many cuisines, including mirepoix in France (celery, onion, carrot), soffrito in Italy (celery, onion, carrot, and parsley), and the Cajun "Holy Trinity" (celery, onion, and green pepper), goes with almost everything. And its natural saltiness makes it an essential part of many soups and stews. Rhubarb, on the other hand, has such a unique and assertive flavor that it can clash with other ingredients. Kohlrabi brings a fresh, delicate flavor, like that of tender broccoli stems, to raw salads. Like fennel and asparagus, it comes to life with a touch of acidity from citrus or mild vinegar.

ASPARAGUS: lemon, Parmesan, garlic, ginger, sesame, eggs, cream, ham

CELERY: dill, tarragon, mayonnaise, blue cheese, curry, onions, carrots, parsley

FENNEL: orange, lemon, Parmesan, almonds, olives, parsley, thyme, tomatoes

KOHLRABI: lemon, mustard, Swiss cheese, dill, cream

RHUBARB: strawberries, ginger, orange, raspberries, mint, cinnamon, crème fraîche

Steamed Asparagus, Three Ways

Nothing says spring like the first appearance of local asparagus, which needs only brief cooking (or none at all) to be at its best. We especially like it when simply steamed, with little embellishment other than a few classic flavor pairings, like the ones below. Choose asparagus that is uniform in size for even cooking.

SERVES 6

2 bunches asparagus (2 pounds), trimmed

Coarse salt

Place asparagus in a steamer insert set in a pot filled with 1 inch of water. Cover and bring to a boil. Steam until tender, 2 to 6 minutes (depending on thickness). Remove from heat and season with salt. Top as desired.

1
WITH
MINT BUTTER

Melt 1 stick unsalted butter in a small saucepan over medium heat with ½ cup packed finely chopped mint leaves, and season with coarse salt and freshly ground pepper. Heat until just bubbling around edges. Drizzle mint butter over asparagus, and toss gently to coat. Garnish with whole mint leaves.

2
WITH
EGGS MIMOSA

In a small bowl, whisk together 1 tablespoon white-wine vinegar and 2 teaspoons Dijon mustard, then season with coarse salt and freshly ground pepper. Add 3 tablespoons extra-virgin olive oil in a slow, steady stream, whisking until combined. Pass 1 large peeled hard-cooked egg through a fine-meshed sieve into another bowl. Spoon vinaigrette over asparagus, and top with sieved egg.

3
WITH
LEMON AÏOLI

Chop 2 garlic cloves on a cutting board, and add a pinch of coarse salt. Mash into a paste with knife's flat side (or in a mortar and pestle). Whisk 2 large egg yolks with ½ teaspoon salt in a bowl. Slowly add 1 table-spoon each fresh lemon juice and water, and whisk until thoroughly blended. Add 1¾ cups extra-virgin olive oil in a slow, steady stream, whisking until com-bined. Stir in garlic mixture. Serve as a dip for steamed asparagus. (Aïoli can be refrigerated, covered, up to 2 days. If aïoli separates, whisk 1 egg yolk with 1 table-spoon tepid water in a bowl; gradually whisk into aïoli until combined, then whisk in ¼ cup oil.)

TIP
An asparagus steamer allows the spears to stand upright, so the tougher parts cook faster than the tips, but you can use a regular steamer insert and a pot; you may need to trim the spears to fit in the basket, so they can lay flat.

Egg, Asparagus, and Mushroom Stir-Fry

There may be no better partner for asparagus than egg—you will often find asparagus in omelets and frittatas, in eggs benedict (in place of spinach), topped with mimosa (as on page 144) or a poached egg, and in quiches and custards. This egg and asparagus stir-fry includes garlic and scallions, as well as woody, flavorful oyster mushrooms.

SERVES 4

6 large eggs, room temperature

Coarse salt and freshly ground black pepper

2 tablespoons safflower oil

2 tablespoons minced peeled fresh ginger (from a 2-inch piece)

1 tablespoon minced garlic (from 2 to 3 cloves)

1 bunch scallions, trimmed and thinly sliced on the bias

12 ounces asparagus, trimmed and sliced on the bias into 3-inch pieces

6 ounces oyster mushrooms, separated into individual caps, large caps halved lengthwise

1 hot red chile pepper, very thinly sliced into rounds

2 tablespoons low-sodium soy sauce

3 tablespoons fresh lime juice (from 2 to 3 limes)

1. Whisk eggs with ½ teaspoon salt. Heat a large nonstick skillet over medium high. Swirl in 1 tablespoon oil. Add eggs and cook, undisturbed, until bottom and edges are set, about 30 seconds. Lift up edges of eggs with a heatproof flexible spatula, swirling and tilting pan so runny eggs slide underneath. Cook until eggs are golden in places along the bottom but still very wet on top, about 1 minute more. Gently slide eggs onto a cutting board. Roll them up like a cigar and slice crosswise into ½-inch-thick strips.

2. Wipe skillet clean; return to high heat with remaining 1 tablespoon oil. When oil shimmers, add ginger, garlic, scallions, asparagus, and mushrooms. Cook, stirring frequently, until vegetables are tender and golden brown in places, 4 to 5 minutes. Stir in chile and season with black pepper; cook 30 seconds. Add soy sauce, lime juice, and egg strips to skillet, tossing to evenly coat. Serve immediately.

Asparagus and Potato Flatbread

Other than serving shaved asparagus raw in a salad, we like to use it as a topping for flatbread, along with thinly sliced potato and crumbled goat cheese. (The dish makes a nice starter for Easter dinner.) Plump stalks of asparagus yield the optimal number of shavings.

MAKES 2 FLATBREADS

FOR THE DOUGH

- ¼ teaspoon sugar
- 1 envelope (¼ ounce) active dry yeast
- 1 cup warm water (about 110°F)
- 2¾ cups unbleached all-purpose flour, plus more for dusting
- 1 teaspoon coarse salt
- ¼ cup extra-virgin olive oil, plus more for bowl
- Fine cornmeal, for dusting

FOR THE TOPPINGS

- 1 Yukon Gold potato, peeled and very thinly sliced
- 2 tablespoons extra-virgin olive oil
- Coarse salt and ground pepper
- 1 bunch asparagus (1 pound), trimmed and shaved with a vegetable peeler
- 4 ounces fresh goat cheese, crumbled (1 cup)

1. Make the dough: In a small bowl, sprinkle sugar and yeast over the warm water; stir with a fork until yeast and sugar dissolve. Let stand until foamy, about 5 minutes. In a food processor, pulse together flour and salt to combine. Add yeast mixture and 2 tablespoons oil; pulse until mixture comes together but is still slightly tacky. Dough should pull away cleanly from your fingers after it's squeezed. Turn out dough onto a lightly floured work surface; knead four or five times, until a smooth ball forms. Place in a lightly oiled bowl, smooth side up. Cover with plastic wrap; let rise in a warm place until doubled in bulk, about 40 minutes.

2. Punch down dough. Fold dough back onto itself four or five times, then turn smooth side up. Replace plastic wrap; let dough rise again in a warm place until doubled in bulk, 30 to 40 minutes.

3. Preheat oven to 500°F, with racks in middle and lower thirds. Punch down dough; turn out onto a lightly floured work surface. Using a bench scraper or knife, divide dough into two pieces. Knead each four or five times, then form two smooth balls. Return one ball to oiled bowl; cover with plastic wrap. Pat remaining ball into a flattened disk; cover with wrap; let rest 5 minutes. Using your hands or a rolling pin, press or roll out dough balls into two 6-by-16-inch ovals, working from center outward. Transfer to two parchment-lined baking sheets. Brush each with 1 tablespoon oil.

4. Make the toppings: In a bowl, toss potato with 2 teaspoons oil and season with salt and pepper. Arrange slices on dough, leaving a ¼-inch border. Bake until edges of crusts are golden and potato is beginning to crisp around edges, about 12 minutes, rotating halfway through. Reduce heat to 450°F. Toss asparagus with 2 teaspoons oil; season with salt and pepper. Top flatbread with asparagus; bake until asparagus is crisp-tender, about 5 minutes. Top with cheese; bake until cheese is warmed through, about 3 minutes more. Drizzle each flatbread with 1 teaspoon oil, then cut into wedges.

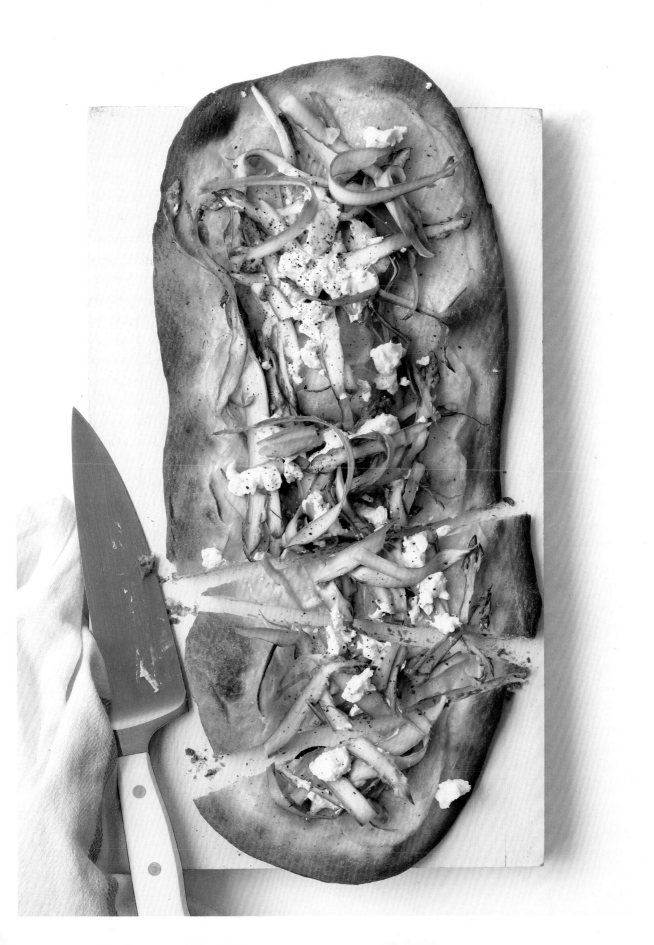

Rhubarb Chutney with Pork Roast

Pies and pastries are not the only ways to enjoy rhubarb. The tart stalks also work wonders as an accompaniment to savory foods. They're excellent pickled, or cooked in a chutney, here with brown sugar, orange zest, and fresh ginger, plus celery (another stalk). Try the chutney as a toast topping along with sliced sharp cheese.

SERVES 6

FOR THE CHUTNEY

- ½ red onion, cut into ¼-inch-thick rounds
- ¼ cup golden raisins
- 1 teaspoon finely grated peeled fresh ginger
- Finely grated zest of 1 orange
- ½ cup dry white wine, such as Sauvignon Blanc
- ¼ cup white-wine vinegar
- 1 cup packed light-brown sugar
- 1 pound rhubarb, trimmed and cut into 4-inch lengths
- 2 celery stalks, cut into 4-inch lengths

FOR THE ROAST PORK

- 1 small boneless pork loin (about 3 pounds), tied
- Coarse salt and freshly ground pepper
- ½ cup loosely packed fresh sage or basil leaves
- 2 tablespoons extra-virgin olive oil

1. Make the chutney: Bring onion, raisins, ginger, orange zest, wine, vinegar, and brown sugar to a simmer in a saucepan over medium heat.

2. Add rhubarb and celery; cover; reduce heat. Simmer gently until rhubarb is tender but not falling apart, about 5 minutes. Transfer rhubarb to a bowl with a slotted spoon.

3. Continue to simmer liquid until it has thickened and reduced and celery is tender, about 10 minutes more. Transfer to bowl with rhubarb. Let cool, and chill until needed. (Chutney will keep several weeks refrigerated in an airtight container.)

4. Make the pork: Preheat oven to 400°F. Pat pork roast dry and season all over with salt and pepper. Tuck herbs under twine. Heat oil in a large ovenproof skillet over medium. Add pork, fat side down, and cook until golden brown, about 5 minutes. Flip pork and transfer to oven. Cook until an instant-read thermometer inserted into middle reaches 150°F, about 20 minutes. Let rest 10 minutes before slicing and serving with chutney.

TIP
Sample the finished chutney: If it's too tart, add more brown sugar. If too sweet, add a little more vinegar.

Asparagus, Artichoke, and Farro Salad

To really appreciate the faintly earthy taste of white asparagus, eat it raw, preferably combined with comparably flavored baby artichokes—in other words, in this bright, crisp grain salad. Fresh mint and dill, lemon, and feta round out the flavors.

SERVES 6 TO 8

1¼ cups semipearled farro

Zest and juice of 1 lemon

¼ cup extra-virgin olive oil

½ cup chopped red onion

Coarse salt and freshly ground pepper

1 pound baby artichokes, trimmed (see Prepping, page 239)

1 bunch white (or green) asparagus (1 pound)

¼ cup fresh mint leaves

⅓ cup chopped fresh dill

6 ounces feta cheese

1. Cover farro with 3 inches of water in a large saucepan. Bring to a boil over high heat. Reduce heat to medium, and cook until tender but still slightly chewy, 25 to 30 minutes.

2. Meanwhile, combine lemon zest and juice, oil, and onion in a large bowl, then season with salt and pepper. Drain farro and immediately toss with dressing. Let cool completely.

3. Trim and peel asparagus; then slice, on the bias, into ½-inch-thick pieces, leaving tips whole. Add to farro along with mint and dill, tossing to combine. Add feta, drizzle with additional oil, if desired, and serve.

Fennel and Smoked Salmon Salad

Fennel's mild licorice flavor has an affinity for salty, briny foods, including olives, capers, smoked fish, and sardines. Here, we toss thinly sliced fennel and snipped fronds with lemon zest and juice to create a tart topping that cuts through the richness of smoked salmon. It's a great dish for brunch or a holiday open house, or to serve with cocktails.

SERVES 4

1 medium fennel bulb, trimmed and thinly sliced, plus ¼ cup fennel fronds

½ teaspoon grated lemon zest, plus 4 teaspoons lemon juice

Coarse salt and freshly ground pepper

4 ounces thinly sliced smoked salmon

1 tablespoon extra-virgin olive oil

Toss sliced fennel and fronds with lemon zest and juice in a bowl; season with salt and pepper. Arrange salmon on a platter. Top with fennel mixture, drizzle with oil, and serve.

Clam Pan Roast
with Fennel and Sausage

Many of the seafood stews of the world—bouillabaisse, cioppino, and caldeirada de peixe (from Portugal), among others—all share a common ingredient: fennel. Essentially a creamy stew, the shellfish pan roast is most famously made with oysters, but clams are just as traditional, and often appear in combination with sausage; we include two types, sweet Italian and kielbasa. Pernod and tarragon add more licorice flavor.

SERVES 6

1 garlic clove, minced

1 pound sweet Italian sausage, casing removed

¼ pound kielbasa, cut into ½-inch cubes

12 small red potatoes, halved

3 small fennel bulbs, trimmed and cut into ¼-inch-thick slices

1 small leek, cut into ¼-inch rounds, rinsed well

¼ cup Pernod or other anise-flavored liqueur

1½ cups bottled clam juice (unsalted)

Coarse salt and freshly ground pepper

2½ pounds littleneck clams, scrubbed

2 large tomatoes, cut into 8 wedges each

¼ cup tarragon leaves

1. Cook garlic and Italian sausage in a Dutch oven or heavy pot over medium heat, stirring and breaking up meat with a spoon, until sausage is no longer pink, about 5 minutes; transfer to a bowl with a slotted spoon. Drain all but 1 tablespoon fat from skillet. Cook kielbasa until crisp, stirring occasionally, 8 to 10 minutes. Add to bowl.

2. Arrange potatoes in pan, cut side down; cook until golden brown, 5 to 7 minutes. Flip potatoes; cook until just tender, about 5 minutes. Scatter fennel over potatoes. Cook until fennel is tender, stirring frequently, about 10 minutes.

3. Add leek, Pernod, and clam juice. Season with salt and pepper. Cook until vegetables are tender, stirring occasionally, about 5 minutes. Return sausage mixture to pan; stir to combine. Add clams, cover, and cook 5 minutes. Add tomatoes; cook, covered, until clams open, about 8 minutes.

4. Discard any unopened clams, and remove pan from heat. Stir in tarragon and serve.

TIP
To clean clams, rinse them under cold running water and scrub the shells with a stiff sponge or vegetable brush. Discard any that are chipped or open.

Celery, Cilantro, and Almond Salad

For some people, the tender leaves that top the inner celery stalks are the best part.
In pretty shades of yellow and green, they have a delicate celery flavor.
They also make a wonderful salad "green" that can be tossed with vinaigrette.

SERVES 4

¼ cup almonds

6 small celery stalks
(from 1 bunch),
thinly sliced on the bias,
tender leaves reserved

1½ cups fresh cilantro leaves

⅔ cup dried cherries

3 tablespoons extra-virgin
olive oil

1 tablespoon plus 1 teaspoon
fresh lemon juice

Coarse salt

1. Preheat oven to 350°F. Toast almonds on a rimmed baking sheet until fragrant and darkened, tossing occasionally, 10 to 12 minutes. Transfer to a plate; let cool, then coarsely chop.

2. Combine celery (stalks and leaves), cilantro, dried cherries, and almonds in a bowl. Drizzle with oil and lemon juice, and season with salt. Toss to coat and serve.

TIP Always seek out celery bunches with the most leaves at farmstands and greenmarkets (and even at some supermarkets).

Braised Celery

A long, slow braise transforms the taste and texture of celery so it's more mellow and almost silken. Here, the heads are left intact and halved lengthwise, exposing the hearts. (Be sure to peel the outer stalks to remove the strings.) Finishing the dish under the broiler results in a nicely browned top. Serve with roast turkey or pork.

SERVES 8 TO 10

2 large heads celery,
    outer stalks removed

    Coarse salt and freshly
    ground pepper

4 to 6 large thyme sprigs

6 tablespoons unsalted butter,
    cut into small pieces

2½ cups low-sodium
    chicken broth

¼ cup extra-virgin olive oil

1. Preheat oven to 375°F, with rack in upper third. Cut each head of celery in half lengthwise, and peel larger stalks with a vegetable peeler. Trim ¼ inch from bases (keeping heads intact), then trim tops so each half is about 12 inches long. Arrange celery in a single layer, cut sides up, in a 9-by-13-inch baking dish. Season generously with salt and pepper, scatter with thyme, and dot with butter. Pour in broth and oil.

2. Cover with parchment-lined foil. Bake until celery is tender and easily pierced with the tip of a knife, 40 to 45 minutes. Turn oven to broil, and remove foil. Spoon braising juices over celery, and broil until lightly charred in places, 5 to 10 minutes.

PODS

We keep what's precious stashed away safely, in boxes and cases, chests and trunks. Plants do, too. In the case of beans, peas, and okra, this means enclosing and protecting their precious seeds in little capsules until the time is right for them to be sent forth into the future. Edible pods and their contents, known collectively as *legumes,* have been part of human agriculture since the earliest days—and continue to be a significant aspect of diets the world over. Because it turns out that those same seeds in which the plant has invested its hope and nourishment for the next generation are full of good things for our bodies, too.

Unlike most plants grown for food, which have just a single phase of ripe edibility, legumes have been cultivated to be eaten at every stage of maturity. This is true whether they grow on bushes or vines (or poles). Some varieties are harvested when the shells are sweet and tender and the seeds barely formed (as with snow peas, okra, and green beans), others when the seeds are fully grown but still delicate, and the pods coarse (as with English peas, edamame, and fava beans). Still others come to market dried hard as pebbles. One phase American cooks are less familiar with is the fresh-shelled one, when the husks turn papery around the seeds, which are mature but not yet dried. These beans and peas are a buttery, nutty revelation—and just one more treasure to be found nestled inside a pod.

EDAMAME

—

ENGLISH PEAS

—

FAVA BEANS

—

GREEN BEANS

—

OKRA

—

SHELL BEANS

—

SNAP PEAS

—

SNOW PEAS

THE BASICS

SEASONALITY

Fava bean pods are lined with a velvety fuzz, which must help keep the beans warm as they germinate and grow in winter. By early spring, they're ready to eat; look for favas in late April and May. English peas, sugar snap peas, and snow peas follow close on their tails; you'll find them throughout spring and early summer. Green beans and okra are warm-weather plants, and are harvested throughout the summer. Shell beans, like cranberry and lima, turn up in greenmarkets just as summer moves to fall. Once their season has passed, dried beans are a fine substitute. Be sure to buy them from a shop with a high turnover (preferably sold in bulk) or directly from specialty sources such as Rancho Gordo or Zürsun Idaho Heirloom Beans.

BUYING

Look for green beans and fresh peas of all sorts that are a bright green with no yellowing (unless you are buying wax beans), and make sure the shells are tender. Green beans and snow peas should never feel leathery or hollow, and the seeds should be small and fully embedded in the pod's interior, rather than rattling around. English peas, fava beans, and other fresh shelling beans should bulge slightly within their pods—neither too big nor too small. Because these vegetables begin to lose freshness the moment they are harvested, buy them as recently picked as you can—at a farmstand or greenmarket. Okra should be velvety and vivid in color.

NOTABLE VARIETIES

Green and wax beans: Green beans, including purple-colored varieties and yellow wax beans, are the most common of the bush or pole beans. Haricots verts are also a familiar option, while Romano beans are among the more common heirloom varieties. It's worth seeking out purple varieties, such as Royal Burgundy or purple Romano beans, for serving raw, and also for their distinctive flavors.

Shell beans: Those dried beans in your pantry started out as shell beans, which you can buy in their pods during their brief season. Fresh ones have an incomparably creamy texture, don't need to be soaked prior to cooking, and cook more quickly than dried. Among the most widely available are mottled cranberry beans, edamame, and lima beans. Also, keep your eye out for heirloom varieties (and their descriptive names): Jacob's Cattle, scarlet runner, Pink Half-Runner, Black Calypso, borlotti, and Tongues of Fire, to name a few chefs' favorites.

STORING

Refrigerate pods, loosely wrapped in a plastic bag—but not for long. Tender, fresh green beans and peas are the most ephemeral of vegetables. That's because their shells are designed to transfer moisture and sugars into the seeds, which are themselves working on transforming the sugars into starch—processes designed to benefit future generations of the plant, but not cooks or eaters. Fresh shell beans can be stored in a paper bag in the refrigerator for up to three days.

PREPPING

With green beans, snap peas, and snow peas, trim only the stem end and not the tapered—and delectable—tip. It's the same with sugar snap and snow peas. When shelling English peas, edamame, and shell beans, twist the pod gently to crack it open and release the tasty contents. One pound of pods equals about a cup of peas and beans. (We find frozen peas to be a fine substitute for fresh; thaw them quickly in a colander under running tepid tap water.) Fava bean pods can be similarly opened, but the seeds require a further step before becoming edible: Blanch them for a minute in boiling water, plunge them into an ice bath, then peel off the milk-white membrane encasing each one. (Unless, of course, you grill them, as we do on page 180.) Okra pods are covered in a fuzz that can become prickly with age; wrap several at time in a kitchen towel, and rub gently to remove fuzz before cooking.

COOKING

If you've ever tasted a sugar snap pea or green bean plucked straight from the vine, you know that the best legumes need never see the inside of a kitchen. But since most vegetables travel to reach our tables, cooking them is in order. Usually, all they need is a quick dip in rapidly boiling, salted water—but "quick" can be anywhere from one to seven minutes depending on age and variety, so sample as you cook, then drain and plunge into ice water to stop the cooking and brighten their color. Okra, traditionally

used to thicken stews, tastes wonderful battered and fried. And okra, along with green beans, is a classic for pickling.

HOW TO STEAM
(For all pods except shell beans)
Remove English peas and fava beans from the pods and peel favas; trim green beans, okra, and snap and snow peas. Place in a steamer basket (or colander) set in a pot filled with 1 inch of water; bring to a boil. Cover and steam until pods are tender and color brightens, 2 to 7 minutes. Drizzle with olive oil, season with salt, and squeeze a halved lemon over the top.

HOW TO BRAISE
(For fava beans, green beans, okra, shell beans)
Remove fava and shell beans from pods and peel favas; trim green beans and okra. Heat olive oil or butter in a skillet over medium high, then cook finely chopped onion and minced garlic until softened. Add vegetables and season with salt and pepper, then add enough liquid (chicken or vegetable broth, supplemented with a splash of wine or vinegar if desired) to cover by 1 inch along with a bay leaf. Simmer, with pan partially covered, until tender and liquid has thickened, 8 to 10 minutes for fava, okra, and green beans, 30 minutes for shell. Sprinkle with fresh herbs, such as parsley or thyme, and shaved cheese such as Pecorino Romano (spike okra with hot-pepper sauce).

HOW TO ROAST
(For green beans and okra)
Trim green beans and okra. Drizzle with olive oil on a rimmed baking sheet, and season with salt and pepper. You can also add some whole

peeled garlic cloves or thinly sliced peeled fresh ginger. Toss to combine and spread evenly. Roast at 400°F until tender and browned in spots, tossing halfway through, 15 to 20 minutes. Sprinkle with chopped fresh mint or cilantro.

HOW TO GRILL
(For all pods except English peas and shell beans)
Trim green beans, okra, and snap and snow peas. Grill vegetables in a vegetable grilling pan or threaded on skewers (to keep them from slipping through the grates) until charred in spots, 2 to 7 minutes, turning as needed.

HOW TO BLANCH
(For all pods except shell beans)
Remove English peas and fava beans from the pods, and peel favas; trim green beans, okra and snap and snow peas. Bring vegetables and enough water to cover to a boil in a pot; add salt and boil until vegetables are tender, 2 to 5 minutes. Drain and season while warm; or plunge into an ice-water bath to stop the cooking, then drain again.

HOW TO SIMMER
(For shell beans)
Remove beans from the pods. Place beans in a pot with enough water to cover by 4 inches. Season generously with salt, and bring to a boil, then reduce heat and simmer until beans are tender and creamy, 20 to 30 minutes, depending on type of bean. Drain well. Drizzle with olive oil, sprinkle with chopped parsley or thyme, and season with red-pepper flakes or top with grated or shaved Parmesan cheese.

FLAVOR PAIRINGS

Toss cooked young beans and peas with butter and a pinch of salt, adding gently torn herbs like mint or marjoram if you like—these springtime babies need little to taste sublime. And the buttery, nutty, or earthy flavors of shell beans can stand up to bold late-summer ingredients and rich fall flavors, including hearty greens.

EDAMAME: garlic, ginger, chili peppers, orange zest, soy sauce, tomatoes, corn

ENGLISH PEAS: mint, parsley, butter, bacon, onions, cream, lettuce

FAVA BEANS: olive oil, olives, basil, parsley, sheeps'-milk cheeses, peas, lamb

GREEN BEANS: basil, tomatoes, parsley, lemon zest, ginger, garlic, thyme

OKRA: tomatoes, vinegar, corn meal, bell peppers, shrimp

SHELL BEANS: garlic, sausage, bitter greens, Parmesan, rosemary, tomatoes

SNAP PEAS: dill, carrots, ginger, basil, lemon, chiles, garlic

SNOW PEAS: sesame, peanuts, ginger, garlic, soy sauce, bell peppers

Blanched Sugar Snap Peas, Three Ways

Fresh from the garden or farmstand, sugar snap peas are tender and sweet enough to eat raw, as a snack or with dips as crudités. They're also delicious blanched, which leaves the flavor intact as it brightens the color. We like to serve sugar snaps with simple sauces, made with the pod's favorite flavors: fresh herbs and lemon.

SERVES 4

Coarse salt

1 pound sugar snap peas

In a large pot of boiling salted water, cook snap peas until crisp-tender and bright green, about 2 minutes. Drain and toss with desired sauce.

1
DILL BUTTER

Melt 2 tablespoons unsalted butter in a small saucepan over medium-low heat. Remove from heat and stir in ¼ cup chopped fresh dill. Toss with warm peas.

2
PESTO

Sprinkle ¼ teaspoon coarse salt over 1 peeled garlic clove on a cutting board, then coarsely chop; using a flat side of the knife, crush into a thick paste. Transfer to a food processor; add ¼ cup toasted pine nuts (or walnuts), 3 cups packed fresh basil leaves, and 1 tablespoon extra-virgin olive oil. Pulse until finely chopped. With machine running, add ½ cup more oil in a slow, steady stream, until combined. Add ¼ cup grated Parmigiano-Reggiano cheese and pulse to combine. Season with salt and pepper. (Pesto can be stored in an airtight container, with a layer of olive oil on top, up to 1 week in the refrigerator.) Toss with warm peas.

3
LEMON-CILANTRO

Toast 2 tablespoons coriander seeds in a dry skillet over medium heat, shaking pan frequently, until fragrant, 2 to 3 minutes. Transfer to a plate and let cool, then lightly crush with the flat side of a chef's knife. Combine with strips of zest of 1 lemon, 2 tablespoons rice vinegar (unseasoned), and ¼ cup chopped fresh cilantro. Toss with warm peas.

TIP
You can use any of these sauces with snow peas. Blanch as directed above.

Risi e Bisi

One of our favorite ways to showcase fresh peas is in this traditional Venetian dish ("rice and peas"). Prepared properly, it's slightly soupier than risotto, and according to culinary lore, it is supposed to contain one pea for every grain of rice—meaning the dish is just as much about the peas as the rice. That's just the way we like it, topped with grated lemon zest and freshly grated Parmesan.

SERVES 4

1 cup shelled green peas (from 1 pound in pods), or 1 cup thawed frozen peas

Coarse salt and freshly ground pepper

6 cups low-sodium vegetable broth

¼ cup extra-virgin olive oil

1 small onion, finely chopped

1 cup Arborio rice

½ cup dry white wine, such as Sauvignon Blanc

1 teaspoon finely grated lemon zest plus 2 tablespoons fresh lemon juice, plus more zest for serving

½ cup finely chopped fresh flat-leaf parsley

½ cup finely grated Parmigiano-Reggiano cheese, plus more for serving

1. Blanch fresh peas in a pot of salted boiling water until just tender and bright green, 3 to 4 minutes. Transfer to an ice-water bath and let cool completely. Drain. (If using frozen peas, skip this step.)

2. Bring broth to a simmer in a medium saucepan; cover to keep warm.

3. Heat 2 tablespoons oil over medium in another saucepan. Cook onion, stirring frequently, until soft, 6 to 7 minutes. Add rice, cook, stirring, until edges are translucent, 2 to 3 minutes. Add wine; cook, stirring, just until evaporated.

4. Add ½ cup hot broth; cook, stirring, until almost absorbed. Continue adding ½ cup broth in this manner until liquid is creamy and rice is al dente, about 20 minutes total (you may not need to add all the broth). Add peas about 1 minute before risotto is finished cooking.

5. Remove from heat; stir in lemon zest and juice, parsley, cheese, and remaining 2 tablespoons oil. Season with salt and pepper. Serve immediately, topped with more cheese and lemon zest.

Green-Pea Burgers with Harissa Mayo

Because their season is so fleeting, it makes sense to have a number of ways in which to enjoy fresh garden peas, especially one or two unexpected options. Peas not only lend bright-green vegetable burgers a lovely flavor (and color), they also help keep them moist. These pack a lot of protein (here aided by a half cup of chickpeas). Serve the burgers on brioche rolls with baby greens, cucumber slices, and harissa-spiked mayonnaise.

SERVES 4

1 cup shelled green peas (from 1 pound in pods), or 1 cup thawed frozen peas

Coarse salt

½ cup cooked chickpeas (rinsed and drained)

½ small onion, finely chopped

2 tablespoons fresh flat-leaf parsley, chopped

1 large egg, whisked

1 cup fresh breadcrumbs (from 3 to 4 slices white bread)

2 tablespoons extra-virgin olive oil

½ cup mayonnaise

2 tablespoons harissa

4 brioche rolls, split and toasted

1 cup mixed baby greens

½ English cucumber, cut into thin rounds

1. Blanch fresh peas in a pot of salted boiling water until just tender and bright, 3 to 4 minutes. Transfer to an ice-water bath, and let cool completely. Drain. (If using frozen peas, skip this step.)

2. In a food processor, pulse peas and chickpeas until coarsely chopped. Transfer to a bowl and stir in onion, parsley, egg, and breadcrumbs. Season with salt. Form into four patties, each about ¾ inch thick.

3. Heat oil in a large nonstick skillet over medium. Cook burgers until golden and crisp, about 4 minutes per side.

4. Stir together mayonnaise and harissa in a small bowl until combined. Spread on brioche rolls. Divide the burgers, baby greens, and cucumber among rolls; serve.

Cranberry Bean Salad with Delicata Squash and Broccoli Rabe

Simmered cranberry beans—also called Roman beans, with a flavor similar to chestnuts—are the foundation of this hearty fall salad that includes roasted delicata squash, sautéed broccoli rabe, and crumbled bacon. It makes a delicious side dish for a family-style meal. Skip the bacon and you have a wonderful vegetarian main dish.

SERVES 6

1 medium onion

1 dried bay leaf

4 or 5 whole black peppercorns

2½ pounds fresh cranberry beans, shelled (about 3 cups)

¼ cup plus 1 tablespoon extra-virgin olive oil, plus more for brushing

Coarse salt and freshly ground pepper

1 small delicata squash (about 1¾ pounds), cut into ½-inch-thick slices

4 slices bacon (4 ounces)

4 garlic cloves, minced

1 bunch broccoli rabe, washed and trimmed (about 1 pound)

1. Using a sharp knife, slice off stem end of onion, and score shallow slits all over, making sure onion stays intact. Place in a large saucepan with the bay leaf and the peppercorns; fill with 3 quarts water. Bring to a boil; reduce heat, and simmer 20 minutes. Add beans; simmer until cooked through, about 15 minutes. Drain beans, reserving cooking liquid. In a bowl, toss beans with 1 tablespoon each oil and cooking liquid; season with salt and pepper.

2. Meanwhile, preheat oven to 425°F. Arrange squash on a rimmed baking sheet, brush with oil, and season with salt and pepper. Roast until tender and golden brown, about 20 minutes.

3. While squash is roasting, cook bacon in a large skillet over medium heat until crisp, turning occasionally, about 8 minutes. Transfer bacon to paper towels to drain. Wipe skillet clean.

4. Heat 3 tablespoons oil in the same skillet over medium. Add garlic, and sauté until just golden, 1 to 2 minutes. Add broccoli rabe; sauté until wilted and heated through, about 5 minutes. Season with salt and pepper.

5. Add beans and squash to skillet, and cook just until heated through. Drizzle with remaining tablespoon of oil, and season with salt and pepper. Sprinkle reserved bacon on top and serve.

Skillet Edamame, Corn, and Tomatoes with Basil Oil

Pop edamame out of their pods, and use as you would garden peas, lima beans, or fava beans. They replace limas in this update on succotash, a classic summertime side dish.

SERVES 4 TO 6

1 cup fresh basil leaves

¼ cup plus 2 tablespoons extra-virgin olive oil

Coarse salt

4 scallions, finely sliced

3 garlic cloves, minced

3¼ cups corn kernels

⅔ cup shelled edamame (thawed, if frozen)

½ pound cherry tomatoes

2 tablespoons white balsamic vinegar

1. Blanch basil in a small pot of boiling water for 10 seconds. Transfer to an ice-water bath until cool, then drain and squeeze dry. Purée basil, ¼ cup oil, and ½ teaspoon salt in a blender or food processor until smooth.

2. Heat remaining 2 tablespoons oil in a large skillet over medium high. Add scallions and garlic; cook, stirring, until fragrant, about 30 seconds. Add corn and edamame, and season with salt. Cook, stirring occasionally, until corn starts to caramelize, about 10 minutes (reduce heat if overbrowning). Add tomatoes (halved, if large) and vinegar; cook, stirring occasionally, until tomatoes start to collapse, about 8 minutes. Drizzle basil oil on vegetables, stir to combine, and serve.

Roasted Wax Beans
with Peanuts and Cilantro

Roasting beans until tender and caramelized brings out their sweetness. Try them as a snack, or in this side dish, tossed with a savory sweet sauce, peanuts, and cilantro.

SERVES 4

1 pound wax beans, trimmed

1 tablespoon safflower oil

Coarse salt and freshly ground pepper

2 teaspoons low-sodium soy sauce

¼ teaspoon finely grated peeled fresh ginger

¾ teaspoon fresh lemon juice

½ teaspoon light-brown sugar

¼ cup unsalted peanuts

¼ cup fresh cilantro leaves

1. Preheat oven to 450°F. On a rimmed baking sheet, toss together wax beans and oil, and season with salt and pepper. Roast until browned in spots and tender, tossing halfway through, about 15 minutes.

2. In a large bowl, combine soy sauce, ginger, lemon juice, and sugar. Add roasted beans, peanuts, and cilantro. Toss to combine and serve.

Green Bean, Shell Bean, and Sweet Onion Fattoush

In late summer, fresh green beans and shell beans make a wonderful pair, one sharp and crisp-tender, the other buttery and plump. They're the beginnings of our version of fattoush, a Middle Eastern bread salad that's a fine way to enjoy summer produce. You can blanch the beans in the same pot: first the green beans, and then the shell (and not the other way around, since shell beans release a lot of starch).

SERVES 4

2 lemons, 1 zested and both juiced

2 garlic cloves, crushed

Coarse salt and freshly ground pepper

½ cup extra-virgin olive oil, plus more for brushing

½ pound haricots verts, trimmed

¾ cup shelled fresh shell beans, such as limas

3 pita breads (6-inch)

½ large Vidalia onion, coarsely chopped

1 English cucumber, quartered and cut into 1-inch pieces

4 ounces feta cheese, crumbled

½ cup coarsely chopped fresh mint, plus more for garnish

⅓ cup coarsely chopped fresh flat-leaf parsley

1. Whisk together lemon zest, lemon juice, and garlic, and season with salt. Whisking constantly, pour in oil in a slow, steady stream and whisk until emulsified. Season with pepper. Let stand 15 minutes; discard garlic.

2. Blanch haricots verts in a pot of salted boiling water until crisp-tender and bright green, about 1 minute. Transfer beans to an ice-water bath (reserve pot of water); let cool, then remove and pat dry. Place in a large bowl.

3. Return water to a boil. Blanch shell beans until just tender, 18 to 20 minutes. Transfer to ice bath; let cool, then drain in a colander and pat dry. Combine with haricots verts.

4. Heat a grill (or grill pan) to medium. Split each pita in half. Brush both sides of pita halves with oil; season with salt and pepper. Grill pita, turning once, until golden and crisp, about 1 minute per side. Let cool, then tear into 1-inch pieces.

5. Add onion, cucumber, feta, herbs, and pita to the beans; drizzle with ½ cup vinaigrette; toss well to combine. Season with salt and pepper; garnish with mint. Let stand at least 10 minutes and up to 1 hour before serving.

TIP
The pita is charred on the grill (or under the broiler) to make it sturdy enough to soak up the vinaigrette without falling apart. The longer the salad sits before serving (up to an hour), the better the flavors and textures will be.

White Beans with Dandelion Greens and Crostini

Many a delicious meal can be built around fresh shell beans. The Italians are masters of this art, cooking the beans with simple seasonings and then serving them with wilted greens and grated cheese on top. Serve with toasted bread, mashing some of the beans on top as you go.

SERVES 4

1 pound fresh cannellini beans, shelled (about 1¼ cups)

6 garlic cloves, 5 left whole and 1 minced

½ cup and 2 tablespoons extra-virgin olive oil, plus more for drizzling

¼ cup fresh thyme leaves

Coarse salt and freshly ground pepper

1 bunch dandelion greens, tough stems trimmed

1 tablespoon red wine vinegar

Crostini, for serving

Finely grated Parmigiano-Reggiano cheese, for serving

Fresh basil, for serving

1. Combine beans, whole garlic cloves, ½ cup oil, and thyme in a large pot with enough water to cover. Bring to a boil, then reduce heat and simmer until beans are tender, 30 to 35 minutes. Season with salt, and continue cooking 5 more minutes. Let cool completely in cooking liquid, then drain.

2. Meanwhile, heat remaining 2 tablespoons oil in a large skillet over medium high. Add minced garlic, and cook, stirring frequently, until softened, about 2 minutes. Add dandelion greens, and cook, tossing, just until wilted, about 1 minute. Season with salt and pepper, and add vinegar.

3. Serve beans with dandelion greens and crostini. Drizzle with oil, sprinkle with cheese, and top with basil.

TIP
Leftover beans can be frozen, in an airtight container, for up to three months; thaw overnight in the refrigerator before using.

Grilled Fava Beans

Generally speaking, fava beans have to be shelled and skinned, a time-consuming (but rewarding) process. Here's a wonderful shortcut: You can simply grill them in their pods, then pop out the beans, no peeling required. Serve them with a minty herb sauce, and sprinkle more mint and fresh lemon juice over the top.

SERVES 4

1 pound fava beans
(still in pods)

1 cup finely chopped fresh
mint, plus more for serving

½ cup extra-virgin olive oil

Coarse salt and freshly
ground pepper

Juice of ½ lemon,
plus wedges for serving

1. Heat grill to high. Clean and lightly oil hot grill. Grill favas directly on grates, turning, until charred, 10 to 12 minutes. Let cool slightly.

2. Meanwhile, stir together mint and oil in a small bowl, and season with salt and pepper.

3. To serve, sprinkle favas with lemon juice and more mint, and season with salt. Serve with herb sauce and lemon wedges on the side.

Creamy Fava Beans

Simmering fava beans with chicken broth and a little heavy cream makes a delectable accompaniment for pan-seared, poached, or grilled chicken breast, as shown here. This takes just long enough for the favas to become crisp-tender and for the liquids to reduce slightly to form a sauce.

SERVES 4

1 pound fava beans, shelled

2 tablespoons unsalted butter

1 leek (white and pale-green parts only), thinly sliced, rinsed well

¼ cup low-sodium chicken broth

1 tablespoon heavy cream

2 tablespoons fresh lemon juice

Coarse salt and freshly ground pepper

1. Prepare an ice-water bath. Blanch fava beans in a pot of boiling water until bright green, about 1 minute. Transfer to ice-water bath using a slotted spoon. Let cool, then slip beans from skins (discard skins).

2. Heat butter in a large skillet over medium high. Sauté leek until softened, stirring frequently, about 5 minutes. Add favas and broth; cook, stirring, 1 minute. Stir in cream, and simmer for 2 minutes. Remove from heat, and stir in lemon juice. Season with salt and pepper when ready to serve.

Beef and Snap-Pea Stir-Fry

As their name suggests, these peas literally snap when broken, thanks to their firmness. That's why they're often used in stir-fries, in which case they are cooked lightning fast, just until crisp and bright (they'll lose that snap if cooked too long). Thinly sliced steak is also a good choice for stir-frying, as it browns quickly in a hot pan. Here, scallions, fresh ginger, red-pepper flakes, and lime juice round out the flavors.

SERVES 4

1 pound sirloin steak, thinly sliced crosswise, halved if long

1 tablespoon cornstarch

Coarse salt and freshly ground pepper

2 teaspoons safflower oil

12 ounces snap peas

5 to 6 scallions, white and green parts separated, both thinly sliced on the bias

1 tablespoon grated peeled fresh ginger

¼ to ½ teaspoon red-pepper flakes

¾ cup water

2 tablespoons fresh lime juice

White or brown rice, or rice noodles, for serving

1. Place steak in a bowl. Sprinkle with cornstarch, and season with salt and pepper; toss to coat. In a large wok or skillet, heat oil over medium-high. Cook half the steak until browned on one side, 1 to 2 minutes (steak will cook further in step 2); transfer to a plate. Repeat with remaining beef.

2. Add snap peas, white parts of scallions, ginger, red-pepper flakes, and the water to wok; season with salt and pepper. Cook until snap peas turn crisp-tender and bright green, 1 to 2 minutes. Return steak to wok and cook until cooked through, 1 to 2 minutes. Remove from heat, mix in green part of scallions and the lime juice, and serve over rice or noodles.

Green Bean and Watercress Salad

Consider this an upgrade on the beloved green-bean casserole, one in which the flavor of the pods really shines through. Crisp, golden fried shallots are sprinkled on top.

SERVES 8

1 pound green beans, trimmed

Coarse salt and freshly ground pepper

1 cup safflower oil

3 shallots, thinly sliced crosswise into rings

2 teaspoons all-purpose flour

2 tablespoons fresh lemon juice

2 tablespoons Dijon mustard

3 tablespoons extra-virgin olive oil

1 bunch watercress, tough stems trimmed

1. Blanch green beans in a large pot of salted boiling water until crisp-tender and bright green, 2 to 3 minutes. Transfer to an ice-water bath to cool. Drain and pat dry.

2. Heat safflower oil over medium low in a small saucepan until shimmering. Meanwhile, in a small bowl, toss shallots with flour. Working in batches, fry shallots in oil until brown and crisp, 2 to 4 minutes. Transfer shallots to paper towels with a slotted spoon or mesh spider and season generously with salt.

3. Whisk together lemon juice, mustard, and olive oil in another bowl; season with salt and pepper. Place watercress on a serving platter, and drizzle with half the dressing. Top with green beans and remaining dressing. Serve sprinkled with fried shallots.

Tempura Green Beans

Green beans make excellent candidates for tempura, since you get a nice contrast of light, puffy crust and tender beans that retain some of their trademark crispness.

SERVES 4

1¼ cups Dijon mustard

⅛ teaspoon dry mustard

4 teaspoons hot sauce

3 tablespoons soy sauce

¾ cup honey

Grapeseed or safflower oil

4 large egg whites

3 cups all-purpose flour

2¾ cups plus 2 tablespoons club soda or seltzer (from a new bottle)

1 pound green beans, trimmed

Coarse salt

1. Heat mustards, hot sauce, soy sauce, and honey in a pan over low, whisking, until smooth and heated through, about 5 minutes. Transfer to a bowl; let cool.

2. Heat 4 inches of oil in a large pot over medium high until oil reaches 350°F on a deep-fry thermometer. Meanwhile, whisk egg whites to soft peaks. Whisk in flour and club soda just until combined, with lumps remaining.

3. Working in batches, dip beans into batter, letting any excess drip off, then carefully place in hot oil. Cook, stirring occasionally to keep beans from sticking together, until light golden brown, about 3 minutes. Transfer beans to paper-towel-lined plate to drain; season with salt. Repeat with remaining beans, returning oil to 350°F between batches. Serve immediately, with dipping sauce.

Quick-Pickled Pods

Try quick-pickling when you have a bounty of peak-of-season summer crops; the vegetables maintain their bite while taking on the flavor of the seasonings. Here, wax beans, green beans, and okra are pickled with the same brine. If you're unfamiliar with okra, pickling is a wonderful way to get to know (and love) this Southern staple.

MAKES 2 QUARTS

1 pound wax beans, green beans, or okra, trimmed

4 thyme sprigs

4 cups white-wine vinegar

2 cups sugar

4 garlic cloves

1 teaspoon fennel seeds

1 teaspoon coriander seeds

1 teaspoon mustard seeds

½ teaspoon whole black peppercorns

1 cup water

1. Divide pods into two quart-size glass jars, arranging pods upright; place 2 thyme sprigs in each jar.

2. In a small saucepan, bring vinegar, sugar, garlic, fennel seeds, coriander seeds, mustard seeds, peppercorns, and the water to a boil. Reduce heat and simmer 10 minutes. Let cool completely.

3. Pour cooled brine over beans or okra, leaving a ½-inch space at the top of each jar. Cover and refrigerate at least 3 days (and up to 2 months) before serving.

SHOOTS

Whether destined to become pea or pumpkin, a vegetable seed begins life the same way. When conditions are right, it drops anchor, sending out a little root sprout to secure it to the soil. Next, it raises a slender cotyledon, a leaf shoot that's already present inside each seed. Its tiny wings thus outstretched, the plant can begin taking in the minerals, water, and sunlight it needs to pursue its vegetable destiny.

We humans find deliciousness wherever nature hides it, so it's no wonder we enjoy these earliest stages of plant life. The pale, crisp sprouts that show up in pad thai are infant roots from mung or soybean seeds; the fluffy green sprouts piled up on sandwiches come typically from alfalfa or radish seeds. And the beautiful tangles of miniature leaves crowning many restaurant creations consist of pea shoots or microgreens, the first true leaves of peas, beets, and other vegetables. Even ferns may be eaten at this infant stage of development—as fiddleheads, the tightly spiraled fronds of plants that actually turn toxic when full grown.

Shoots reward impatience: most can be eaten within a week of planting. But speed isn't their only virtue; microgreens are dense with flavor and nutrients. When you harvest these crops young, the nutrients are more concentrated than in a full-grown plant. The flavors in shoots are intensified, too: Radish sprouts taste like radishes; sunflower greens are nutty. So you can let nature prepare these vegetables for you, and transform something inedible into a nourishing treat.

FIDDLEHEAD
FERNS
—
MICROGREENS
—
PEA SHOOTS
—
SPROUTS

THE BASICS

SEASONALITY

Fiddleheads are available April through June. Pea shoots turn up in spring and fall if they've been thinned from pea crops; but if you find a purveyor who cultivates them as a crop in their own right, they may be offered year-round, which is also true of most microgreens. Sprouts, too, are grown indoors and available year-round.

BUYING

Look for crisp, brightly colored pea shoots and microgreens at farmers' markets and specialty stores. Certain purveyors will harvest them on the spot, cutting the tiny plants from the trays in which they germinated. Often foraged rather than cultivated, fiddleheads also show up most often at greenmarkets; select small, tightly coiled fronds with little to no stalk, and *only* from the ostrich fern—other species should be avoided. As for sprouts, look for those with crisp, white "necks" without a trace of browning or wilting, and be sure to buy from a reputable source; the same warm, moist conditions that allow seeds to germinate can also breed pathogens. (That's why the Centers for Disease Control and Prevention and other federal agencies charged with food safety advise children, the elderly, pregnant women, and persons with weakened immune systems to avoid eating raw sprouts of any kind, including alfalfa, clover, radish, and mung bean sprouts. In these instances, cook sprouts thoroughly to reduce the risk of illness. Cooking should kill the harmful bacteria.)

NOTABLE VARIETIES

Microgreens: You can find micro-crops of many different herbs, vegetables, even grains at gourmet grocers and farmers' markets. Cress is intensely flavorful with subtle spice; arugula has a mild peppery flavor; beet greens, broccoli, and kale are all mild and slightly sweet with tender leaves on a crunchy stem; mustard greens taste like horseradish; mizuna is fairly mild; tatsoi has a mild, sweet, cabbage-like flavor. Herb microgreens taste like concentrated versions of the herbs; basil, chervil, cilantro, dill, and garlic chives are all worth seeking out. Sunflower greens are nutty and delicious; amaranth is mildly spicy and a vibrant shade of pink-red.

Sprouts: While alfalfa sprouts are by far the most common (and easiest to find), there are many others that are sold at natural-food stores and farmers' markets. Clover sprouts are similar in appearance and flavor to alfalfa; radish sprouts are considered the spiciest; lentil sprouts have a peppery taste; sunflower sprouts are mild and slightly sweet, similar to alfalfa; mung bean sprouts are crisp and nutty; garbanzo sprouts, which look just like the beans, are very crunchy and beany; adzuki sprouts have a pronounced leafy flavor.

STORING

Shoots, sprouts, microgreens, and fiddleheads should be eaten within a day of purchase. Store sprouts wrapped in paper towels in an open plastic bag in the refrigerator. Shoots, microgreens, or fiddleheads may be enclosed in a loosely folded plastic bag.

PREPPING

Wash sprouts thoroughly, first submerging them in several changes of cool water, then rinse and dry well. Gently rinse pea shoots and microgreens and spin dry. With fiddleheads, first brush off any fuzzy or papery sheaths, then submerge them in a bowl filled with cool water mixed with a squeeze of lemon and a dash of salt.

COOKING

Eaten raw, microgreens and pea shoots show off their intense, green vitality; add them to salads or sprinkle them over main dishes such as fish or steak. They can also be stirred into risottos and other stews at the last minute, where they will wilt in the residual heat. Delicate sprouts such as alfalfa and radish are best in salads and sandwiches, while crisper mung and soy bean sprouts are often sautéed with stir-fries a minute or two before serving, in addition to being used as a garnish. Fiddleheads are best lightly steamed or blanched, then sautéed in oil or butter.

FLAVOR PAIRINGS

Fiddleheads have echoes of asparagus and green beans and can be used in similar ways to both of those "grassy" vegetables—namely in egg dishes, salads, and with lamb or fish. Think of pea shoots as sprightly versions of peas and pair them accordingly (with other spring produce, salty hams, rich cheeses, rice, and other grains). In the case of flavor partners, there are basically two kinds of sprouts: those that are delicate in texture (alfalfa and radish) and the sturdier bean sprouts (mung and chickpea). As for microgreens, use them wherever you want the flavor of the mature vegetable—peppery arugula or cress, say, or sweet, earthy beet greens—minus the bulk.

BEAN SPROUTS: lime, soy sauce, fish sauce, ginger, sesame, garlic, scallions, cucumber, cilantro, peanuts, shrimp

DELICATE SPROUTS: lemon, tomato, cucumber, radish, carrot, avocado, goat cheese

FIDDLEHEADS: butter, eggs, sharp cheese, lemon, vinaigrette, basil, tarragon

MICROGREENS: eggs, lemon, goat cheese, blue cheese, almonds, fennel

PEA SHOOTS: bacon, prosciutto, feta cheese, wild mushrooms, salmon, ginger, radish, mint

Sesame Salmon with Shiitake Mushrooms and Shoots

Shoots make a refreshing change of pace from tender herbs such as parsley, mint, or basil, and their taste is just as versatile. Here, fresh shoots serve as a last-minute (but essential) garnish for steamed salmon and shiitakes; black sesame seeds are also sprinkled on top. The heat from the fish helps to release just enough of the shoots' flavor.

SERVES 4

2 tablespoons low-sodium soy sauce

1 tablespoon plus 1 teaspoon finely grated peeled fresh ginger

1 tablespoon plus 1 teaspoon fresh lemon juice

4 cups thinly sliced shiitake mushrooms (8 ounces)

4 boneless, skinless salmon fillets, preferably wild sockeye (each 5 ounces and 1 inch thick)

Coarse salt

2 teaspoons toasted sesame oil

1 teaspoon black sesame seeds

2 ounces microgreens, radish sprouts, or pea shoots

1. Preheat oven to 400°F. Cut four 12-by-17-inch pieces of parchment. Fold each in half crosswise to form a crease, then open and place on work surface.

2. Combine soy sauce, ginger, and lemon juice in a small bowl. Add mushrooms and toss to combine. Divide evenly among parchment pieces, arranging mixture on one side of each crease. Lay one salmon fillet on top of each pile. Season with salt and drizzle with sesame oil. Fold parchment over ingredients, then make overlapping pleats to seal.

3. Bake on two baking sheets (two packets per sheet), 10 to 11 minutes for medium rare or 12 minutes for medium. Carefully open the packets. Top salmon with sesame seeds and shoots, and serve.

Fiddlehead and Potato Hash with Eggs

The shoots of the ostrich fern (Matteuccia struthiopteris)*, fiddleheads get their name from their shape: The tight coils resemble the scroll carving at the top of a violin. They grow near streams and rivers in the eastern half of the United States and Canada, and they are harvested by hand. Here they are blanched, then cooked in a skillet with potatoes and eggs for a great one-pot meal.*

SERVES 4

1½ pounds small potatoes, scrubbed and halved

Coarse salt and freshly ground pepper

8 ounces fiddlehead ferns, cleaned and trimmed

2 tablespoons extra-virgin olive oil

1 shallot, thinly sliced

4 large eggs

1. Bring potatoes and enough water to cover to a boil in a medium pot; add salt and cook until potatoes are knife-tender, about 8 minutes. Add fiddleheads and cook just until bright green, about 1 minute more. Drain potatoes and fiddleheads.

2. Heat oil in a large skillet over medium high. Cook shallot until golden, stirring frequently, about 2 minutes. Add potatoes and fiddleheads, and cook, stirring occasionally, until golden brown, about 4 minutes.

3. Push potatoes and fiddleheads to one side, then crack eggs into pan on the other side. Season with salt and pepper. Cook, undisturbed, 4 minutes. Remove from heat; let stand until whites are set but yolks are still runny, about 4 minutes more. Serve immediately.

Kale and Lentil Bowl with Sprouts

Alfalfa and other sprouts have long been used to lend any dish instant health-food credibility. That's still true today, as in this of-the-moment macro bowl. Thinly sliced raw kale and tender lentils may be the feature players, but sprouts (we use sunflower) are just as necessary to the blend of flavors and textures. A creamy avocado-garlic dressing, sliced sharp cheddar, and chopped almonds make this hearty and substantial.

SERVES 4

Coarse salt

1¼ cups de Puy lentils, picked over and rinsed

1 ripe avocado, halved, pitted, and peeled

1 teaspoon minced garlic

2 tablespoons minced shallot

¼ cup fresh lemon juice, plus cut lemons for serving

¼ cup extra-virgin olive oil

1 bunch Tuscan (or Lacinato) kale (10 ounces), stems trimmed, leaves thinly sliced

4 ounces sunflower or radish sprouts

Slices of extra-sharp cheddar, for serving

Chopped roasted salted almonds, for serving

1. In a medium saucepan of salted boiling water, cook lentils until tender but not mushy, about 20 minutes. Drain, rinse under cold water to stop the cooking, and drain again.

2. Pulse together avocado, garlic, shallot, lemon juice, oil, and 1 teaspoon salt in a blender or food processor until smooth.

3. Toss two-thirds of dressing with kale in a bowl. Divide dressed kale among four serving bowls. Add lentils, sprouts, cheddar, and almonds to each bowl. Serve, with remaining dressing and lemons on the side.

Sautéed Snow Peas and Pea Shoots

The edible shoots and curly tendrils of pea plants can withstand brief cooking. Just 30 seconds is all it takes for the shoots to wilt and take on the flavors of accompaniments like garlic and red-pepper flakes. Here they are paired with snow peas, part of the category of legumes known as mange-touts—or "eat all."

SERVES 4

1 tablespoon extra-virgin olive oil

1 garlic clove, sliced

Pinch of red-pepper flakes

8 ounces snow peas, trimmed

8 ounces pea shoots

1 tablespoon water

Coarse salt

½ lemon, for serving

1. Heat oil in a large skillet over medium high. Add garlic and red-pepper flakes, and cook, stirring, until garlic is golden, about 1 minute. Add snow peas and cook, stirring, until bright green and still crisp, about 1 minute.

2. Add pea shoots in batches along with the water. Cook, stirring, until just wilted, about 30 seconds. Season with salt, squeeze lemon over top, and serve.

Avocado-and-Sprout Club Sandwiches

One of the golden rules of sandwich making is to use contrasting flavors and textures. Consider the classic California vegetable sandwich, which wouldn't be the same without crunchy sprouts, creamy avocado, sharp radish, and tangy goat cheese.

SERVES 4

Assorted vegetables, such as cucumbers, red onions, lettuce, carrots, and radishes

2 ripe but firm avocados, halved, pitted, and peeled

12 slices whole-grain bread, toasted

4 ounces alfalfa, clover, or garbanzo sprouts

8 ounces fresh goat cheese, room temperature

Olive oil, for drizzling

Coarse salt and freshly ground pepper

1. Slice vegetables into thin rounds or matchsticks, as desired; tear lettuce and slice avocados. Dividing evenly, layer vegetables on 8 toast slices. Top with sprouts. Spread goat cheese on remaining 4 toast slices; then drizzle with oil, and sprinkle with salt and pepper.

2. Stack sandwiches so that each has two layers of vegetables and one of cheese (cheese side down). Cut in half and serve.

Pad Thai

Bean sprouts, which are made from sprouting mung beans, are a traditional component of many Thai dishes, including pad thai. In this version, some of the sprouts are stir-fried with the noodles just until wilted, and the rest are used as a crisp, cool garnish along with sliced radishes, cilantro sprigs, and lime wedges.

SERVES 4

4 ounces boneless pork loin, cut into ¼-inch slices, then into 1½-inch pieces

1 teaspoon sugar

2 tablespoons tamarind concentrate

2 tablespoons low-sodium soy sauce

2 tablespoons Thai fish sauce (*nam pla*)

4 tablespoons peanut or safflower oil

2 or 3 garlic cloves, minced

2 to 3 ounces pressed tofu, cut into ¼-inch slices, then into 1½-inch pieces

3 large eggs, lightly beaten

Coarse salt

8 ounces dried rice-stick noodles, soaked (see tip below)

8 ounces bean sprouts, rinsed and drained (about 4 cups)

3 scallions, trimmed, flattened with the side of cleaver, and cut into 1½-inch pieces

1 tablespoon dried shrimp, chopped

1 cup dry-roasted peanuts, coarsely chopped

Thinly sliced radishes, sliced Thai chiles, cilantro leaves, and lime wedges, for serving

1. Toss pork with sugar in a small bowl to mix. Combine tamarind concentrate, soy sauce, and fish sauce in another small bowl.

2. Heat a large wok or skillet over medium-high until very hot. Add 2 tablespoons oil and swirl to coat. Cook garlic, turning, until golden, about 15 seconds. Add pork, spreading into a single layer. Cook until golden on all sides, about 1 minute total. Add tofu and sear, pressing it against sides of wok, 10 to 20 seconds. Transfer to a plate.

3. Season eggs with salt and pour into wok. Cook until starting to set, about 1 minute. Using a spatula, cut into large pieces, and transfer to plate.

4. Raise heat to high and heat wok until sizzling hot. Add 1 tablespoon oil and swirl to coat. Cook noodles, tossing frequently and pressing against sides of wok to sear, until softened, 2 to 3 minutes.

5. Push noodles up sides of wok and add remaining tablespoon oil to bottom, along with 2½ cups bean sprouts and the scallions. Cook, tossing, until wilted, 1 to 2 minutes. Add dried shrimp and toss briefly to heat through. Add soy-sauce mixture. Cook, tossing, about 30 seconds. Incorporate noodles. Add pork mixture, eggs, and ½ cup peanuts; toss gently to combine.

6. Divide among bowls and top with remaining 1½ cups bean sprouts and ½ cup peanuts, and assorted garnishes.

TIP Rice-noodle sticks don't have to be cooked before using; just soak them in boiling water until tender, according to package instructions.

LEAVES

The glory of leaves lies in their fresh green simplicity. Tossed in nothing but a dollop of dressing, their bright grassy notes enliven any meal. But just because they demand so little from a cook—a rinse, a tear, maybe a splash of vinaigrette—does not mean they give little in return. Whether mild or bitter, crisp or tender, spiky or round as thumbprints, leafy vegetables are essential to any culinary repertoire. Learning to prepare them is one of the easiest ways to grow as a cook.

Leafy vegetables make your own vitality grow as well. After all, in nature it is a plant's leaves that perform the prodigious task of harnessing sunlight and converting it into the fuel that powers almost every living creature on the planet. It's a punishing job, and in order to fulfill it, leaves are loaded with phytochemicals that prevent and repair the damage caused by basic cellular processes. Our own bodies benefit enormously from the hard work that leaves do—utilizing those protective phytochemicals to mend, cleanse, and restore our own cells.

As nature's ubiquitous and most abundant source of nourishment, it's no wonder, then, that leaves—in the form of lettuce and cabbage—are also one of humankind's earliest foods, cultivated as early as some 5,000 years ago. Maybe a tossed salad, far from being a sidekick to lunch or dinner, is actually our first and most fundamental meal. It's sunlight transformed into wild, green deliciousness.

CABBAGES
—
CHICORIES
—
ENDIVES
—
LETTUCES
—
SPINACH
—
SPRING AND
WILD GREENS

THE BASICS

SEASONALITY

Leafy greens prefer cool, mild weather; intense sunlight and heat trigger the plants' impulse to "bolt," sending up a seed-bearing stalk that turns the leaves tough and bitter. So look for local lettuces and other leafy greens in spring, early summer, and fall. Some hardier leaves, like spinach, chicories, and cabbages, turn sweet late in fall after a cold snap, and can form the basis for salads throughout the winter. Imported and greenhouse-grown leaves are available year-round.

BUYING

Tender, delicate leaves don't travel well, so shop farmers' markets for the freshest choices and to find unusual foraged or heirloom specialties. However, leaves can flourish in greenhouses, so many are available year-round in grocery stores, including hardy romaine, iceberg, endives, and cabbages. When selecting lettuces and spinach, look for dark, firm leaves, which generally contain more nutrients, and avoid any that are limp or wilted, or streaked with brown along the ribs. When buying leaves by the head—including romaine, butterhead, and iceberg lettuces, plus chicories, endives, and cabbages—inspect the base; it should appear freshly cut, pale and dry rather than dark or slimy. If you buy pre-packaged greens (such as spinach or mesclun), gently shake the container to check that there are no dead leaves clinging to the others or the container itself—they're almost impossible to clean off at home. Hardier leaves, such as endive, radicchio, and cabbage, should be vividly colored or brightly hued and the heads should feel firm rather than squishy or spongy. Avoid endive and radicchio whose outer leaves are brown at the edges.

NOTABLE VARIETIES

Lettuces: Green Salad Bowl is an all-purpose buttery lettuce; others include Oakleaf (red or green varieties) and Tango. Lollo Biondo is a peppery green loose-leaf lettuce. Mâche, also known as corn salad or lamb's lettuce, is also tender and mild. Colorful lettuces include Marvel (or Red Besson), Rossa di Trento, Red Grenoble, Red Riding Hood, Red Salad Bowl, Loose-Leaf Garnet, Lollo Rossa, Rubens Romaine, and Amaranth (botanically a grain but the leaves can be used like lettuces). You can also find red romaine, which tends to be more tender than green, as well as baby romaine and other lettuces, which are all harvested young.

Spring and wild greens: The hearty leaves of stinging nettle turn almost nutty when cooked; chickweed has a mild, earthy flavor; lamb's quarters are slightly more delicate in taste and texture than spinach; purslane tastes of citrus; dandelions are mildly bitter; both types of sorrel (wood and sheep's) are refreshingly sour. Watercress is the most popular type of cress sold in the United States; others include pepper cress, curly cress, land cress, and upland cress. All have a similar peppery taste, though it varies in intensity.

Spinach: There are three types of spinach: Savoy spinach, such as Regiment and Bloomsdale, has thick, deeply crinkled, dark green leaves; Flat-Leaf (or Smooth-Leaf) spinach has more tender, smooth leaves and includes such varieties as Red Cardinal and Red Kitten, usually harvested for baby greens; Semi-Savoy spinach is a hybrid of Savoy and Flat-Leaf and has a texture that's between the two—varieties include Indian Summer Hybrid, Teton, and Catalina. Orach, also known as mountain spinach, has a mild flavor; it is botanically unrelated to spinach but can be used in the same way.

Chicories and endives: You can find Belgian endive in creamy white or red; full-heart endive has a mild, slightly bitter flavor. Of all the varieties of radicchio, Radicchio Rosso and Chioggia are the most common; Radicchio Caesar is one of many Italian varieties, with vibrant red leaves and a bitter, almost tart flavor. Others include Treviso, which looks and tastes similar to endive; Treviso Tardivo, a more intensely flavored, firmer version of Treviso; Castelfranco, with speckled white leaves; and Puntarelle, the edible part of another type of Italian chicory (sometimes referred to as "chicory hearts") that has long pale-green stalks with spiky dark green leaves. Blanched frisée is spikier than other frisées.

Cabbages: Savoys have a more delicate flavor than basic green cabbages. Their broad leaves work well as wrappers for ground meat and other stuffings. Napa cabbages include several varieties—some pale and compact, others green and leafy; they may be labeled Chinese cabbage, celery cabbage, wong bok, or Peking cabbage. Red (purple, really) cabbages are crunchy and mildly peppery; look for miniature varieties at farmers' markets.

STORING

Remove any twist ties or rubber bands—they'll bruise the leaves and speed deterioration—then handle gently. Leaves should be stored loosely in a plastic bag left open at the top or poked with holes to allow for some air circulation. Adding a barely damp paper towel to the bag increases humidity and can prolong freshness. Tender lettuces should be eaten within two days of being washed, so refrain from pre-washing if you're not sure when you'll get around to consuming them. Hardier leaves (frisée, escarole) can be washed and dried in a spinner before being refrigerated for up to five days. Kept whole, iceberg lettuce can last a week, and cabbages can remain a month or more, loosely wrapped in a plastic bag in the refrigerator.

PREPPING

The best way to wash leaves is to fill a sink with very cold water. Add the leaves, swish gently, then allow to sit a few minutes so dirt sinks to the bottom. Gently lift out the leaves, and repeat the process—once if they're fairly clean to start with and up to four times if they're quite sandy or dirty. (Even leaves labeled "triple-washed" should be washed before eating.) Spin lettuce dry, filling the spinner no more than halfway at a time; check to ensure that no moisture remains, since dressings won't cling to wet lettuce. Don't cut or tear until just before serving. Which technique is better? Large, delicate leaves, such as butterhead and Batavian, should be torn rather than cut to preserve cell structure and limit wilting. Firm leaves can be sliced or chopped. And small, tender leaves are best left whole, as are especially shapely ones, such as endive.

COOKING

All leaves, even the mildest lettuces, may be braised or sautéed or added to soups. Some, including spinach, dandelion, and romaine, can be juiced or whirred into smoothies. And large, pliable leaves make excellent wraps for a variety of fillings, as well as pretty beds for composed salads. But surely the simplicity of these leaves is their greatest gift to the cook—a green salad can be quickly tossed together. Take the time to master a few versatile dressings at home. Start by rubbing a pinch of salt into the leaves to infuse them with flavor. Then use a light vinaigrette for mild lettuces, a thicker dressing for sturdier leaves—and always add it just before serving. Pour the dressing around the sides of the bowl rather than right on top of the leaves, and toss from the bottom up. Or whisk together the dressing in the bottom of your salad bowl, then add the leaves and toss to combine (but here you want to make sure you don't make too much dressing).

HOW TO BRAISE
(For all leaves)
Cut heads (such as romaine, cabbage, radicchio, and endive) into quarters, leaving wedges intact. Cut or tear other types of leaves (dandelion, watercress, spinach, and arugula) into 2-inch pieces. Heat olive oil in a large high-sided skillet over medium low. Add wedges, cut sides down; add leaves in batches, tossing and adding more as they wilt. Cook until wedges are golden underneath or leaves are just wilted, 5 to 10 minutes (5 minutes for spinach). Add enough liquid (broth or water) to cover, and bring to a simmer. Cover and cook until very tender, 10 to 15 minutes, depending on vegetable (10 minutes for spinach). Season with salt and pepper.

HOW TO SAUTÉ
(For all leaves)
Cut heads (such as romaine, cabbage, radicchio, and endive) into quarters, leaving wedges intact. Cut or tear other types of leaves (dandelion, watercress, spinach, and arugula) into 2-inch pieces. Heat butter or olive oil in a large skillet over medium; butter should start to brown. Add wedges, cut sides down; add leaves in batches, tossing and adding more as they wilt. Cook, stirring occasionally, just until tender, 3 to 5 minutes. Season with salt and pepper.

HOW TO ROAST

(For all leaves)

Cut heads (such as romaine, cabbage, radicchio, and endive) into quarters, leaving wedges intact. Cut or tear other types of leaves (dandelion, watercress, spinach, and arugula) into 2-inch pieces. Drizzle with olive oil, season with salt and pepper, and toss to combine. Place wedges, cut sides down, on a rimmed baking sheet; scatter leaves in a single layer. Roast at 400°F, turning once, until leaves are wilted and slightly charred, about 15 minutes for wedges, 2 to 5 minutes for more tender pieces. For Italian flavors, drizzle with balsamic vinegar and top with finely grated Parmesan.

HOW TO GRILL

(For sturdy lettuces: romaine and iceberg)

Cut heads into halves or quarters, leaving wedges intact, and brush cut sides with olive oil. Grill on medium high, cut sides down, until charred in spots, 2 to 3 minutes. Serve warm, drizzled with olive oil and a flavorful vinegar, or top with crumbled croutons and grated Parmesan.

FLAVOR PAIRINGS

The words *salad* and *salt* have the same Latin root—no accident, as it happens. A judicious amount of salt has long been the key to a successful dressing. That's because salt interferes with our ability to taste bitterness, and all leaves are slightly bitter. (Even the most abrasive of today's cultivated leaves are mild compared with their wild forebears, however.) Acidity in the form of vinegar or citrus heightens the taste of freshness in all plant foods, and fat—whether olive oil or bacon renderings—is the best harmonizer and conveyer of subtle flavors to the tongue. In addition to oil, acidity, salt and pepper, try these pairings in your salads:

ARUGULA: almonds, goat cheese, grapes, pears, fennel, lemon, Parmesan

CABBAGE: bacon, apples, caraway, juniper, red onions, ginger, garlic, soy, cashews, chiles, lime, radishes, carrots

CHICORIES AND ENDIVES: bacon, asiago, blue cheese, walnuts, garlic

MESCLUN LEAVES: goat cheese, nuts, mushrooms, dried fruits

MILD/SWEET LETTUCE (BIBB, BOSTON): shallots, citrus, chervil, tarragon, avocado, sour cream/yogurt (in dressing)

ROMAINE: anchovies, Parmesan, garlic, eggs, Dijon mustard, tomatoes, capers

SPINACH: bacon, egg, Dijon mustard, shallots, lemon, dill, mushrooms, pine nuts

WATERCRESS: buttermilk, blue cheese, beets, bell peppers, ginger, lemon, shrimp

Watercress and Asparagus Pizza

It's common practice by now to top pizza with a heap of arugula when it comes out of the oven, as a sort of pizza-and-salad-in-one. With a similar spicy, peppery taste, watercress works well on pizza, too. Here, we've combined upland cress with asparagus and red onion to create a springy, savory pie for dinner.

SERVES 4

1 bunch asparagus, tough ends trimmed and spears thinly sliced on the diagonal

1 small red onion, thinly sliced

¼ cup plus 1 tablespoon extra-virgin olive oil

Coarse salt and freshly ground black pepper

Pizza dough (see recipe on page 304; use 1 ball; reserve other for another use)

8 ounces ricotta cheese

4 ounces mozzarella cheese, shredded

2 cups upland cress or watercress, tough stems removed

Red-pepper flakes

1. Preheat oven to 450°F with rack in lower third. Toss together asparagus, onion, and 1 tablespoon oil in a medium bowl. Season with salt and black pepper.

2. Brush a rimmed baking sheet with 2 tablespoons oil. Using your hands, gently stretch dough from all sides to approximate size of baking sheet. Place dough on baking sheet, stretching and fitting it to edges.

3. Brush dough with remaining 2 tablespoons oil, then spread with ricotta, leaving a ½-inch border. Top with asparagus mixture; sprinkle with mozzarella.

4. Bake until crust is golden brown and asparagus is tender, about 20 minutes. Top with cress, season with salt, and sprinkle with red-pepper flakes. Cut into pieces and serve.

TIP
We especially like the sharp flavor and heat of upland cress; look for it at farmers' markets and specialty grocers.

Endive and Fennel Salad

Belgian endive leaves are crisp and sharp—just right for perking up salads during the winter months. The taste is often described as bittersweet, and the same could be said for fennel and walnuts, both used here. Pomegranate seeds add vibrant color.

SERVES 8

2 fennel bulbs, halved, cored, and thinly sliced, plus ¼ cup lightly packed fennel fronds

1 pound Belgian endive (preferably red), trimmed and leaves separated

½ cup pomegranate seeds

½ cup chopped walnuts, toasted

⅓ cup extra-virgin olive oil

1 tablespoon fresh lemon juice

Coarse salt and freshly ground pepper

1. Scatter fennel and endive on a large platter, and sprinkle with pomegranate seeds, walnuts, and fennel fronds.

2. Whisk together oil and lemon juice in a small bowl, and season with salt and pepper. Drizzle over salad and serve.

Shredded Napa Cabbage Salad

With its long, slender, open head, napa cabbage—or Chinese cabbage (napa is loosely translated from Chinese as "leaf")—definitely stands out from more familiar cabbages. It's a milder-tasting, less-crunchy option for making slaws like this one.

SERVES 6

¼ cup white-wine vinegar

2 tablespoons Dijon mustard, preferably whole grain

2 tablespoons sugar

½ small head napa cabbage, cored and shredded

4 or 5 radishes, thinly sliced and cut into matchsticks

½ cup golden raisins

1 tablespoon thinly sliced fresh chives

Coarse salt and freshly ground pepper

Whisk together vinegar, mustard, and sugar in a small bowl. Toss together cabbage, radishes, golden raisins, and chives in a large bowl. Drizzle dressing over salad, and season with salt and pepper. Toss to combine and serve.

Pork Scaloppine
with Radicchio

Here, breaded cutlets are served with a sauce made by deglazing the pan with a splash of Marsala, one of the simplest and most beloved Italian preparations. The dish usually features sautéed mushrooms; we substitute roasted portobellos and add roasted radicchio, which tastes less bitter than the raw vegetable.

SERVES 4

1 pound boneless pork tenderloin, cut on the bias into ⅓-inch-thick slices

1 head radicchio, halved, cored, and cut into ¾-inch-thick slices

1 pound fresh portobello mushrooms, stemmed and cut into ¼-inch-thick slices

1 tablespoon extra-virgin olive oil, plus more for drizzling

Coarse salt and freshly ground pepper

Wondra (instant) flour or all-purpose flour, for dredging

⅓ cup fresh sage leaves

1 tablespoon unsalted butter

⅔ cup Marsala wine

1. Preheat oven to 425°F. Place pork between layers of waxed paper and pound to an even thickness (about ⅛ inch).

2. Spread radicchio on half of a rimmed baking sheet and mushrooms on other half. Drizzle with oil; season with salt and pepper. Roast until just starting to turn tender, 10 to 12 minutes.

3. Lightly dredge pork in flour. Heat a large straight-sided skillet over medium high. Add oil, swirl to coat, and cook sage until just crisp, about 1 minute. Remove from skillet.

4. Swirl butter into skillet and cook pork in two batches until lightly browned around edges, 1 to 2 minutes on each side. Return all pork to skillet. Pour in wine and simmer until reduced to a glaze, stirring up browned bits from bottom of pan, about 1 minute. Add radicchio and mushrooms, coat with sauce, and serve.

TIP
You could substitute veal, chicken, or turkey cutlets for the pork.

Spinach and Fontina Strata

When brunch is in the forecast, make strata—this one is built around the long-running combination of spinach and eggs (think soufflés, omelets, and quiches). The spinach is seasoned with nutmeg, another classic flavor partner, and is paired with two terrific cheeses: young fontina, a superb melting variety, and Parmesan.

SERVES 8

- 2 tablespoons extra-virgin olive oil
- 1 small onion, finely chopped
- Coarse salt and freshly ground pepper
- 2 pounds spinach, stems trimmed and leaves coarsely chopped
- ¼ teaspoon freshly grated nutmeg
- Unsalted butter, room temperature, for baking dish
- 1 pound challah loaf, sliced ½ inch thick
- 8 ounces young Italian fontina cheese, grated
- ⅓ cup finely grated Parmigiano-Reggiano cheese
- 8 large eggs
- 2⅔ cups whole milk

1. Heat oil in a large sauté pan over medium until shimmering. Add onion and season with salt; cook, stirring occasionally, until translucent, about 3 minutes. Fill pan with as much spinach as will fit; cook, stirring, and adding remainder a handful at a time as space allows. When all the spinach is wilted, season with pepper and stir in nutmeg. Drain spinach in a sieve. When cool enough to handle, squeeze excess moisture from spinach by hand.

2. Butter a 3-quart baking dish. Place a third of the bread slices in a single layer in dish. Top with half the spinach mixture and a third of the cheeses. Repeat layering with a third of the bread, remaining spinach mixture, and a third of the cheeses, then top with remaining bread (reserve remaining third of the cheeses).

3. Whisk together 6 eggs and 2 cups milk, season with salt, and carefully pour over bread. Cover with parchment, and gently press down with hands until egg mixture soaks through top of bread. Cover parchment with foil, and refrigerate at least 8 hours (and up to 2 days).

4. Preheat oven to 350°F. Meanwhile, remove strata from refrigerator, uncover, and let stand 30 minutes. Whisk together remaining 2 eggs and ⅔ cup milk, and pour over strata, gently pressing between layers of bread with a spoon or spatula to ensure that egg mixture seeps to bottom. Sprinkle with remaining cheeses.

5. Bake until puffed and golden brown in spots, 45 to 50 minutes. Let cool 15 minutes before serving.

TIP
Young fontina has a softer texture than aged varieties and is often labeled as "semi-firm" or "table cheese"; you can find it at cheese shops and specialty grocers. Regular fontina will also work here.

Garden Greens with Chopped Eggs

Baby spinach is much more tender and mild tasting than mature varieties, and needs only a quick rinse (and no stemming) before serving. While you can find it in clamshell packages, seek out baby spinach in bunches for superior flavor and freshness.

SERVES 4

8 ounces haricots verts, trimmed

Coarse salt and freshly ground pepper

8 ounces snap peas, trimmed

4 anchovy fillets, minced

1 tablespoon fresh lemon juice

2 tablespoons sour cream

¼ cup extra-virgin olive oil

4 cups baby spinach

4 large eggs, hard-cooked

¼ cup fresh tarragon leaves

1 cup fresh flat-leaf parsley leaves

1. Prepare an ice-water bath. Working in batches, blanch haricots verts in a pot of generously salted boiling water until bright green and crisp-tender, about 2 minutes. Transfer to ice bath and let cool; remove. Return water in pot to a boil, and blanch snap peas, in batches, about 1 minute. Transfer to ice bath until cool; remove snap peas, and cut in half.

2. Whisk together anchovies, lemon juice, and sour cream in a bowl. Slowly add oil in a steady stream, whisking until combined. Season with salt and pepper.

3. Divide spinach, haricots verts, and snap peas among four plates, and top each with chopped eggs and herbs. Drizzle with dressing, season with salt and pepper, and serve.

Spinach and Garlic Soup

In this chilled spring soup, spinach is paired with two forms of garlic:
fresh garlic is roasted to bring out the natural sugars; and green garlic, which has
no bulb, is briefly sautéed, to preserve its delicate flavor.

SERVES 6

2 cups plain yogurt

4 heads roasted garlic (see How to Roast, page 16)

¼ cup extra-virgin olive oil, plus more for drizzling

6 to 10 green garlic stems, sliced ¼ inch thick

1½ cups chicken broth

½ pound baby spinach

¼ cup fresh basil leaves, plus small leaves for garnish

1 tablespoon plus 1 teaspoon fresh lemon juice

Coarse salt

1. Stir together ¼ cup yogurt and 2 teaspoons roasted garlic in a bowl; cover and refrigerate up to 1 day.

2. Heat ¼ cup oil in a saucepan over medium high. Cook green garlic until translucent, stirring frequently, about 3 minutes. Add broth and bring to a boil. Reduce heat and simmer 5 minutes; let cool.

3. Transfer broth mixture to a blender. Add remaining 1¾ cups yogurt and half the spinach, and purée until smooth. Add remaining spinach, the basil, and 2 tablespoons roasted garlic (reserve remainder for another use), and purée. Add lemon juice, and season with salt. Refrigerate, covered, at least 2 hours (and up to 1 day). To serve, top with roasted-garlic yogurt and more basil.

Escarole and Bean Soup

When you have a head of escarole (and a half hour to spare), make a quick beans-and-greens soup. This member of the chicory family has a pleasant bitterness and sturdy leaves that become tender after only a brief simmer. We include two types of legumes—chickpeas and kidney beans—for contrasting tastes and textures in this hearty one-pot meal.

SERVES 4

3 tablespoons extra-virgin olive oil

4 garlic cloves, smashed

Pinch of red-pepper flakes, plus more for serving

1 small head escarole, leaves torn into 2-inch pieces (about 12 cups)

Coarse salt

1 can (15.5 ounces) red kidney beans, rinsed and drained

1 can (15.5 ounces) chickpeas, rinsed and drained

4 cups low-sodium chicken broth

2 cups water

Toasted bread and lemon wedges, for serving

1. Heat a large saucepan over medium; add oil and swirl to coat. Add garlic and red-pepper flakes; cook, stirring, until fragrant, about 1 minute. Add escarole, toss to coat, and season with salt. Cook until escarole is just wilted, stirring frequently, about 2 minutes.

2. Add kidney beans, chickpeas, broth, and the water. Bring to a simmer. Cook until heated through, stirring occasionally, about 5 minutes. Season with salt; remove garlic. Top with red-pepper flakes. Serve immediately, with lemon wedges and toasted bread.

Frisée and Roasted Pear Salad

SERVES 8

2 tablespoons honey

5 tablespoons sherry vinegar

5 tablespoons extra-virgin olive oil

Coarse salt and freshly ground pepper

3 Bosc pears, cored, each cut into eighths (unpeeled)

8 shallots, halved lengthwise

1 teaspoon Dijon mustard

⅓ cup water

1 large head frisée, trimmed (about 8 ounces)

2 heads endive, trimmed

¾ cup walnut halves, toasted

1. Preheat oven to 400°F. Whisk together honey, 3 tablespoons vinegar, and 2 tablespoons oil; season with salt and pepper. Arrange pears and shallots in a single layer in a roasting pan; toss with honey mixture to coat. Roast 20 minutes, turning pears and shallots halfway through. Continue roasting until shallots are easily pierced with the tip of a paring knife, about 10 minutes more.

2. Meanwhile, whisk together remaining 2 tablespoons vinegar and 3 tablespoons oil with the mustard in a heatproof bowl; season with salt and pepper.

3. Remove roasted pears and shallots from roasting pan and place pan over high heat; add the water, and scrape up any browned bits with a wooden spoon. Let liquid reduce by half, then whisk mixture into vinaigrette.

4. Toss frisée and endive with vinaigrette. Transfer to a platter, top with pears, shallots, and walnuts, and serve.

Baby Greens with Pine Nuts and Pancetta

You can often find a mix of so-called Asian greens sold at supermarkets,
but it's fun to assemble your own; baby mizuna, baby tatsoi,
and chrysanthemum greens are among the most widely available varieties.

SERVES 4

4 ounces assorted delicate salad greens, such as baby tatsoi, baby mizuna, and chrysanthemum greens (about 8 cups)

8 very thin slices pancetta

2 tablespoons extra-virgin olive oil

2 shallots, thinly sliced crosswise

3 tablespoons pine nuts

3 tablespoons sherry vinegar

Coarse salt and freshly ground pepper

1. Combine greens in a serving bowl. Heat a skillet over medium; cook pancetta, turning once, until crisp, 2 to 4 minutes per side. Transfer with tongs to paper towels; drain.

2. Pour off half of the fat from skillet. Add oil to skillet; place over medium-low heat. When fat is hot but not smoking, add shallots and pine nuts. Cook, stirring, until pine nuts are golden brown, about 2 minutes. With a slotted spoon, transfer pine nuts and shallots to serving bowl.

3. Remove skillet from heat. Immediately add vinegar; scrape up browned bits with a wooden spoon. Drizzle warm dressing over salad. Season with salt and pepper, and toss to combine. Top with pancetta and serve.

Arugula and Stone Fruit Salad with Balsamic Lamb Chops

The peppery, mustardy taste of arugula complements so many other flavors, including the earthy lamb and sweet fruits in this summer main course (inspired by Moroccan tagines). And arugula has a particular affinity for mint (and other fresh herbs, like basil or cilantro). A mix of aged balsamic vinegar and olive oil does double duty as a marinade for the chops and a dressing for the salad.

SERVES 4

3 tablespoons pepitas (hulled pumpkin seeds)

¼ cup balsamic vinegar, preferably aged

½ cup extra-virgin olive oil

Pinch of sugar

8 bone-in rib lamb chops, frenched (each about 4 ounces and 1 inch thick)

Coarse salt and freshly ground pepper

1 bunch arugula (about 8 ounces), trimmed

2 plums or nectarines, or a combination, pitted and sliced into wedges

¼ cup packed fresh mint leaves

1. Heat a medium skillet over medium high. Toast pepitas, shaking pan frequently, until darkened and fragrant, 3 to 5 minutes.

2. Whisk together vinegar, oil, and sugar in a bowl. Reserve ¼ cup of the mixture; transfer remaining marinade to a sealable plastic bag. Season lamb with salt and pepper and add to the bag, turning to coat. Let marinate in refrigerator, turning occasionally, at least 1 hour and up to 4 hours.

3. Let chops stand at room temperature 30 minutes. Heat a large skillet over medium. Working in batches, remove lamb from marinade, letting excess drip off, and add to pan. Cook, flipping once, until an instant-read thermometer inserted in thickest part (avoiding bone) registers 125°F, about 8 minutes. Transfer to a plate and let stand 10 minutes.

4. Whisk reserved vinegar mixture to combine. Divide arugula, fruit, pepitas, and mint among four plates. Season with salt and pepper; drizzle with reserved vinegar mixture. Top with lamb, dividing evenly; serve immediately.

Fig and Arugula Crostini

These appetizers show how even a little bitter arugula can go a long way in balancing the sweetness of other ingredients (in this case, caramelized onions and fresh figs). Sharp Parmigiano-Reggiano, arugula's frequent partner, is shaved over the top.

SERVES 6

2 tablespoons extra-virgin olive oil

2 large onions, thinly sliced

Coarse salt and freshly ground black pepper

1 tablespoon sugar

⅛ teaspoon cayenne pepper

12 ounces fresh figs, halved lengthwise

12 slices baguette, toasted

3 cups baby arugula

1 ounce Parmigiano-Reggiano cheese, shaved

1. Preheat oven to 400°F. Heat oil in a large skillet over low. Add onions, season with salt, and cook, stirring occasionally, until soft and golden, 45 minutes. Raise heat to medium low and cook until lightly browned and caramelized, about 10 minutes. Remove from heat; let cool slightly.

2. Combine sugar, cayenne, and a generous pinch of salt in a bowl. Place figs, cut side up, on a rimmed baking sheet. Sprinkle with sugar mixture. Roast until tender and caramelized, about 10 minutes.

3. Dividing evenly, top each slice of bread with some caramelized onions (reserve extra for another use), figs, arugula, and cheese. Serve immediately.

Charred Romaine Salad

Sturdy romaine leaves stand up beautifully to the heat of the grill. The salad is best when the romaine is hot off the grill, topped with radishes, shallot, and buttermilk dressing.

SERVES 4

1 bunch radishes, quartered

1 shallot, thinly sliced

⅔ cup water

½ cup plus 2 tablespoons red-wine vinegar

2 tablespoons sugar

Coarse salt and freshly ground pepper

½ cup buttermilk

¼ cup plus 2 tablespoons sour cream

1 large head romaine lettuce, halved lengthwise

Safflower oil, for brushing

1. Place radishes and shallot in a bowl. Bring the water, ½ cup vinegar, the sugar, and 2 teaspoons salt to a boil in a small saucepan. Pour over radishes and shallot; refrigerate.

2. Meanwhile, whisk together buttermilk, sour cream, and remaining 2 tablespoons vinegar in a bowl. Season with salt and pepper.

3. Heat grill (or grill pan) to medium high. Brush romaine halves with oil, and season with salt and pepper. Grill until charred but still crisp, about 4 minutes per side. Drizzle dressing over romaine. Drain radish-shallot mixture, scatter over romaine, and serve.

Free-Form Lasagna with Edible Weeds

Once thought of as pesky intruders, edible weeds—sorrel, dandelion, lamb's quarters, chickweed, purslane, and stinging nettle, among others—boast a diversity of flavors, from sweet to savory, tart to nutty, and spicy to bitter. Use just one or any combination in this lasagna. The weeds are sautéed with garlic and combined with golden raisins and lemon juice, then layered with zesty ricotta and pasta sheets.

SERVES 4

Coarse salt and freshly ground pepper

2 tablespoons extra-virgin olive oil, plus more for drizzling

1 cup fresh ricotta cheese

1 teaspoon finely grated lemon zest, plus 1 to 2 tablespoons fresh lemon juice

8 square fresh lasagna noodles (each about 5 inches)

2 garlic cloves, thinly sliced

12 ounces edible weeds, such as sorrel and lamb's quarters, thick stems removed, large leaves coarsely chopped

¼ cup golden raisins

1. Bring a large pot of water to a boil; add a generous amount of salt and 1 tablespoon oil. In a bowl, stir together ricotta and lemon zest; season with salt and pepper. Working with a few at a time, cook lasagna noodles until al dente, according to package instructions. Using tongs, transfer to a baking sheet, laying each square flat. Cover with plastic wrap.

2. In empty pot, heat remaining 1 tablespoon oil over medium high. Add garlic and cook, stirring frequently, until tender, 1 to 2 minutes. Add weeds; season with salt and pepper. Cook, tossing, until tender, 6 to 8 minutes. Stir in raisins and lemon juice; season with salt and pepper.

3. On each of four serving plates, top one lasagna noodle with about ¼ cup weed mixture and 2 tablespoons ricotta mixture. Top with another noodle, ¼ cup weeds, and 2 tablespoons ricotta. Drizzle with oil and serve immediately.

TIP
Fresh lasagna noodles can be found at specialty shops and Italian markets; you can also boil dried sheets as directed on the package, then drain and cut into squares.

Braised Red Cabbage

The compound that gives red (and purple) cabbage its beautiful color will also turn it blue when it's cooked with an alkaline substance, such as chicken broth, so don't omit the vinegar or another acid (like lemon juice); the acid counterbalances the alkaline.

SERVES 8

3 tablespoons olive oil

1 medium onion, thinly sliced

2 tablespoons brown sugar

½ cup apple cider vinegar

2 cups pure apple cider

1 cup chicken broth

1 cinnamon stick

1 dried bay leaf

Coarse salt and freshly ground pepper

1 small head red cabbage, cut into 8 wedges, core intact

1. Preheat oven to 350°F. Heat oil in a large, wide, heavy ovenproof pot over medium. Add onion and cook, stirring occasionally, until edges start to caramelize, 10 to 12 minutes. Add sugar and cook, stirring, 1 minute more. Add vinegar and bring to a boil, scraping up browned bits with a wooden spoon. Stir in cider, broth, cinnamon, and bay leaf; season with salt and pepper. Add cabbage, arranging in a single layer. Bring to a boil. Cover; transfer to oven and braise until cabbage is tender, 40 to 45 minutes.

2. Transfer cabbage to a serving platter using a slotted spoon; discard cinnamon stick and bay leaf. Bring remaining liquid in saucepan to a simmer over medium-high heat. Cook until reduced by half, about 10 minutes. (You will have about 1 cup sauce.) Spoon sauce over cabbage, and serve.

Creamed Green Cabbage

Cabbage is delicious when drenched in a creamy béchamel sauce, blanketed with grated cheese, and baked. Serve it with roast pork or sausages, like kielbasa or bratwurst.

SERVES 6

Coarse salt and freshly ground pepper

1 **small head green cabbage (about 2½ pounds), cored and shredded (10 cups)**

3 **tablespoons unsalted butter**

¼ **cup all-purpose flour**

2 **cups whole milk, warmed**

¼ **cup plus 1 tablespoon finely grated Pecorino Romano cheese**

1 **tablespoon finely grated lemon zest (from 2 lemons)**

1. Preheat oven to 350°F. Bring 1 inch of water to a boil in a pot; add salt. Add cabbage and cook until tender, about 5 minutes. Drain and let cool slightly. Squeeze out excess water using a clean kitchen towel.

2. Melt butter in a medium saucepan over medium heat. Stir in flour, and cook until bubbling but not browning, 1 to 2 minutes. Slowly whisk in milk. Cook, stirring, until sauce is thick enough to coat the back of a wooden spoon, about 5 minutes. Remove from heat; add ¼ cup cheese and the lemon zest. Immediately fold cabbage into sauce. Season with salt and pepper.

3. Spoon mixture into a shallow casserole dish. Sprinkle with remaining tablespoon cheese. Bake until bubbling, 30 to 35 minutes. Let stand 5 minutes before serving.

Fried Chicken with Puntarelle Salad

Here's Southern fried chicken and greens, Italian style: Buttermilk-battered strips of meat are topped with a salad (à la Milanese) of bitter leaves and basil. If you can find a head of puntarelle, a chicory that's a specialty of Rome, by all means use it here. First, peel back and trim the leaves, and reserve the celery-like heart for another use. Otherwise, use any bitter leaves you like.

SERVES 6

FOR THE SALAD

- 10 cups bitter leaves, such as puntarelle, dandelion greens, arugula, escarole, or chicory, torn or sliced if large
- ¾ cup torn fresh basil leaves
- 5 scallions (white and pale-green parts only), thinly sliced
- 2 garlic cloves

  Coarse salt
- 3 oil-packed anchovy fillets
- ¼ cup fresh lemon juice
- ¼ cup plus 2 tablespoons extra-virgin olive oil

FOR THE CHICKEN

- 2 cups buttermilk
- 2 large eggs
- 2 teaspoons baking powder
- 1 teaspoon baking soda
- 2 cups all-purpose flour

  Coarse salt and freshly ground pepper

  Safflower oil, for frying (about 8 cups)
- 3 skinless, boneless chicken breast halves (1½ pounds), cut into 1-by-3-inch strips

  Flaky sea salt, such as Maldon, for sprinkling

  Lemon wedges, for serving

1. Make the salad: Toss together greens, basil, and scallions in a large bowl. Mash garlic and a pinch of coarse salt into a paste using a mortar and pestle or using the flat side of a chef's knife. Add anchovies and mash. Transfer mixture to a small bowl, and stir in lemon juice. Gradually add oil, whisking constantly, until emulsified.

2. Make the chicken: Combine buttermilk, eggs, baking powder, and baking soda in a bowl. Whisk flour with coarse salt and pepper in another bowl.

3. In a medium pot, heat a few inches of oil over medium until oil reaches 380°F on a deep-fry thermometer. Dip each piece of chicken into buttermilk mixture to coat, shaking off excess, then dredge in flour mixture, patting it onto chicken as you work to coat completely.

4. Working in batches, carefully fry chicken until deep golden brown, about 3 minutes. Use tongs to transfer to paper-towel-lined plates to drain. Sprinkle with sea salt.

5. Toss salad with half the dressing in a large bowl. Season with coarse salt and pepper. Divide chicken strips among six plates, and top each with salad. Serve with lemon wedges and remaining dressing on the side.

Mini Asian Meatballs in Lettuce Cups

Lettuce is an entirely authentic wrapper for Asian meatballs, and it doesn't detract from the flavorings the way that bread can. Soft, tender lettuces like Bibb and Boston work best, but green and red leaf lettuces are fine here, too. Don't skip the accompanying lime mayonnaise; it's so easy to mix, and really completes the dish, as do the other garnishes.

SERVES 4

½ cup chopped garlic (from 10 to 12 cloves)

3 tablespoons chopped peeled fresh ginger (from a 3-inch piece)

¼ cup chopped scallions (from 2 to 3 scallions)

1 pound ground beef, turkey, or pork, or a combination

1 teaspoon fish sauce, such as *nam pla* or *nuoc mam*

1 teaspoon coarse salt

1 tablespoon toasted sesame oil

¼ cup mayonnaise

1 tablespoon fresh lime juice, plus lime wedges, for serving

Bibb lettuce leaves, for serving

Assorted garnishes, such as cilantro, sliced Thai chiles, chopped roasted peanuts, and hot sauce such as Sriracha

1. Finely chop together garlic, ginger, and scallions. In a bowl, gently combine garlic mixture with ground beef, fish sauce, and salt. Form mixture into 1-inch meatballs.

2. Heat sesame oil in a large skillet over high. Working in batches, fry meatballs until browned and cooked through, about 5 minutes per batch.

3. In a small bowl, mix mayonnaise and lime juice. Serve meatballs in lettuce cups, with lime mayonnaise, assorted garnishes, and lime wedges.

FLOWERS & BUDS

In the flower garden, a bud speaks of beauty's promise, and a blossom of its bright fulfillment. But in the vegetable patch, where deliciousness trumps gorgeousness, flowers and buds are far less prized, for they rarely embody a plant's crowning flavors or nutrients.

Not so in the case of artichokes, broccoli, and cauliflower—all vegetables that are actually buds. The artichoke, a relative of the thistle, consists of tightly furled petals (referred to, erroneously, as leaves), which cradle a layer of tender flesh near its base; that bud's heart and stem are also delectable when harvested young. Cauliflower and broccoli are dense clusters of tiny buds proliferating within a loose head of cabbage-like leaves. Brussels sprouts, meanwhile, are not actual sprouts, but instead are budlike heads that sprout along a thick stem.

Flowers eaten in full bloom tend to be quite fragile—not surprising, for they are seldom designed to support weight greater than that of a honeybee—and they are delicate in flavor as well. Chive blossoms taste like a whisper of onion. Nasturtiums have a mildly spicy, velvety quality. Among edible flowers, only voluptuous squash blossoms are substantial enough to be cooked and eaten as true vegetables rather than as a garnish.

In nature, buds are transitory and flowers are fleeting, which makes the stop-time quality of the edible varieties all the more wonderful—a promise come to delicious fruition.

ARTICHOKES
—
BROCCOLI
—
BRUSSELS SPROUTS
—
CAULIFLOWER
—
CHIVE BLOSSOMS
—
EDIBLE FLOWERS
—
SQUASH BLOSSOMS

THE BASICS

SEASONALITY

Broccoli, cauliflower, and brussels sprouts are members of the crucifer (cabbage) family, all of which like cool weather. Although these vegetables are available throughout much of the year, connoisseurs swear they taste best after a cold snap in fall. Look for them at farmers' markets once sweater season is under way. Artichokes also like cool weather, and their peak seasons are in spring and early fall. Squash blossoms open throughout early and midsummer—a single plant will keep producing them over the course of several weeks. As for other flowers, they may bloom in spring, summer, or early fall, depending on variety.

BUYING

Look for artichokes, broccoli, and cauliflower that are dense and firm; their flavors start to deteriorate the moment the buds burst open and begin to blossom. Baby artichokes are actually buds that sprout lower on the stalk than full-size ones; reduced sun exposure keeps them from developing the rough chokes and sharp barbs that can make prepping full-size ones arduous. Broccoli and brussels sprouts should be a bluish green, the latter with a coating of natural wax. The best way to buy brussels sprouts is when they are still on the stalk, available at farmer's markets (and some supermarkets) during the spring and fall. With flower blossoms, the most important criterion may be one you can't see: They must be grown without the pesticides that saturate most commercial flowers. So buy them at greenmarkets, or grow them yourself.

NOTABLE VARIETIES

Artichokes: Baby purple artichokes are milder and slightly sweeter than the regular variety. Violetta di Chioggia is a smaller variety and more oval shaped than globe artichokes, with mottled purple leaves and a pronounced flavor. Benicarló, a highly prized variety from Valencia, Spain, has a full, meaty flavor.

Broccoli: Purple broccoli has a head beaded with indigo florets that turn a shade of olive green when cooked; the flavor is milder than green broccoli. Romanesco broccoli, also known as cavolo broccolo Romanesco, or simply cavolo Romano, has tight, bright green spiraling heads; the taste is mellow and slightly nutty. Broccoflower, a broccoli-cauliflower hybrid, looks like a lime-green cauliflower and tastes a little like both its parents.

Broccolini and Chinese broccoli are close relatives of broccoli, as all are members of the cabbage family (unlike broccoli rabe, which is not related to broccoli at all; see page 110 for more information). Broccolini is actually a hybrid of broccoli and Chinese broccoli, with tight florets, long stalks, and tender leaves (all edible); the flavor is milder and sweeter than regular broccoli. Chinese broccoli, on the other hand, is slightly bitter and has thicker stems and flatter, sturdier leaves than broccolini.

Brussels sprouts: The most common types of sprouts are Diablo and Dimitri, two hybrids that bear the hallmark green color and mild taste. It's worth looking for more robust-flavored heirloom varieties, such as Long Island, Catskill, and gorgeous, purplish-red Rubine.

Cauliflower: Stunning heirloom varieties of cauliflower in a range of colors are now being cultivated. Orange cauliflower, sometimes referred to as cheddar cauliflower, has the same taste and texture as white, while purple cauliflower is milder, sweeter, and nuttier. Miniature cauliflowers (often called baby cauliflower) the size of fists can be prepared the same way as the full-size variety.

Edible flowers: There are dozens of flower blossoms that can be used for culinary purposes: Calendula or marigolds range from spicy to bitter, tangy to peppery, with a golden-orange hue that makes them a good substitute for saffron; white and red clover blossoms are sweet and taste of licorice; dandelions are sweetest when picked young, and the buds are tastier than the flowers; hibiscus has a citrusy flavor; sweet woodruff is sweet and grassy; violets are sweet and fragrant. The flowers of most herbs and vegetables are also generally edible: we especially like flowering basil, borage, chives, dill, lavender, lemon verbena, mint, and thyme, as well as the flowers from arugula, okra, radish, and scarlet runner beans.

STORING

Broccoli, cauliflower, brussels sprouts, and artichokes should all be kept in the refrigerator, loosely wrapped in a plastic bag; depending on how fresh they are to begin with, they will keep anywhere from a couple of days to a week. If you can't use fresh blossoms right away, store them like any flowers: with their stems in a vase of cool water, in the refrigerator.

PREPPING

To ready baby artichokes, simply remove the tougher outer leaves and trim the stems. Slice very thinly on a mandoline to eat raw. Full-size artichokes take more work to prepare for cooking: Strip away the tough outer leaves, then cut roughly ½ inch off the top. Using kitchen scissors, trim away the tips of remaining leaves to remove thorns. At this point the artichoke is ready for boiling; but to roast or sauté, slice it lengthwise into quarters or wedges, and use the tip of a paring knife to cut out the fuzzy, pinkish choke. As you work, place prepped artichokes in a bowl of water acidulated with lemon juice (3 tablespoons per quart of water) or white vinegar (2 tablespoons per quart); cut surfaces quickly darken when exposed to air.

You can break a head of cauliflower or broccoli into florets with your bare hands, or use a knife to chop it down to the right size for a recipe, or to eat raw. To make cauliflower or broccoli "steaks," simply trim one end from stalks, then slice down vertically through the heads into thick slabs (anywhere from a half inch to an inch). If you plan to eat the stalks, pare away the tough outer layer with a peeler or knife; then continue to shave them with the peeler, or slice thinly on the diagonal, to use raw in salads and slaws. Handle cauliflower with care; it bruises easily. Use the potato-eye scoop on a vegetable peeler to cut out any black spots. Blossoms need nothing but a gentle rinse.

Brussels sprouts only require pulling off the outer leaves, which are often bruised or blemished, and trimming the short stems. If you plan to eat brussels sprouts raw, simply separate the tender, inner leaves or slice very thinly. Otherwise, you can halve or quarter larger sprouts before cooking so they are of a more uniform size.

COOKING

People who adore broccoli, cauliflower, and brussels sprouts often question those who don't, and vice versa: *How can they . . . ?* Blame generations of cooks who boiled these vegetables, then served them as is, often at room temperature. That's not to say that steamed and blanched versions can't be wonderful—they are, when combined with other flavorful ingredients in stir-fries, salads, and the like, or dipped in sauces. But for serving alone as a side dish, these vegetables generally taste better when roasted or sautéed. Baby artichokes are wonderful left whole (or halved, as desired) and fried or roasted. The large ones are best steamed or boiled, so that they can be taken apart, petal by petal, when eaten. Fragile blossoms should

be added to dishes at the last minute to minimize wilting. Squash blossoms can be sliced or chopped, and added to recipes where you use zucchini—or the beautiful bell-shaped flowers can be stuffed and fried whole.

HOW TO STEAM
(For artichokes, broccoli, brussels sprouts, cauliflower)
Trim artichokes as described on page 239 (leave baby artichokes whole or cut in half). Trim stalks from broccoli and cauliflower, and cut heads into large florets. Trim brussels sprouts and leave whole or halve. Place in a steamer basket set in a pot with 2 inches of water. Bring to a boil; cover and steam until just tender and broccoli and brussels sprouts are bright green, 6 to 8 minutes. Toss with butter or olive oil; season with salt and pepper.

HOW TO SAUTÉ
(For artichokes, broccoli, brussels sprouts, cauliflower)
Trim artichokes as described on page 239; cut into quarters (leave baby artichokes whole or cut in half). Trim other vegetables, peeling outer layer of any stalks. Separate broccoli and cauliflower into small florets, or cut diagonally into 1-inch slices and cut stalks into same-size pieces. Halve or quarter sprouts. Heat olive oil or butter in a large skillet over medium high. Add vegetables, season with salt and pepper, and cook, stirring occasionally, until golden brown and caramelized, 8 to 10 minutes. Add a little water (about ⅓ cup for 2 pounds of vegetables) and cook, stirring up browned bits from bottom of pan, until evaporated, about 2 minutes. Sprinkle with lemon juice.

HOW TO ROAST

(For baby artichokes, broccoli, brussels sprouts, cauliflower)

Trim baby artichokes, and leave whole or cut in half. Trim 1 inch from stalks of broccoli and cauliflower and peel outer layer of stalk. Cut diagonally into 1-inch-thick slices. Separate florets into bite-size pieces. Trim brussels sprouts and halve or quarter. Drizzle with olive oil, season with salt and pepper, and toss to combine. Spread evenly on a rimmed baking sheet. Roast in a 425°F oven until tender and browned, tossing once or twice, 15 to 20 minutes.

HOW TO BRAISE

(For artichokes, broccoli, brussels sprouts, cauliflower)

Trim artichokes as described on page 239; halve lengthwise (leave baby artichokes whole). Trim broccoli and cauliflower stems and separate heads into large florets. Trim brussels sprouts. Heat olive oil or butter in a large skillet over medium high. Add vegetables and enough liquid (chicken or vegetable broth, or water) to cover. Bring to a boil, reduce heat, and cover. Simmer until fork-tender, 8 to 10 minutes (20 minutes for full-size artichokes). Season with salt and pepper and serve with lemon wedges.

HOW TO GRILL

(For artichokes, broccoli, cauliflower)

Trim full-size artichokes as described on page 239. Steam for 20 minutes, then halve and scoop out the choke. Trim baby artichokes, and leave whole or cut in half. Trim broccoli and cauliflower stems and peel outer layer of stalks. Cut diagonally into ½-inch-thick slices. Brush cut sides of vegetables with olive oil; season with salt and pepper. Grill over medium, directly on grates or in a grill basket, turning as needed, until tender and charred in spots, 5 to 12 minutes, depending on size.

FLAVOR PAIRINGS

Broccoli, cauliflower, and brussels sprouts are strong-tasting vegetables whose flavor is brought to new life by other potent ingredients—bacon, garlic, and mustard are all good examples. Artichokes have a subtler taste. Commonly paired with butter, they are also enlivened by herbs and lemon. One thing not to serve with artichokes is wine: the artichokes block your taste buds' ability to appreciate the wine. Mild blossoms will enliven any dish featuring the herb or vegetable they bloom from—but can be overwhelmed by strong flavors, so reserve them for subtler combinations.

ARTICHOKES: butter, toasted breadcrumbs, garlic, Parmesan, onions, parsley, thyme

BROCCOLI: garlic, anchovy, red-pepper flakes, lemon, mustard, cheddar, Parmesan, sausage

BRUSSELS SPROUTS: bacon, walnuts, lemon, Pecorino, mustard, parsley, apple cider

CAULIFLOWER: cheddar, mustard, curry, apple, garlic, parsley, saffron, raisins, anchovy

CHIVE BLOSSOMS: eggs, ricotta, potatoes, salads, cream soups, salmon, crème fraîche

SQUASH BLOSSOMS: basil, ricotta, Parmesan, mozzarella, eggs, tomato, cilantro, shrimp

Nasturtium Salad with Artichokes and Asparagus

Nasturtium blossoms and leaves make beautiful, tasty additions to soups, pasta dishes, and salads, including this harbinger-of-spring dish that features artichokes and purple potatoes. You can find nasturtiums in a range of hues at farmers' markets.

SERVES 4

1 lemon, halved

4 large artichokes, trimmed (see Prepping, page 239)

Coarse salt and freshly ground pepper

12 ounces small potatoes, preferably purple or blue, scrubbed

12 ounces asparagus, tough ends trimmed and spears cut on the bias into 2-inch pieces

4 cups spicy mixed salad greens, such as tatsoi, arugula, and watercress

1 cup nasturtiums and chive blossoms, plus more for garnish

1 bunch radishes, thinly sliced

¼ cup Dijon mustard

¼ cup rice-wine vinegar (unseasoned)

¾ cup safflower oil

1. Bring 1 inch of water to a boil in a large pot. Squeeze juice of lemon into pot. Set a steamer basket in pot. Add artichokes, season with salt, cover, and steam 20 minutes. Add potatoes to steamer. Continue steaming until potatoes and artichokes are easily pierced with the tip of a sharp knife, 12 to 15 minutes. Let cool to room temperature.

2. Meanwhile, bring 2 inches of water to a boil in a saucepan. Generously season with salt. Add asparagus and boil until crisp-tender, about 1 minute. Transfer to an ice-water bath until cool. Drain and pat dry.

3. Remove petals from artichokes and reserve. Scoop out chokes from hearts with a spoon, then slice hearts lengthwise into quarters. Slice potatoes into ¼-inch-thick rounds. Divide artichoke hearts, potatoes, asparagus, greens, flowers, and radishes among four plates.

4. Whisk together mustard and vinegar in a bowl. Add oil in a slow, steady stream, whisking constantly, until dressing is emulsified. Season generously with salt and pepper.

5. Lightly drizzle salads evenly with some of the dressing and garnish with more flowers. Serve remaining dressing with reserved artichoke petals on the side.

Bucatini with Cauliflower, Capers, and Lemon

We've taken some liberties with the Italian pairing of cauliflower and pasta in the cooking method here. First, the pasta is simmered in an ovenproof skillet with water, oil, and seasonings, then it's topped with cauliflower, capers, and Parmigiano-Reggiano, and broiled to finish. You could use this same technique with broccoli, too.

SERVES 4

1 pound bucatini

5 cups water

¼ cup extra-virgin olive oil, plus more for drizzling

Fresh oregano sprigs, plus 1 tablespoon chopped leaves

¼ teaspoon red-pepper flakes, plus more for serving

Coarse salt

1 teaspoon finely grated lemon zest and 2 tablespoons fresh lemon juice, plus wedges for serving

1 head cauliflower, stem trimmed and florets finely chopped (about 4 cups)

3 tablespoons capers, preferably salt-packed, rinsed and drained

½ cup finely grated Parmigiano-Reggiano cheese, plus more for serving

1. Heat broiler with rack 8 inches from heating element. Combine pasta, the water, 2 tablespoons oil, 1 oregano sprig, red-pepper flakes, and 2 teaspoons salt in a large, straight-sided ovenproof skillet. Bring to a boil over medium-high heat; continue cooking, stirring occasionally, until sauce is mostly reduced and pasta is al dente, according to package instructions, about 8 minutes. Remove from heat; stir in lemon zest and juice.

2. In a bowl, toss cauliflower with remaining 2 tablespoons oil, ½ teaspoon salt, the capers, cheese, and oregano leaves. Sprinkle over pasta in skillet. Broil until cauliflower is golden in spots and pasta is heated through, about 5 minutes. Toss to combine. Serve with more cheese and red-pepper flakes, a drizzle of oil, oregano sprigs, and lemon wedges.

Oven-Fried Baby Artichokes

Once you remove the outer leaves and trim the stems, you can eat baby artichokes in their entirety (there's no choke to remove). They also don't take long to cook, meaning you can quickly fry them (here, in the oven) until tender inside but golden brown outside.

SERVES 6

1 large egg yolk

½ teaspoon finely grated lemon zest plus 2 tablespoons lemon juice

½ teaspoon minced garlic

2 tablespoons salt-packed capers, rinsed and drained

⅔ cup extra-virgin olive oil

Flaky sea salt and freshly ground pepper

18 baby artichokes, trimmed (see Prepping, page 239)

1. Preheat oven to 500°F with rack in lowest position and a rimmed baking sheet on rack (this helps crisp artichokes).

2. Purée yolk, lemon zest and juice, garlic, and capers in a blender until smooth. With motor running, slowly add ⅓ cup oil in a steady stream; blend until mixture is thick and creamy. Season generously with salt and pepper. Transfer caper aïoli to a serving bowl.

3. Toss artichokes with remaining ⅓ cup oil in a bowl. Place upside down on hot baking sheet, and roast until petals are crisp and artichoke hearts are tender, 8 to 13 minutes. Sprinkle with salt, and serve immediately with caper aïoli.

Smoky Brussels Sprouts Gratin

*This holiday-worthy side dish will win over even the brussels sprouts averse. The sprouts
are blanched then combined with grated smoked Gouda in a rich, creamy gratin.*

SERVES 8

2 tablespoons unsalted butter

2 tablespoons all-purpose flour

2 cups whole milk

Coarse salt and freshly
ground pepper

⅔ cup coarsely grated smoked
Gouda cheese (2 ounces)

1½ pounds brussels sprouts

⅔ cup finely grated aged
Gouda cheese (2 ounces)

Pinch of flaky smoked
sea salt, such as Maldon

1. Preheat oven to 375°F. Melt butter in a saucepan over medium heat. Add flour and whisk until mixture bubbles slightly
but has not started to brown, about 2 minutes. Gradually
whisk in milk. Raise heat and bring to a boil, whisking often.
Reduce heat to low, and cook, stirring occasionally with
a wooden spoon, until thickened, 12 to 15 minutes. Season
with coarse salt and pepper. Remove from heat. Add smoked
Gouda; stir until melted and smooth.

2. Meanwhile, blanch brussels sprouts in a pot of salted
boiling water until just tender, 3 to 4 minutes. Drain, and
transfer to a 2-quart baking dish.

3. Pour cheese sauce over sprouts, and sprinkle with aged
Gouda and smoked sea salt. Bake, uncovered, until bubbling
and golden, about 25 minutes. Serve immediately.

Broiled Striped Bass with Cauliflower and Capers

Broiling cauliflower is a faster way than roasting to achieve a similar golden-brown tenderness. We combine cauliflower with salty capers and sweet golden raisins, for a dish with Italian flavors. To make it a meal, the cauliflower is topped with striped bass and broiled some more. Another firm-fleshed fish, such as halibut or salmon, can be substituted for the striped bass.

SERVES 4

1 small head cauliflower, trimmed and cut into ½-inch-thick slices

3 tablespoons extra-virgin olive oil, plus more for serving

Coarse salt and freshly ground pepper

4 skin-on striped bass fillets (each about 6 ounces)

2 tablespoons salt-packed capers, rinsed and drained

3 tablespoons golden raisins

2 tablespoons sherry vinegar

Mixed fresh herbs, such as parsley, tarragon, and chives

1. Heat broiler with rack 6 inches from heating element. Place cauliflower on a rimmed baking sheet and drizzle with 2 tablespoons oil; season with salt and pepper, then toss to combine. Spread in a single layer and broil until crisp-tender and golden brown in spots, about 10 minutes.

2. Drizzle fish with remaining 1 tablespoon oil; season generously with salt and pepper. Place on top of cauliflower, skin side up, and add capers to sheet. Broil until fish is just opaque throughout, 5 to 7 minutes. Add raisins and broil just until plump and hot, about 30 seconds. Drizzle fish and vegetables with vinegar, and divide evenly among four plates. Serve sprinkled generously with herbs and drizzled with more oil.

TIP
Broilers vary in heat intensity; move the rack to a lower position if the cauliflower or fish is browning too quickly, or to a higher rack if too slowly.

Roasted Cauliflower with Herb Sauce

When roasting cauliflower, the transformation from sturdy and bitter to tender and mildly sweet is a revelation. Here, the whole head is wrapped in parchment and then steam-roasted till it's tender enough to scoop with a spoon.

SERVES 8

1 large head cauliflower

¾ cup extra-virgin olive oil

Coarse salt and freshly ground pepper

½ cup packed chopped fresh flat-leaf parsley

½ cup packed chopped fresh cilantro leaves and stems

½ teaspoon minced garlic

1½ teaspoons Dijon mustard

2 tablespoons sherry vinegar

1. Preheat oven to 450°F. Place cauliflower on a large parchment-lined rimmed baking sheet. Brush with ¼ cup oil; season with salt and pepper. Pull short sides of parchment over cauliflower and fold one end over other a few times to seal. Fold long ends of parchment under cauliflower to create a packet. Roast until knife-tender; about 40 minutes. Tear open parchment at top; continue to roast until golden brown, 15 to 20 minutes more.

2. Stir together parsley, cilantro, garlic, mustard, vinegar, and remaining ½ cup oil in a small bowl to combine. Season with salt and pepper. Serve cauliflower warm, with herb sauce alongside.

Crisped Brussels Sprout Leaves

Roasting brussels sprout leaves turns them crisp and crunchy. Simple seasonings are all that's needed; sprouts do well with bright flavors like lemon zest and rich ingredients such as hazelnuts and nutty cheeses (here, Pecorino Romano). As great as this is as a side dish, the leaves also make a tasty topping for pizza.

SERVES 6

1 pound brussels sprouts, trimmed, leaves separated

1 tablespoon extra-virgin olive oil

1 tablespoon finely grated lemon zest, plus lemon wedges for serving

¼ cup hazelnuts, coarsely chopped

Coarse salt and freshly ground pepper

¼ cup finely grated Pecorino Romano cheese (1 ounce)

Preheat oven to 375°F. On a rimmed baking sheet, toss brussels sprout leaves with oil, zest, and hazelnuts. Season with salt and pepper. Roast until leaves are crisp and golden around edges, 10 to 12 minutes. Sprinkle with cheese and serve with lemon wedges.

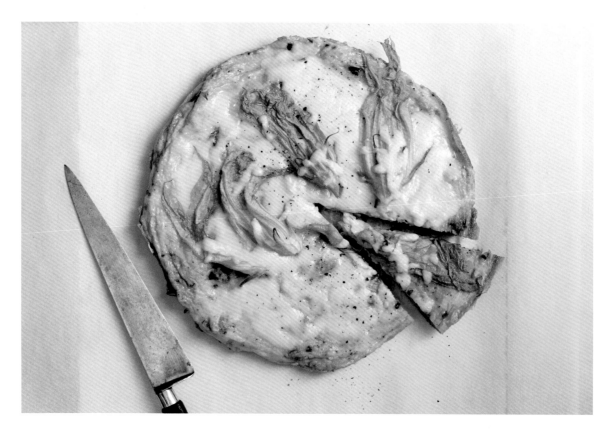

Squash-Blossom Frittata

Anyone who has ever planted zucchini knows it's hard to keep up with the steady supply (or onslaught!) of vegetables and flowers. Thus, gardeners are always looking for new ways to prepare them both. For this simple and beautiful frittata, half the blossoms are stirred into the eggs, and the rest are scattered over the top along with mozzarella.

SERVES 4 TO 6

2 tablespoons extra-virgin olive oil

1 medium onion, thinly sliced

2 tablespoons minced fresh cilantro

10 squash blossoms

10 large eggs, lightly beaten

Coarse salt and freshly ground pepper

4 ounces fresh mozzarella cheese, sliced

1. Preheat oven to 375°F. Heat oil in a large nonstick oven-proof skillet over medium. Add onion, cilantro, and half the squash blossoms, and cook, stirring, 1 minute. Add eggs, season with salt and pepper, and transfer to oven.

2. Bake until just set, about 10 minutes. Top with mozzarella and remaining squash blossoms. Return to oven until cheese melts and frittata is golden in spots, about 5 minutes more. Serve warm.

Goat Cheese with Edible Flowers and Arugula

When you have a bunch of edible blossoms, let their vibrant colors do the work for you. Simply mix chopped flowers (petals and leaves) into softened goat cheese, then shape into rounds and pat more flowers on top. Any edible flower will work; peppery nasturtium, borage, and pansy are shown here.

SERVES 12

2 large logs (11 ounces each) fresh goat cheese, room temperature

1 cup packed arugula, coarsely chopped

Freshly ground pepper

2 cups loosely packed edible blossoms and leaves, coarsely chopped

Crackers or thinly sliced baguette rounds, for serving

1. Stir one goat-cheese log in a bowl until smooth. Mix in arugula, and season with pepper. In another bowl, stir remaining goat-cheese log until smooth. Mix in 1½ cups flowers and leaves, and season with pepper.

2. Form each mixture into two or three disks (each about ½ inch thick). Roll in remaining blossoms. Place disks on a parchment-lined baking sheet, cover, and refrigerate until chilled, about 30 minutes. Serve with crackers or baguette rounds.

Broccoli, Shrimp, and Shiitake Stir-Fry

The brief high-heat cooking of stir-frying suits broccoli, since you want it to retain some of its crunch, and the color brightens as well. Here, broccoli is combined with shiitake mushrooms and shrimp; you'll want to use the simple garlic-ginger-soy-sauce mixture in other stir-fries, too. Serve over steamed white or brown rice.

SERVES 4

1 garlic clove, thinly sliced

1 teaspoon finely grated peeled fresh ginger

3 tablespoons rice vinegar (unseasoned)

2 tablespoons low-sodium soy sauce

¼ teaspoon red-pepper flakes

2 tablespoons safflower oil

1 pound fresh shiitake mushrooms, stemmed and halved (large ones quartered)

1 pound large shrimp (16 to 20 count), peeled and deveined

1 head broccoli, separated into small florets (2 cups)

2 scallions, finely chopped, for serving

1. Stir together garlic, ginger, vinegar, soy sauce, and red-pepper flakes in a small bowl.

2. In a wok or large skillet, heat oil over medium high. Add mushrooms and cook, stirring, just until tender, about 5 minutes. Stir in garlic mixture and cook until slightly reduced, about 2 minutes.

3. Add shrimp and broccoli, and cook, stirring, until shrimp are opaque throughout and broccoli is crisp-tender, 3 to 4 minutes. To serve, top with scallions.

Braised Chicken and Brussels Sprouts

After years of being overcooked, underappreciated, and generally scorned, brussels sprouts are finally getting their due. Instead of boiling them (to death), cooks have championed a host of ways to prepare them, including roasting (page 76) and shaving into slaws and salads (page 115). This one-pan dinner presents another option: Sauté halved sprouts until golden, then oven-braise with chicken until perfectly tender.

SERVES 4

1 tablespoon extra-virgin olive oil

1 whole chicken (3 to 4 pounds), cut into 10 pieces

Coarse salt and freshly ground pepper

1 pound brussels sprouts, trimmed and halved

2 medium shallots, thinly sliced

1 tablespoon Dijon mustard

¼ cup apple cider vinegar

½ cup low-sodium chicken broth

2 tablespoons heavy cream

1. Preheat oven to 375°F. In a large ovenproof skillet, heat oil over medium high. Season chicken all over with salt and pepper. Working in batches, cook chicken until browned, about 6 minutes per side. Transfer to a plate, then add brussels sprouts and shallots to pan. Sauté until golden brown, about 3 minutes. Stir in mustard and cook, stirring, 1 minute. Add vinegar and broth, return chicken to pan, and bring to a rapid simmer.

2. Transfer pan to oven and braise until chicken is cooked through, 20 to 25 minutes. Remove from oven. Add heavy cream to pan and swirl to combine; season with salt and pepper, and serve.

Capellini with Chive Blossoms

The lovely purple blossoms that appear when chives have matured taste just like the herb, only in flower form. Such an eye-catching component instantly makes any dish— scrambled eggs, creamy soups, mashed potatoes, even pasta—more appealing.

SERVES 4 TO 6

1 cup crème fraîche

¼ cup minced chive blossoms, plus more for garnish

¼ cup snipped fresh chives, plus more for garnish

1 to 2 teaspoons lemon juice

Coarse salt and freshly ground pepper

8 ounces capellini pasta

1 tablespoon unsalted butter

1 jar (4 ounces) whitefish caviar

1 hard-cooked egg, yolk and white separated

1. Stir together ¾ cup crème fraîche, the chive blossoms, chives, and lemon juice to taste in a bowl. Season with salt.

2. Cook pasta in a large pot of salted boiling water until al dente, according to package instructions. Reserve ¾ cup pasta water; drain pasta. Toss pasta with butter and crème-fraîche mixture, adding enough pasta water to make a light sauce. Season with salt and pepper.

3. Place a small dollop of remaining crème fraîche in each of four to six dishes, and sprinkle with chive blossoms and chives. Divide pasta among dishes. Top with caviar and more crème fraîche. Press egg white and yolk through a sieve, then sprinkle over pasta. Serve immediately.

Roasted Broccoli with Grated Manchego

There's boiled and steamed broccoli blanketed with melted cheese, and then there's this upgrade. Roasting turns broccoli brown and tender and delicious. We cook the florets and the (peeled and thinly sliced) stalks together, then finish with a spritz of lemon juice and a dusting of Manchego—a nutty sheep's-milk cheese from Spain.

SERVES 6

2 large heads broccoli

4 garlic cloves, smashed

2 tablespoons extra-virgin olive oil

¼ to ½ teaspoon red-pepper flakes

Coarse salt

1 tablespoon fresh lemon juice, plus wedges for serving

⅓ cup finely grated Manchego cheese, for serving

1. Preheat oven to 450°F with racks in upper and lower thirds. Trim 1 inch from end of broccoli stalks. Cut off florets, and separate into large pieces. Using a vegetable peeler or paring knife, peel outer layer of stalks; thinly slice crosswise.

2. Divide broccoli (stalks and florets), garlic, oil, and red-pepper flakes between two large rimmed baking sheets; season with salt. Toss to combine, then spread evenly on sheets. Roast until broccoli is crisp-tender and beginning to brown, 20 to 25 minutes, rotating sheets from top to bottom and tossing broccoli once halfway through.

3. Sprinkle broccoli with lemon juice; toss to coat. Serve, topped with cheese and lemon wedges.

FRUITS

It's a riddle befitting the Mad Hatter, this when-is-a-vegetable-not-a-vegetable question. But it takes more than just tea-party nonsense to make tomatoes, peppers, and avocados qualify as botanical fruits. By definition, fruits are seed packages—a plant's bid for future generations—wrapped in delectable, fragrant flesh, covered by a skin whose color appeals to hungry animals. A form of communication not just between species but also across taxonomic kingdoms, fruits tempt mobile creatures into acting as agents for the plant, carrying the seeds in their digestive tracts, and then depositing them far from home. Even the fieriest chiles utilize the services of birds to distribute their seeds; certain species of tropical birds are immune to the chiles' heat.

So why do we call certain fruits vegetables? The answer is surprisingly unscientific. Sometimes it has to do with their sugar content. Tomatoes, for example, are about 3 percent sugar, while peaches and plums are 10 percent. But that rule doesn't apply to winter squashes such as butternuts and pumpkins, which are not only sweet but also as comfortably at home on the dessert plate as on the dinner plate. In those cases, the classification seems to have to do with the fact that we never eat them raw, as we do with other fruits. Yet avocados and cucumbers are almost always eaten raw, and we consider them vegetables; in their case, it's back to the sugar content. Ultimately, one fact escapes confusion: These fruits are among the most popular in the vegetable kingdom.

AVOCADOS
—
CUCUMBERS
—
EGGPLANTS
—
PEPPERS AND CHILES
—
SUMMER SQUASHES
—
TOMATILLOS
—
TOMATOES
—
WINTER SQUASHES

THE BASICS

SEASONALITY

Nearly all these fruits/vegetables are summer babies, turning bright and plump in the hot sun of July and August. Sweet peppers and chiles ripen into early fall. And, as their name implies, winter squashes mature in cool weather; harvested September through November ("autumn squashes" would be a more apt name), they are sold throughout the winter, when their rich, earthy flavors are appreciated.

BUYING

Fruits acquire flavors, sugars, and nutrients from the parent plant, so the best ones are allowed to ripen in the field and sold close to where they're grown. In other words, this category is especially worth seeking out at farmstands and greenmarkets. Look for cucumbers, peppers, tomatoes, summer squash (including zucchini), and eggplants that feel taut and smooth-skinned, and are heavy for their size, with vivid, deep color. The same criteria apply to winter squash such as hubbard, butternut, and kabocha. As for size, it doesn't much matter except with eggplants and summer squash—the smaller ones are far superior in texture because their cell walls toughen and fill with water as they grow, becoming stringy, bland, and watery. As for tomatillos, select those with loose, papery husks and no bruises. The exception to the close-to-home rule is avocados: They originated in Mexico and Guatemala, and so the best U.S.-grown ones come from California and Florida. Avocados are picked hard and they ripen only after harvest. Because they bruise easily when ripe, it's best to buy them when they're still firm and let them soften at home, placing them in a paper bag on the kitchen counter until barely soft.

NOTABLE VARIETIES

Avocados: At any time of year, there will be an avocado in season, and it's worth looking for them at farmers' markets in California and Florida, and at specialty food stores everywhere else. Most California varieties originated in Guatemala: the well-known Hass avocado; pear-shaped Fuerte, with skin that remains bright green, even when very ripe; and round Reed, with thick green skin that's easy to peel. In Florida, you are more likely to find West Indian varieties such as Booth, Lula, and Taylor, which come into season in the middle of summer. Mexican varieties tend to be on the smaller side; the most popular are the Bacon (slightly brownish skin that's easy to peel) and the Zutano (jade green skin and creamy yellow flesh).

Cucumbers: Many so-called slicing cucumbers are cultivated to have seeds that are barely perceptible, with very tender skins, meaning no seeding or peeling is required. Besides English cucumbers, there are little Persian cucumbers and striking Armenian cucumbers with pale striped skin, smooth-skinned Mediterranean (or Lebanese) cucumbers, and long, dark-green Japanese cucumbers, which resemble English ones but have bumpy skins. Pickling cucumbers tend to be shorter, thicker, and bumpier; Kirby and Liberty are the most common of these.

Eggplants: This fruit is cultivated around the world in a range of colors, shapes, and sizes that go beyond the hefty dark-purple globes found in our grocery stores. Italian breeds include Barbarella, which can grow up to half a foot wide and nearly as long; squat, oval Beatrice, which is mild and creamy; streaky, thick-skinned Nubia; and white Clara eggplants, which are meaty and mild. Chinese and Japanese eggplants are typically long, slim, and delicate tasting, while the smaller, rounder Asian varieties such as Calliope (or Indian) and Kermits (or Thai) are fast cooking and rarely bitter. You'll know Graffiti eggplants by their violet and white stripes with velvety flesh; at a mere 2 to 4 inches, Fairy Tales are less seedy than globes and, hence, less bitter.

Peppers and chiles: These come in many different shapes, colors, and heat levels. Among bell peppers, there are Purple Bell, Chocolate Beauty, and Dove (white- or ivory-skinned). Hot chiles include: Anaheim, from New Mexico; Cascabel; Cayenne; Chilaca, the name for a green fruit of a pasilla pepper, which translates as "little raisin" owing to its dried dark-brown pods; Chiltepin, the closest thing to the original wild pepper (and, when dried, the world's second-most-expensive spice, after saffron); Cubanelle, a long sweet pepper that's also known as Italian frying pepper; Manzano; Padrón (or shishito) peppers; and Asian chiles such as Thai Hot and Thai Bird. Wax peppers, so called for their shiny, polished-looking skins, include Hungarian Wax, Sante Fe Grande, and Yellow Banana.

Summer squashes: The vast range may come as a surprise to many of us. Crookneck squash such as Horn of Plenty are so-named for their curvaceous shapes. Pattypan squash such as Butter Scallop are also named for their squat shapes. Baby squash, including Butterstick and Sunburst, are picked when young. Of the straight-necked varieties, there's Zebra Zuke, a striking zucchini with light- and dark-green stripes, and two-toned Zephyrs. Then there are round varieties, including Ronde de Nice, an heirloom zucchini with creamy flesh and tender skin; Cousa, used in Middle Eastern cooking, which is tender and sweet; and Tatuma, a Mexican variety that resembles Cousa but with a very thin skin (and very few seeds).

Tomatoes: Everyone's favorite summer fruit begs to be explored; start with exceptionally sweet Sun Gold, a type of cherry tomato with a golden-orange flesh. Then there are hundreds of heirloom varieties: Brandywine has excellent flavor and slightly purple skin when ripe; round Black Russian has a rich flavor, while Purple Russian is a meaty plum tomato; Cherokee Purple is a beefsteak-style tomato prized for its exceptional flavor; Speckled Roman is another excellent plum tomato; Big Rainbow is rich and melony; Black Cherry is complex and mild, with a slight acid tang; Green Doctor is sweet, with good acidic balance; Reisetomate has strong tomato flavor; Green Zebra and Yellow Peach are slightly tart; and Jaune Flamme is wonderfully fruity.

Winter squashes: Similar to gourds that are harvested in the summer, those that are found in fall and winter come in an arresting array of shapes, colors, textures, and sizes. Calabaza (or West Indian Pumpkin) has a sweet, juicy golden flesh similar to butternut; delicata has fine, creamy flesh and tender skin that can be eaten (as with acorn squash); bumpy-skinned hubbards have thick, sweet meat; Hokkaidos are choice Japanese varieties with dry, flaky, sweet flesh; kabocha is another Japanese variety with a similar taste and texture; New England Pie (or Small Sugar Pumpkin) has smooth, very sweet flesh that's ideal for pie making; single-serving-size Sweet Dumplings have two-toned skins; Cheese Pumpkin (named for its shape, which resembles a flattened cheese box) is fine-grained and sweet; Cushaw has sweet, moist, pale-yellow flesh; White Swan is an acorn-type squash in shape and flavor, with creamy-white skin; Rouge vif d'Etampes, also known as Cinderella, is an heirloom French variety with dense, flavorful flesh.

STORING

The rule of thumb with storing fruits is to mimic the climate in which they ripen. Tomatoes, avocados, eggplant, tomatillos, and peppers are all hot-weather, full-sunshine crops, and they suffer cell damage if refrigerated—tomatoes turn mealy; eggplants and avocados grow spongy and gray-brown inside. Because zucchini and cucumbers grow in the cool shade of their plants' broad leaves, they can withstand a brief spell of refrigeration. Winter squashes prefer cool temperatures around 50°F, but won't be harmed by a few days in the refrigerator, if you can't eat them right away.

PREPPING

Cut avocados lengthwise around the pit and twist to separate the halves, then use a large spoon to scoop out the flesh, or peel away the skin and slice the flesh—dousing it with citrus juice or vinegar as you work to keep it from browning.

Depending on variety, cucumbers may be seedy or seedless (as with English cucumbers), and may be thin-skinned or thick; the latter should be peeled before use (especially if they're waxed). To remove seeds, cut in half lengthwise, then scoop out with a teaspoon. Don't dress or salt cucumbers until just before serving or they will turn watery.

Examine summer squash closely: many need only a good rinse, but if they lay against the dirt as they ripened, they might need a gentle scrub.

The skin of winter squashes can be linoleum-hard; if your recipe calls for skinless wedges or chunks, it may be necessary to slice the squash into wedges before paring the skin away with a small knife or peeler.

Water between the cell walls gives eggplant its spongy texture; roasting or baking evaporates it, but if you're frying eggplant or using it in stews, you can make the flesh firmer by salting the slices first, and laying them in a colander or on a rack to drain.

To cut raw sweet peppers, stand them on end and cut the flesh from top to bottom; remove ribs and seeds with a knife. When cutting chiles, always use gloves, and don't touch your eyes or nose or any other sensitive areas until you've washed your hands. Leave ribs and seeds unless you prefer a milder heat.

Remove tomatillos' papery husks before cooking, and rinse off the sticky coating (from bitter-tasting saponins) on the fruits' skin.

As for tomatoes, if you wish to remove their skins, cut a small, shallow X into the skin at the rounded end, dunk them in rapidly boiling water for 15 seconds, then transfer to an ice-water bath. The skin will easily peel away. Otherwise, to remove the seedy flesh, core and quarter tomatoes lengthwise, flatten each piece with the inside up, and scrape it clean with a knife; then you can easily cut those pieces into a fine dice or as desired.

COOKING

Most fruits are incredibly versatile when it comes to cooking. Even avocados can be grilled or broiled until charred (perfect for topping toasts), and cucumbers take well to sautéing. Summer squash responds well to a range of treatments, and is also excellent grated and fried into crisp cakes or fritters, or baked into quick breads. Tomatoes and peppers can be cooked almost any which way—stewed, baked, roasted, simmered, puréed. Although tomatillos are related to tomatoes, they're much less versatile and best used to make sauces and salsas; try roasting the tomatillos first until blackened to add a smoky, charred flavor. Eggplant, too, is fussy about how it's prepared; its spongy flesh quickly becomes waterlogged or leaden with oil if drenched. However, roasting or grilling—dry heat techniques—compresses its flesh and undoes the mealiness. If you start with whole or halved roasted eggplants, you can scoop out the creamy insides to make baba ganoush and other purées; slices or chunks turn almost meaty, and can be tossed into sauces and spreads, or used to top pizza. Winter squashes can be roasted (whole or cut into pieces), simmered in soups and stews, braised, baked (with or without stuffing), boiled and mashed or puréed, or steamed.

HOW TO STEAM
(For eggplants, summer squashes, winter squashes)
Cut eggplant and summer squash into 1-inch-thick rounds; peel and seed winter squash and cut into 1-inch pieces. Place in a steamer basket

(or colander) set in a pot with 2 inches water. Bring to a boil, cover, and steam until tender, 5 to 10 minutes. Drizzle with olive oil and season with salt and pepper.

HOW TO ROAST
(For eggplants, summer squashes, winter squashes)
Cut eggplant and summer squash into uniform pieces (cubes, rounds, or lengthwise strips). Peel winter squashes (except acorn and delicata, which do not need to be peeled) and remove seeds. Drizzle with olive oil, season with salt and pepper, and toss to combine. Spread evenly on a rimmed baking sheet and roast at 450°F, tossing once or twice, until tender and golden brown, 20 to 30 minutes.

(For peppers and chiles)
Roast whole peppers and chiles directly over the flame of a gas burner until blackened and blistered, turning with kitchen tongs (alternately, roast under the broiler). Place in a bowl, cover, and let steam about 10 minutes. Rub off skin with paper towels; use a paring knife for stubborn spots. Cut as desired or specified in a recipe and remove ribs and seeds of bell peppers; leave ribs and seeds in chiles for more heat. Toss with olive oil and salt and pepper, to taste.

(For tomatoes)
Halve plum tomatoes and arrange, cut side up, on a rimmed baking sheet. Brush with olive oil, and season with salt and pepper; add a few herb sprigs, such as thyme or oregano, along with some sliced garlic cloves. Slow-roast in a 350°F oven until softened, about 1 hour. Let cool and refrigerate, covered, up to 5 days.

HOW TO SAUTÉ
(For all fruit except avocados)
Leave cherry or grape tomatoes whole or cut in half; halve plum tomatoes, scoop out pulp if desired, and then finely chop flesh. Halve cucumbers lengthwise and scoop out any seeds. Halve peppers and chiles, and remove ribs and seeds from peppers. Husk and rinse tomatillos. Peel and seed winter squash. Cut vegetables into 1-inch pieces; summer squash can also be grated on the large holes of a box grater. Heat olive oil or butter in a large skillet over medium high. Add vegetables; season with salt and pepper. Cook, stirring occasionally, until tender and golden brown, 10 to 15 minutes, depending on size of pieces. Sprinkle with lemon juice or vinegar, season with salt, and top with chopped fresh herbs.

HOW TO GRILL
(For avocados)
Brush a halved avocado (peeled and pitted) with lime juice and olive oil. Grill over medium heat, cut side down, 1 to 2 minutes. Rotate to create cross-hatch marks, and grill 1 minute more. Season with salt and pepper.

(For eggplants and summer squashes)
Cut eggplant and summer squash into ½-inch-thick slices. Brush both sides with olive oil, and season with salt and pepper. Grill over medium-high heat until charred in spots, about 5 minutes; flip slices and cook until charred on other side, about 5 minutes more. Drizzle with more oil and sprinkle with chopped herbs.

(For peppers and chiles)
Halve bell peppers lengthwise, and remove ribs and seeds. Grill over medium-high heat, cut sides down, until beginning to soften, about 5 minutes; flip peppers and cook until charred in spots, about 5 minutes more. Cut into thin strips. Toss with olive oil, and season with salt and pepper to taste.

(For tomatoes)
Halve plum tomatoes lengthwise. Toss with olive oil, and season with salt and pepper. Grill over medium-high heat, cut sides down, until charred in spots, about 5 minutes; flip tomatoes and cook until charred on other side, about 5 minutes more.

FLAVOR PAIRINGS

New World natives—tomatoes, summer squashes, sweet peppers, and chiles—all pair beautifully with one another, and with most Mexican and Central American flavorings: corn, cilantro, onions, lime. But they are equally at home in Mediterranean dishes flavored with olive oil, oregano, thyme, or basil. And they complement a variety of cheeses, including sharp Parmesan, chalky feta and cotija, and mild and milky mozzarella. Combined with eggplant, they become the classic Provençal ratatouille. Eggplant can go in many other directions as well— its smoky, slightly bitter flavor complements deeply umami miso in Japanese dishes or tahini and lemon in Middle Eastern dishes. Tomatillos turn up most often in Mexican sauces, paired with onion, garlic, and sometimes pulverized pumpkin seeds. Buttery avocado is enlivened by all kinds of citrus—grapefruit, lime, lemon, orange—as well as salty bacon and fresh herbs. And chiles, whether fresh or dried, whole or ground, bring heat and flavor to chicken, shrimp, beef, pork, vegetable, and grain dishes the world over, from Thailand to the Caribbean, Italy to India, Mexico to Morocco.

AVOCADO: chiles, cilantro, lime, crab, shrimp, tomato, bacon, red onion

CHILES: tomatoes, lime, cilantro, curry powder, cumin, coconut, onions, garlic, sugar, chicken, shellfish, pork, beef

CUCUMBER: mint, dill, vinegar, onion, yogurt, garlic, lemon, salmon

EGGPLANT: mozzarella, tomatoes, basil, anchovies, soy sauce, sesame, yogurt, lentils

SUMMER SQUASHES: basil, tomato, ricotta, eggplant, chiles, parsley, oregano, garlic

SWEET PEPPERS: onions, garlic, sausage, tomatoes, vinegar, potatoes, goat cheese

TOMATILLOS: cilantro, onion, garlic, tomatoes, tequila, fish, chicken, pork, avocado

TOMATOES: basil, thyme, mint, garlic, onion, peppers, goat cheese, mozzarella, fennel

WINTER SQUASHES: sage, nutmeg, butter, bacon, maple, coconut, ginger

Pasta with Marinated Heirloom Tomatoes

Heirloom tomatoes, designated as such because the seeds have been saved by growers over generations, are celebrated for their imperfections (unlike commercially grown hybrids, bred for durability and uniformity rather than taste).
Here, we marinate them for a half hour with garlic oil and other seasonings to create a no-cook sauce that's tossed with ribbons of pasta.

SERVES 8

5 garlic cloves, thinly sliced

½ cup extra-virgin olive oil

2 pounds assorted heirloom tomatoes, sliced into wedges

¾ cup fresh basil, torn if large

3 tablespoons capers, preferably salt-packed, rinsed and drained, chopped if large

2 teaspoons finely grated lemon zest, plus more for serving

¼ teaspoon red-pepper flakes

Coarse salt and freshly ground black pepper

1 pound flat pasta such as maltagliati, cooked until al dente

1. Warm garlic and oil in a saucepan over low heat until garlic is pale gold, about 10 minutes. Strain; reserve oil and garlic. Let cool.

2. Combine tomatoes, ¼ cup basil, the capers, lemon zest, and red-pepper flakes in a large bowl, and season with salt. Pour garlic oil and garlic chips over tomato mixture. Cover and let marinate, tossing occasionally, 30 minutes.

3. Meanwhile, cook pasta in a pot of generously salted boiling water until al dente, according to package instructions. Drain.

4. Add warm pasta to tomato mixture and toss gently to combine. Top with remaining ½ cup basil and the lemon zest, season with black pepper, and serve.

TIP
For this dish, boil the pasta about five minutes before the tomatoes are ready. The warmth will bring out the flavors of the fresh ingredients.

Blistered Eggplant with Tomatoes, Olives, and Feta

This salad offers a healthier alternative to frying eggplant: The rounds are simply broiled on a wire rack until blistered, then tossed with olive oil.

SERVES 4

1 large eggplant, cut into ¼-inch-thick rounds

¼ cup extra-virgin olive oil, plus more for drizzling

1¾ pounds mixed tomatoes

Coarse salt and freshly ground pepper

6 ounces feta cheese, crumbled

½ cup mixed olives

½ cup lightly packed fresh flat-leaf parsley leaves

1. Heat broiler with rack 6 inches from heat source. Place eggplant rounds on a wire rack set on a rimmed baking sheet. Broil until eggplant is blistered and deep brown on one side, 10 to 12 minutes. Flip and broil until blistered on other side, 10 to 12 minutes. Immediately transfer to a large bowl, toss with oil, and cover with a plate. Let stand until softened, about 10 minutes.

2. Arrange eggplant and tomatoes on a platter, seasoning each layer with salt and pepper and drizzling with oil before adding next layer. Top with feta, olives, and parsley, and serve.

Miso Eggplant

Inspired by a recipe of chef Nobu Matsuhisa, owner of celebrated restaurants around the world, this dish features a savory-sweet, irresistible miso glaze.

SERVES 6 TO 8

¾ cup white (shiro) miso

5 tablespoons sugar

5 tablespoons sake

5 tablespoons mirin

Olive oil, for frying

4 Japanese eggplants (about 6 ounces each), halved lengthwise and flesh scored in a cross-hatch pattern

1 tablespoon sesame seeds, toasted

Small cilantro sprigs, for serving

1. Combine miso and sugar in a heavy-bottomed saucepan. Whisk in sake and mirin. Bring to a simmer over low heat, and cook, stirring frequently, until sugar is dissolved and color begins to darken, 30 to 45 minutes. Remove from heat.

2. Heat broiler with rack 4 inches from heat source. Line a rimmed baking sheet with paper towels. In a large heavy-bottomed saucepan, heat 2 inches of oil to 360°F. Working in batches, place eggplants in pan, skin side up, and fry 1 minute. Flip and fry 30 seconds more. Transfer to baking sheet; let drain. Return oil to 360°F between batches.

3. Transfer eggplants, skin side down, to another baking sheet. Spread each half with 1 heaping tablespoon miso mixture. Broil until miso begins to caramelize, 1 to 2 minutes. Sprinkle with sesame seeds and cilantro, and serve.

Breaded Eggplant with Arugula and Parmesan

Our vegetarian take on veal Milanese is both crisp (thanks to the panko) and tender (thanks to the texture of eggplant). But using eggplant as a stand-in for meat is nothing new; Italian home cooks have a long tradition of building meals around the creamy-fleshed, earthy-tasting fruit, mostly in the interest of frugality.

SERVES 4

1 large eggplant, cut lengthwise into 1-inch-thick slices

Coarse salt and freshly ground pepper

¼ cup all-purpose flour

1 large egg, whisked with 1 tablespoon water

2 cups panko or coarse breadcrumbs

Olive oil, for frying

2 cups baby arugula

Shavings of Parmigiano-Reggiano cheese, for serving

Lemon wedges, for serving

1. Place eggplant in a large colander and season generously with salt. Let stand 30 minutes, then rinse and pat dry.

2. Place flour, egg mixture, and breadcrumbs in three separate shallow bowls. Dredge each eggplant slice in flour, turning to coat and shaking off excess, then dip in egg mixture and coat in breadcrumbs.

3. Heat ½ inch oil in a 12-inch skillet over medium. Working in batches, fry eggplant until golden and crisp, about 4 minutes per side. Transfer to a paper-towel-lined plate and season with salt and pepper.

4. Top each cutlet with arugula and cheese, and serve with a lemon wedge.

Tomato and Mango Salad

Capture the essence of peak-season tomatoes with tomato water, a near-transparent liquid with the sweet taste of the fresh fruit. This summer starter features cherry tomatoes, cucumbers, mango, basil, and thinly sliced chile bathing in tomato essence.

SERVES 4

1 pound very ripe tomatoes, cored and quartered

Coarse salt

1 small ripe mango

1 Kirby or Persian cucumber, cut into matchsticks

1 pint cherry tomatoes, halved or quartered if large

1 red Thai or serrano chile, very thinly sliced on the bias

1 tablespoon extra-virgin olive oil, plus more for drizzling

Thai or Italian basil, for serving

1. Purée tomatoes and ¼ teaspoon salt in a blender until smooth, about 1 minute. Line a colander with four layers of dampened cheesecloth and set over a deep pot. Pour tomato purée into colander, cover with plastic wrap, and refrigerate, stirring occasionally, until 1 to 2 cups tomato water have dripped into pot, about 1 day. Season with salt, if desired.

2. Peel mango and cut flesh from pit; discard pit. Cut flesh lengthwise into ½-inch slices. Toss mango, cucumber, cherry tomatoes, chile, and 1 tablespoon oil. Season with salt and divide salad among four bowls. Divide tomato essence among bowls, top with basil, drizzle with more oil, and serve.

Zucchini-Scallion Fritters

Zucchini is often grated, to use in slaws and raw salads, muffins or quick breads (page 283), or vegetable fritters, as in this recipe. The squash is firm enough to easily shred on the large holes of a box grater, yet it cooks up soft and tender.

SERVES 4

1 pound zucchini (about 2 medium), coarsely grated

Coarse salt and freshly ground pepper

1 large egg

2 scallions, finely chopped

½ cup all-purpose flour

½ cup safflower oil

Sour cream, for serving

1. Place zucchini in a colander and toss with 1 teaspoon salt; let drain 10 minutes. Press out as much liquid as possible with a wooden spoon or flexible spatula.

2. Whisk egg in a large bowl; mix in zucchini, scallions, flour, and ¼ teaspoon pepper until combined. Line a plate with paper towels.

3. Heat oil in a large skillet over medium. Working in batches, drop six mounds of batter (2 tablespoons each) into skillet, then flatten slightly with back of spoon. Cook until browned on first side, 2 to 3 minutes; flip fritters and cook until browned on other side, 2 to 3 minutes more. Transfer to the paper-towel-lined plate; sprinkle with salt. Serve with sour cream.

Pasta with Zucchini, Mint, and Pecorino

You can never have enough recipes for zucchini during the summer, especially if you grow your own or belong to a CSA group—this is one vegetable that flourishes in abundance. Here, grated zucchini is sautéed with a few anchovies until tender, then tossed with al dente pasta and some of its cooking water. Fresh mint and sharp Pecorino Romano add flavorful finishes.

SERVES 4

12 ounces short curly pasta, such as gemelli or fusilli

Coarse salt and freshly ground black pepper

2 tablespoons extra-virgin olive oil, plus more for drizzling

3 anchovy fillets, preferably oil-packed, rinsed and patted dry

2 garlic cloves, minced

2 pounds zucchini (about 5 small), coarsely grated

¼ teaspoon red-pepper flakes, plus more for serving

⅔ cup finely grated Pecorino Romano cheese, plus more for serving

¼ cup lightly packed fresh mint leaves, chopped, plus more whole leaves for serving

1. Cook pasta in a large pot of generously salted boiling water until al dente, according to package instructions. Reserve 1½ cups water; drain pasta.

2. Heat a large skillet over medium high. Add oil and swirl to coat. Cook anchovies and garlic, stirring, just until anchovies break down and garlic turns golden, about 30 seconds. Add zucchini and red-pepper flakes; season with salt. Cook, stirring occasionally, until zucchini is tender, about 5 minutes. Add pasta and 1 cup reserved pasta water. Simmer, stirring occasionally, until liquid is reduced and slightly thickened, 1 to 2 minutes.

3. Remove from heat; stir in cheese and mint. Add more pasta water if needed, a few tablespoons at a time, until sauce evenly coats pasta. Serve immediately, drizzled with oil and sprinkled with mint, black pepper, red-pepper flakes, and cheese.

TIP
Coarsely grating zucchini, rather than slicing or chopping it, helps make sure the vegetable is evenly distributed when tossed with the pasta. Unlike for fritters (page 279), you don't have to salt and drain the zucchini first, since here the extra moisture is a plus.

Zucchini Quick Bread

Zucchini's natural water content makes it an asset when baking cake and quick breads, keeping them exceptionally moist. This no-mixer batter is easy to whisk together and is flavored with ground cinnamon, vanilla, and chopped walnuts. The addition of whole-wheat flour and olive oil makes these loaves more wholesome than those made with only all-purpose flour and butter.

MAKES 2 LOAVES

Unsalted butter, room temperature, for pans

1½ cups all-purpose flour, plus more for pans

1½ cups whole-wheat flour

1 tablespoon baking powder

¼ teaspoon salt

1 tablespoon ground cinnamon

1¼ cups sugar

1 cup extra-virgin olive oil

3 large eggs

2½ cups grated zucchini

1 tablespoon pure vanilla extract

1 cup chopped walnuts

1. Preheat oven to 350°F with rack in the center. Butter two 4½-by-8½-inch loaf pans, then dust with flour, tapping out the excess. Whisk together flours, baking powder, salt, and cinnamon in a large bowl.

2. In another bowl, stir together sugar, oil, eggs, zucchini, and vanilla. Stir zucchini mixture into flour mixture until well blended. Fold in walnuts.

3. Divide batter between prepared pans. Bake until a cake tester inserted into middle of loaves comes out clean, about 40 to 50 minutes. Let cool in pans on a wire rack 15 minutes, then turn out onto racks and let cool completely before serving.

TIP
The loaves will keep well in the freezer for several months; wrap tightly in plastic and store in sealable freezer bags.

Skillet Steak Peperonata

As its name suggests, peperonata is all about the peppers. To make this traditional Sicilian side dish, bell peppers are stewed with onion and garlic until tender; the sweetness is kept in check by a splash of red-wine vinegar. Peperonata is often served with steak, as here (try the combination as a sandwich, too), but also with seared pork chops or sautéed fish, or tossed into salads and pastas.

SERVES 4

3 tablespoons extra-virgin olive oil

1 onion, thinly sliced

1 garlic clove, minced

3 bell peppers, ribs and seeds removed, thinly sliced

1 sprig thyme

1 sprig rosemary

Pinch of red-pepper flakes

2 tablespoons red-wine vinegar

Coarse salt and freshly ground black pepper

1 pound boneless sirloin steak (1 inch thick)

1. Heat 2 tablespoons oil in a large skillet over medium high. Add onion and garlic, and cook, stirring occasionally, until onion turns golden on the edges, about 4 minutes. Add bell peppers, thyme, rosemary, red-pepper flakes, and vinegar; season with salt. Toss to combine, then cover and cook, stirring occasionally, until peppers are tender, about 30 minutes. Transfer to a bowl; cover to keep warm.

2. Wipe out skillet and heat remaining tablespoon oil over medium high. Pat steak dry and season on both sides with salt and black pepper. Cook steak until browned on first side, 3 to 4 minutes. Turn steak and brown on second side, 3 to 4 minutes more for medium rare. Transfer to a cutting board and let rest 10 minutes.

3. Slice steak across the grain into thin strips and return to skillet; add peperonata, toss to combine, and serve.

Pickled Jalapeños and Cucumbers

Pickled jalapeños are a great way to bring a bit of fiery heat to dishes, delivered in a cool, crunchy package. Here, we've combined the chiles with two other classic pickling vegetables, cucumbers and onions. Try them with nachos, tacos, chili, sandwiches, or burgers.

MAKES 2½ QUARTS

2 pounds Kirby cucumbers, sliced ¼ inch thick

4 red jalapeño chiles, sliced ¼ inch thick

3 small onions, cut into ½-inch wedges

3 tablespoons coarse salt

2 cups apple cider vinegar

1¾ cups light-brown sugar

1 tablespoon yellow mustard seeds

¾ teaspoon celery seeds

¾ teaspoon ground turmeric

1. Toss together cucumbers, jalapeños, onions, and salt in a bowl. Cover; refrigerate 2 hours.

2. Cook vinegar, sugar, mustard and celery seeds, and turmeric in a saucepan over medium heat, stirring to dissolve sugar. Rinse and drain cucumber mixture and place in a bowl (or divide among jars). Pour vinegar mixture over cucumbers; let cool completely. Refrigerate, covered, up to 3 weeks before serving.

Blistered Padrón Peppers with Sea Salt

If you spot these bright-green peppers at the market, grab them—they're slightly less sweet than green bell peppers but take on a delicious, smoky flavor when charred in an iron skillet or under the broiler. But be forewarned: While most are mild, one or two in every ten packs a mouthful of fiery flavor.

SERVES 4

2 tablespoons extra-virgin olive oil

1 pound Padrón peppers

Flaky sea salt, such as Maldon

Heat oil in a large, heavy skillet (preferably cast iron) over medium high. Cook peppers in a single layer, turning, until blistered, about 5 minutes. Transfer to a platter, sprinkle with sea salt, and serve.

Whole Baked Trout with Cherry Tomatoes and Potatoes

Here's a delicious way to use the last of the season's crop of cherry tomatoes (or those available any time of year): Roast them, along with Yukon Gold potatoes, until they are softened and juicy, and at the height of sweetness. Then continue to cook them topped with two whole trout; the juices from the fish will flavor the vegetables, which in turn contribute moistness to the fish. It's a win-win proposition.

SERVES 4

2 Yukon Gold potatoes, scrubbed and thinly sliced

1 garlic clove, smashed

1 tablespoon chopped fresh oregano leaves

1 tablespoon plus 1 teaspoon olive oil

12 ounces cherry tomatoes, broken into smaller clusters if on the vine

Coarse salt and freshly ground pepper

2 whole trout (about 9 ounces each), scaled, gutted, and cleaned

8 thin lemon slices (from 1 lemon)

1. Preheat oven to 425°F. Toss together potatoes, garlic, oregano, and 1 tablespoon oil in a bowl, and season with salt and pepper. Arrange potatoes in a 9-by-13-inch baking dish, overlapping them; top with tomatoes.

2. Roast until tomatoes are juicy and potatoes are tender, about 25 minutes. Remove from oven.

3. Rub fish with remaining teaspoon oil, dividing evenly. Season inside and outside of fish with salt; stuff with lemon slices. Arrange fish on top of potatoes, shifting tomatoes alongside. Roast until fish are opaque throughout and flake with a fork, about 20 minutes. Serve immediately.

Zucchini "Pasta" Primavera

Cut into thin strips and briefly cooked, zucchini takes on a texture that mimics al dente pasta. Here, the gluten-free "noodles" are tossed with a sauce of halved cherry tomatoes, capers, and garlic that's sautéed for all of one minute. Each plate is garnished with the flavorful components of pesto: fresh basil, toasted pine nuts, and grated Parmesan.

SERVES 4

- 3 tablespoons extra-virgin olive oil
- 1 pint cherry tomatoes, halved
- 2 tablespoons capers, preferably salt-packed, rinsed and drained
- 1 garlic clove, thinly sliced
- Pinch of red-pepper flakes
- 1 large zucchini, cut lengthwise into thin strands
- Pine nuts, toasted, for serving
- Finely grated Parmigiano-Reggiano cheese, for serving
- Fresh basil leaves, for serving

1. Heat oil in a large skillet over medium high. Add tomatoes, capers, garlic, and red-pepper flakes and cook, stirring frequently, until heated through, about 1 minute. Add zucchini and cook, tossing, until just tender, 1 to 2 minutes.

2. Serve immediately, topped with toasted pine nuts, grated cheese, and basil.

TIP
Use a mandoline, julienne peeler, or sharp knife— or ideally, a spiral slicer—to make the strands of zucchini.

Roasted Bell Peppers

Bell peppers undergo a particularly drastic transformation when roasted: The once-crisp flesh becomes wonderfully tender, and the skins blister and loosen for easy peeling. Serve these dressed ones as a salad, or in sandwiches, pasta dishes, and antipasti.

SERVES 4

4 red bell peppers

Extra-virgin olive oil

1 tablespoon capers,
preferably salt-packed,
rinsed and drained

¼ cup pitted Kalamata olives

½ teaspoon red-wine vinegar

Lemon peel, cut into
fine julienne

Coarse salt and freshly
ground pepper

Fresh basil leaves,
for serving

1. Heat broiler with rack in top position. Place bell peppers on a parchment-lined rimmed baking sheet. Broil, turning occasionally, until charred on all sides and tender, about 10 minutes. Transfer to a bowl, cover tightly with plastic wrap, and let steam 10 minutes. Rub with paper towels to remove skin. Quarter each pepper lengthwise and remove ribs and seeds.

2. Arrange peppers on a serving platter, drizzle with oil, and top with capers, olives, vinegar, and lemon strips. Season with salt and pepper, sprinkle with basil, and serve.

TIP An alternative to broiling peppers is to char them over an open flame (on the stove or a grill) until skin is blistered and charred.

Tomatillo and Chipotle Salsa

Tomatillos have a tart, citrusy flavor all their own. They're also meatier (less watery) than their distant relative, the tomato. You'll find tomatillos, raw and cooked, in many Mexican dishes, most commonly in the form of salsa. Charring the fruit (and garlic) makes this salsa distinctively smoky; adding chipotles also helps.

SERVES 4

6 tomatillos, husked, rinsed, and quartered

3 garlic cloves (do not peel)

4 canned chipotle chiles in adobo sauce, coarsely chopped

¼ teaspoon sugar

Coarse salt

Cilantro leaves, for serving

Tortilla chips, for serving

1. Working in two batches if needed, cook tomatillos and garlic in a large skillet (preferably cast iron) over medium-high heat, turning occasionally, until charred on all sides, 15 to 20 minutes. Transfer to a plate, and let cool slightly. Then peel garlic, and finely chop tomatillos and garlic.

2. Mix tomatillos, garlic, chipotles, and sugar in a bowl, season with salt, and top with cilantro. Serve with tortilla chips.

Chiles Rellenos

*The large, thick-fleshed poblano chile has a nice amount of heat, but not too much,
and an earthy flavor; it also is the right size for stuffing, as in Mexican chiles rellenos.*

SERVES 6

¼ cup extra-virgin olive oil

2 pounds ground chicken

1 white onion, chopped

1 garlic clove, minced

1¾ pounds plum tomatoes,
seeded and diced

2 dried bay leaves

½ cup raisins

½ cup green olives, chopped

2 tablespoons capers,
rinsed and drained

½ cup finely chopped cilantro,
plus small sprigs for serving

½ cup finely chopped
flat-leaf parsley

¼ cup finely chopped mint

½ cup slivered almonds

Coarse salt

12 fresh poblano chiles

Mexican crema or
sour cream, for serving

Lime wedges, for serving

1. Heat 2 tablespoons oil in a large skillet over medium high until almost smoking. Add chicken; cook, stirring frequently, until lightly browned and cooked through, about 8 minutes. Transfer to a bowl.

2. Heat remaining 2 tablespoons oil in same skillet over medium high. Cook onion, stirring occasionally, until translucent, 2 minutes. Add garlic; cook, stirring, 1 minute. Add tomatoes and bay leaves, and reduce heat to medium low; simmer until tomatoes are soft, 15 minutes.

3. Stir in raisins, olives, and capers; cook 3 minutes. Add chicken; cook 5 minutes. Stir in chopped herbs and almonds, and season with salt. Let cool. (Filling may be refrigerated up to 1 day in an airtight container. Before using, bring to room temperature; discard bay leaves.)

4. Preheat oven to 350°F. Roast poblanos directly over the flame of a gas-stove burner or under a broiler, turning often with tongs, until charred on all sides. Place in a bowl, cover with plastic wrap, and let stand for 15 minutes. When cool enough to handle, rub with a paper towel to remove skins, being careful not to tear flesh. Cut a slit down the side of each poblano from stem to tip. Remove seeds, leaving stem intact.

5. Spoon filling into each chile, dividing evenly; arrange in a baking dish. Bake until heated through, 15 minutes. Serve immediately with crema, cilantro sprigs, and lime wedges.

Cucumber, Mango, and Shrimp Escabèche

Put the cooling qualities of cucumber to work in a Spanish escabèche. It requires minimal cooking—just a minute or two to poach the shrimp; the rest is a matter of letting the acidic lime juice infuse the seafood with flavor.

SERVES 4

1 pound shell-on large shrimp (16 to 20 count)

½ cup plus 3 tablespoons fresh lime juice (from 12 limes)

½ English cucumber, cut into thin half-moons

⅔ cup chopped peeled mango

½ cup chopped red onion

1 jalapeño chile, finely chopped

¼ cup plus 3 tablespoons chopped fresh cilantro, plus more for serving

Coarse salt and freshly ground pepper

1. Prepare an ice-water bath. Bring a large pot of water to a boil. Reduce heat to medium; poach shrimp until just opaque throughout, 1½ to 2 minutes. Transfer shrimp to ice bath and let cool completely.

2. Drain shrimp; peel, devein, and slice in half. Toss shrimp with ½ cup lime juice in a nonreactive dish. Refrigerate, covered, 2 hours, stirring halfway through; drain.

3. Toss together shrimp, cucumber, mango, onion, jalapeño, cilantro, 2 tablespoons lime juice, ¾ teaspoon salt, and a pinch of pepper. Refrigerate, 30 minutes. Stir in remaining tablespoon lime juice, top with cilantro sprigs, and serve.

Chilled Melon, Cucumber, and Mint Soup

The high water content and refreshing flavor of cucumbers are just right for making chilled soups. This soup combines seedless cucumbers, honeydew melon, lime juice, and fresh mint—all in lovely shades of green. More mint is sprinkled on top, and Greek yogurt is smeared alongside.

SERVES 8

2 English cucumbers

½ honeydew melon, peeled, seeded, and cut into 1-inch chunks (8 cups)

½ to ⅔ cup fresh lime juice (from 10 to 12 limes), plus wedges for serving

1 cup lightly packed fresh mint leaves, plus more for serving

2 cups crushed ice

Coarse salt

2 cups plain Greek yogurt

Extra-virgin olive oil

1. Peel, halve, and seed cucumbers, then coarsely chop. (You should have about 4½ cups.) Working in batches, purée cucumbers, melon, ½ cup lime juice, the mint, and ice in a food processor or blender. Season with salt and more lime juice. Transfer soup to a bowl, cover, and refrigerate until ready to serve, up to 2 hours.

2. Spoon ¼ cup yogurt into each bowl, smearing up sides. Spoon chilled soup into bowls, drizzle with oil, and top with mint. Serve with lime wedges.

Stuffed Tomatoes with Mozzarella

Tomatoes, zucchini, and bell peppers are perfect for stuffing. Once the flesh and seeds have been scooped out, the remaining shells are firm enough to hold their shape as they cook. Here, tomatoes are filled with sautéed corn and greens (any of the ones in the Greens chapter will do), toasted bread pieces, and mozzarella, which melts and turns deliciously golden under the broiler.

SERVES 4

2 slices rustic bread, torn into small pieces (about ¾ cup)

4 ripe medium tomatoes, halved horizontally

Coarse salt and freshly ground black pepper

2 tablespoons extra-virgin olive oil

Pinch of red-pepper flakes

½ shallot, thinly sliced

1 cup corn kernels (from 1 ear)

3 cups packed chopped greens, such as Swiss chard or beet greens

3 ounces fresh mozzarella cheese, sliced

1. Heat broiler with rack 8 inches from heat source. Toast bread on a rimmed baking sheet, tossing once, until crisp, about 2 minutes.

2. Scoop out seeds and flesh from each tomato into a bowl; reserve. Arrange tomato halves in a broiler-safe baking dish; season with salt and pepper.

3. In a large skillet, heat 1 tablespoon oil over medium. Add red-pepper flakes and shallot; cook, stirring frequently, until just tender, about 2 minutes. Increase heat to high; add reserved tomato flesh and juice. Cook, stirring, until reduced by half, about 2 minutes. Add corn and greens; cook, stirring, until vegetables are tender, about 2 minutes. Season with salt.

4. Fill tomato halves with vegetable mixture, dividing evenly, then sprinkle each half with toasted bread, drizzle with remaining tablespoon oil, and top with mozzarella. Broil until cheese is bubbly and golden in spots, about 2 minutes. Serve immediately.

Salmon and Avocado Tartines

SERVES 6 TO 8

¼ cup plus ¾ teaspoon fresh lemon juice

1 celery stalk

2 sprigs flat-leaf parsley

Sea salt or coarse salt

1 wild salmon fillet (about 1 pound and 1 inch thick), skin on

1 ripe but firm avocado, halved, pitted, and peeled

1 tablespoon wasabi powder, mixed with 1 tablespoon lukewarm water

1 whole-grain baguette

Radish or sunflower sprouts

1. Fill a saucepan wide enough to hold salmon with 2½ inches cold water. Stir in ¼ cup lemon juice, the celery, parsley, and 2 teaspoons salt. Bring to a boil; reduce heat. Add salmon, skin side down. Cover; simmer until just cooked through, 10 to 12 minutes. Transfer to a plate, and let cool 20 minutes. Discard poaching liquid. Flake salmon into large pieces.

2. Pulse avocado, wasabi, and remaining ¾ teaspoon lemon juice until smooth in a food processor; season with salt. Transfer to a bowl, and cover tightly with plastic wrap, pressing directly onto surface. Refrigerate up to 30 minutes.

3. Preheat oven to 425°F. Cut baguette in half, and cut each half lengthwise into three ½-inch-thick slices. Arrange, flat side down, in a single layer on a baking sheet. Toast in oven until lightly golden, about 7 minutes. Let cool 10 minutes. Spread each slice with about 2 tablespoons avocado-wasabi mixture, and top with salmon and sprouts.

Pistachio Guacamole

Guacamole is endlessly adaptable—and universally adored. Toasted pistachios may not be the most obvious choice, but they supply extra richness and crunch to the simple blend of avocado, fresh lime juice, and salt. Just add corn chips.

SERVES 8

1 cup shelled pistachios

6 ripe avocados, halved, pitted, and peeled

3 tablespoons fresh lime juice (from 2 to 3 limes)

Coarse salt

Tortilla chips, for serving

1. Preheat oven to 350°F. Toast pistachios on a rimmed baking sheet until golden and fragrant, stirring once or twice, 10 to 15 minutes. Transfer to a plate and let cool completely. Coarsely chop.

2. In a bowl, mash avocados and lime juice together with a fork. Fold in all but 3 tablespoons chopped pistachios; season with salt. Top with remaining pistachios and serve immediately with tortilla chips.

Roasted-Tomato Hand Pies

The filling for these portable tarts packs an abundance of flavor: Sliced tomatoes are roasted until their flavors are concentrated and the tomatoes have shed much of their moisture (so the tarts won't get soggy). This is a great way to prepare tomatoes even if you don't make the tarts; store them in an airtight container in the refrigerator, covered in a slick of olive oil, then bring to room temperature and serve on crostini, burgers, or pasta.

MAKES 12

FOR THE DOUGH

- 2½ cups all-purpose flour, plus more for dusting
- 1 teaspoon coarse salt
- 1 cup (2 sticks) cold unsalted butter, cut into small pieces
- ¼ to ½ cup ice water

FOR THE FILLING

- 2½ pounds tomatoes, cored and sliced ¼ inch thick crosswise
- 1 medium onion, quartered lengthwise and thinly sliced crosswise
- ¼ cup extra-virgin olive oil
- Coarse salt and freshly ground pepper
- 2 tablespoons finely chopped fresh oregano, plus small sprigs for serving (optional)
- ⅓ cup chopped pitted oil-cured black olives
- 4 ounces feta cheese, crumbled (¾ cup)
- 1 large egg yolk, lightly beaten with 1 tablespoon water, for egg wash

1. Make the dough: Pulse together flour and salt in a food processor until combined. Add butter, and process until mixture resembles coarse meal, about 10 seconds. With machine running, add just enough ice water in a slow, steady stream until dough just comes together (no longer than 30 seconds). Divide dough in half, shape each piece into a square, and wrap in plastic. Refrigerate at least 1 hour or up to 2 days (or freeze up to 1 month; thaw overnight in refrigerator before using).

2. Roll out dough on a lightly floured surface to ⅛ inch thick. Using a paring knife, cut out twelve 4½-inch squares, and fit into cups of a standard muffin tin, leaving an overhang. Chill until firm, about 30 minutes.

3. Make the filling: Preheat oven to 400°F. Divide tomato and onion slices between two rimmed baking sheets. Drizzle with oil, season with salt and pepper, and roast, rotating sheets halfway through, until tomatoes begin to shrivel and onion slices are golden, about 30 minutes. Let cool on sheets, then transfer to a bowl.

4. Preheat oven or lower temperature to 375°F. Divide half the chopped oregano, olives, and feta among the pastry shells. Top with tomato-onion mixture, dividing evenly. Sprinkle with remaining oregano, olives, and feta. Fold corners of dough toward centers. Brush with egg wash.

5. Bake pies until bubbling and top crusts are golden, 50 to 60 minutes. Let cool completely in tin on a wire rack before serving, with oregano sprigs tucked into pies, if desired.

Butternut Squash and Taleggio Pizza

Butternut squash makes a delicious topping for "white" pizza, particularly when combined with nutty Taleggio and sharp Parmigiano-Reggiano cheeses (and little else).

MAKES 2 PIES

FOR THE DOUGH

- ¼ teaspoon sugar
- 1 envelope (¼ ounce) active dry yeast
- 1 cup warm water (about 110°F)
- 2¾ cups unbleached all-purpose flour, plus more for dusting
- 1 teaspoon coarse salt
- 2 tablespoons extra-virgin olive oil, plus more for bowl

  Fine cornmeal, for dusting

FOR THE TOPPINGS

- 3 pounds butternut squash, peeled, seeded, and cut into ½-inch dice
- ¼ cup plus 2 tablespoons extra-virgin olive oil

  Coarse salt and freshly ground pepper
- 1½ pounds Taleggio cheese
- ¼ cup fresh thyme leaves
- ½ cup finely grated Parmigiano-Reggiano cheese

1. In a small bowl, sprinkle sugar and yeast over the warm water; stir with a fork until yeast and sugar dissolve. Let stand until foamy, about 5 minutes.

2. In a food processor, pulse together flour and salt. Add yeast mixture and oil; pulse until mixture comes together but is still slightly tacky. (Dough should pull away cleanly from your fingers after it's squeezed.) Turn out dough onto a lightly floured work surface; knead four or five times, to form a smooth ball. Place in a lightly oiled bowl, smooth side up. Cover with plastic wrap; let rise in a warm place until doubled, about 40 minutes. Punch down dough. Fold dough back onto itself four or five times, then turn smooth side up. Replace plastic; let dough rise again in a warm place until doubled in bulk, 30 to 40 minutes.

3. Punch dough down again; turn out onto a lightly floured work surface. Using a bench scraper or knife, divide dough into two pieces. Knead each piece four or five times, then form a smooth ball. Return one ball to oiled bowl; cover with plastic wrap. Pat remaining ball into a flattened disk; cover with plastic wrap, and let rest 5 minutes. Sprinkle a large wooden peel with cornmeal. Using your hands or a rolling pin, stretch or press dough into desired shape, working from center outward in all directions. Transfer to prepared peel.

4. Meanwhile, make toppings: Preheat oven to 450°F with a rack in lowest position and a pizza stone on rack. Toss squash with 2 tablespoons oil, and season with salt and pepper. Spread evenly on a rimmed baking sheet, and roast, tossing once or twice, until tender, about 12 minutes. Let cool.

5. Arrange half of squash over one piece of dough, leaving a 1-inch border. Dot with half of Taleggio, squeezing it from rind into 1-inch pieces as you go. Sprinkle with half of thyme, and drizzle with 2 tablespoons oil. Top with half of Parmesan.

6. Slide pizza onto heated baking stone. Bake until crust is golden brown and cheese is melted, 15 to 18 minutes. Meanwhile, repeat to make second pizza with remaining ingredients; bake when first pizza is removed from oven.

1

2

3

Roasted Acorn Squash, Three Ways

The beauty of roasted acorn squash, as opposed to butternut or other tough-skinned varieties, is that you can eat the skin (which contains much of the vegetable's nutrients, including fiber and antioxidants). It also takes well to a variety of flavors.

1
WITH SESAME SEEDS AND CUMIN

- 3 tablespoons sesame seeds
- 1½ teaspoons cumin seeds
- 2 small acorn squashes, halved, seeded, and cut into 1-inch wedges
- 3 tablespoons extra-virgin olive oil
- 1 teaspoon ground coriander
- Coarse salt and freshly ground pepper

1. Preheat oven to 400°F. Toast sesame seeds in a skillet over medium-high, shaking pan frequently, until golden brown, 1 to 2 minutes. Add cumin seeds and toast until fragrant, 30 seconds. Transfer seeds to a bowl; let cool.

2. Toss squashes with oil and coriander, and season with salt and pepper on a rimmed baking sheet. Roast in a single layer 10 minutes. Add seeds and toss to coat, then flip slices. Roast until squashes are tender and golden brown, about 15 minutes more; serve.

2
WITH BACON AND MAPLE

- 2 small acorn squashes, halved, seeded, and cut into 1-inch wedges
- ⅓ cup pure maple syrup
- 2 tablespoons extra-virgin olive oil
- ¼ teaspoon cayenne pepper
- Coarse salt
- 3 thick slices bacon, cut crosswise into ¼-inch pieces

1. Preheat oven to 400°F. Toss squashes with maple syrup, oil, and cayenne and season with salt on a rimmed baking sheet.

2. Roast in a single layer 10 minutes. Add bacon, then flip squashes to coat. Roast, flipping once more halfway through, until tender and golden brown, about 20 minutes more; serve.

3
WITH ORANGE AND SAGE

- 2 small acorn squashes, halved, seeded, and cut into 1-inch wedges
- 3 tablespoons extra-virgin olive oil
- Coarse salt
- 2 tablespoons packed thinly sliced fresh sage or whole small sage leaves
- ⅔ cup finely grated Parmigiano-Reggiano cheese (1½ ounces)
- 5 strips orange peel, cut into fine julienne (¼ cup)

1. Preheat oven to 400°F. Toss squashes with oil and season with salt on a rimmed baking sheet.

2. Roast in a single layer 10 minutes. Add sage, cheese, and orange and toss to coat, then flip slices. Roast until squashes are tender and golden brown, about 15 minutes more; serve.

Butternut Squash and Kale Hash

In this skillet supper, butternut squash is roasted with carrots, then mixed with kale and roasted until that's tender. Finally, the vegetables are topped with eggs, which bake until set. The key is to cook the eggs just until the whites are set but the yolks are still runny, so they form a "sauce" that brings the whole dish together in the most delicious manner.

SERVES 4

½ cup extra-virgin olive oil

3 tablespoons fresh lemon juice

½ cup coarsely chopped fresh cilantro

Coarse salt and freshly ground pepper

1 small onion, finely chopped

2 garlic cloves, minced

½ medium butternut squash or 1 acorn squash, halved, seeded, peeled, and cut into ½-inch pieces (3½ cups)

10 ounces carrots, peeled and cut into ½-inch pieces (1½ cups)

1 small bunch kale, stems trimmed and leaves coarsely chopped (2 cups packed)

4 large eggs

1. Preheat oven to 425°F. In a small bowl, whisk together ¼ cup plus 2 tablespoons oil, the lemon juice, and cilantro, then season with salt and pepper.

2. Heat remaining 2 tablespoons oil in a large straight-sided ovenproof skillet (preferably cast iron) over medium high. Add onion and garlic, and cook, stirring occasionally, until softened, about 3 minutes.

3. Add squash and carrots, season with salt and pepper, and transfer to oven. Roast, stirring once, until golden and tender, 20 to 25 minutes.

4. Stir kale into squash mixture, along with ¼ cup cilantro mixture. Return to oven and bake until kale is wilted, about 8 minutes.

5. Make four wells in vegetables and crack an egg into each. Season eggs with salt. Return to oven and bake until whites are set but yolks are still runny, 4 to 6 minutes. Serve, drizzled with more cilantro dressing.

KERNELS

Sweet corn is as democratic a vegetable as there is. It rewards those who prefer cheap-and-easy preparations with as lavish a show of flavor as those who fuss and fret over it. Boil it and slap it with butter and salt, and it becomes a substantial side dish or snack. But you can just as well dress it up for company by folding it into a savory pudding or transforming it into a luscious ice cream for dessert.

Nor does corn's versatility end with the summertime kitchen. We also eat this so-called vegetable as a grain—think cornmeal and corn flour—in breads, tortillas, grits, polenta, and muffins. Similarly, it turns up in cornstarch, corn syrup, corn oil, and whiskey. And, of course, there are varieties grown specifically for making popcorn.

So perhaps it should come as no surprise to learn that this multifaceted vegetable/grain is actually neither, but instead is a fruit. In fact, each little kernel is an individual fruit surrounding a fairly large seed. When young, these relatively tough-skinned little fruits fill up with sugars and juices, as well as a smooth milky substance that allows them to give way with a *pop* of sweet creamy flavor when you bite into them, no matter how they're prepared.

THE BASICS

SEASONALITY

Sweet corn is a summer crop, plain and simple. Ears sold at other times of year have generally been hybridized, genetically modified, traveled long distances—or all three. In the off-season, opt for frozen corn—it's a decent alternative in any recipe, and better than corn from a can.

BUYING

With corn, the familiar exhortation to buy from farmstands is especially worth heeding. That's not just because good sweet corn should travel minimal time and distance from where it was picked, but also because corn hides its age. Even if you peel back the husk (or the purveyor does), you can't easily see whether the sugars inside each kernel have turned to starch. A better test for freshness is to look at the husk itself (it should look green and cling to the ear), examine the stem end (fresh and pale), and the silks at the tip (glossy where they emerge from the husk and never dried out or brown). Many shoppers shun ears with immature kernels at the tips, but you needn't: The rest of the ear will be especially young, tender, and sweet.

NOTABLE VARIETIES

Sweeter varieties include Breeder's Choice, Kandy Korn, Early Xtra Sweet, Sweetie, and Super-Sweet Jubliee. There are many bicolor (white and yellow) varieties, including Butter & Sugar and Concord; white corn, which is very sweet and tender, includes Silver Queen,

Boone County White Corn, and How Sweet It Is. Peruvian purple corn (also called blue corn), Black Aztec Corn, Bloody Butcher Corn, and Calico Corn (multicolored cobs) are all colorful varieties that are cultivated for eating as well as drying for decorations.

STORING

The trick with storing fresh ears of corn is: *Don't*—at least not for long. Place ears in a plastic or paper bag in the crisper drawer of your refrigerator for no more than a day or so. If you want to save fresh corn for later, husk and remove the silks, slice kernels off the cob, then freeze in a heavy-duty sealable bag. To freeze cooked corn, blanch shucked ears in a pot of boiling water for 4 minutes, then drain and pat dry. When cool enough to handle, shave off kernels and freeze in sealable plastic bags (squeeze out excess air before sealing), up to 6 months or longer.

PREPPING

If you plan to boil corn, remove the husks and silks immediately prior. If you want to grill it, many experts will tell you to peel back the husk and remove the silks first, then wrap the husk back around the ear, but that's quite unnecessary: the silks—so irritating to pick away when raw—slip right off once the ear is grilled (or oven roasted). To remove the kernels from the cob, stand the cob on its broader end on a cutting board, hold the tip with one hand, and using a sharp knife, slice downward toward the base of the kernels, rotating the cob as you go. Then flip the knife around and use the back edge to scrape the milk from the cob, if desired.

COOKING

Sweet corn is heavenly when it's lightly boiled or steamed. (Which method you prefer depends largely on what you grew up doing, as the results are very similar. But advocates of steaming say this method preserves the flavor better.) You can also throw the corn on a hot grill, husk and all. The cooking times will depend on the freshness: To test, pop a raw kernel in your mouth—the fresh ones will pop between your teeth, releasing a sweet, fragrant milk; older ones will have a slight popcorn mealiness that will disappear during cooking. Raw kernels can be sautéed in butter or oil or pan-roasted in a dry skillet (to give them a nice smoky char), and then added to grain and vegetable dishes, or mixed into soups. Grilled kernels can also be cut from the cob and tossed into salads and salsas.

HOW TO BOIL
Shuck ears and cook in a large pot of salted boiling water until kernels are knife-tender, 2 to 6 minutes depending on freshness. Serve with softened butter and chopped fresh herbs (or combined in a compound butter).

HOW TO STEAM
Shuck ears and place, stem ends down, in a pot (or in a pasta insert set in pot) filled with 2 inches of boiling water. Cover and steam until kernels are knife-tender, 2 to 6 minutes.

HOW TO SAUTÉ
Shuck ears and slice off kernels. Melt butter in a large skillet. Add corn, season with salt and pepper, and cook over medium-high heat, stirring occasionally, until tender and golden brown, 8 to 10 minutes.

HOW TO PAN-ROAST
Heat a cast-iron skillet over medium high. Cook corn kernels in a dry skillet, stirring occasionally, until browned, 3 to 5 minutes. Season with salt and pepper. This gives the kernels a nice smokiness (similar to grilling).

HOW TO ROAST
Roast unshucked corn directly on the racks of a 400°F oven for 30 minutes. The husks will slip right off—silks and all—and the kernels will be perfectly tender and great for slicing into salads, salsas, and pastas, or, of course, eating straight off the cob.

FLAVOR PAIRINGS

Butter and salt are the classics, and an ear of good summer corn needs nothing more. Recipes might underscore corn's sweet creamy side, pairing it with cheese, cream, and potatoes, or contrast it with bright, hot or acidic flavors, such as tomatoes, peppers, chiles, and lime—which, like corn, originated in Central America, as did black beans, another natural partner. As for herbs, corn likes them all but has a special affinity for basil, lemongrass, cilantro, chives, and thyme.

Grilled Corn, with Three Toppings

Aside from boiling or steaming, a favorite way to enjoy corn is to grill it, then smother it with flavorful toppings. As long as you're grilling the rest of the meal, you may as well grill the corn, too. We took inspiration from wildly popular Mexican grilled corn to come up with three topping combinations: sesame, ginger, and jalapeño; chili powder and fresh lime juice; and crisped bacon, oregano, and mayonnaise.

Safflower oil, for grill

4 ears corn, shucked

Topping of choice (see below)

Heat a grill or grill pan over medium high. Brush hot grates with oil. Grill corn, turning occasionally with tongs, until kernels are just tender when pressed and charred in spots, about 20 minutes. Transfer corn to a platter; while still warm, top as desired.

1
SESAME, GINGER, AND JALAPEÑO

Combine 2 tablespoons toasted sesame oil, ½ teaspoon finely grated peeled fresh ginger, ½ teaspoon minced seeded jalapeño chile, and 2 teaspoons chopped fresh cilantro; season with salt and pepper. Transfer grilled corn to a platter. Dividing evenly, spread mixture over grilled cobs, sprinkle with 2 teaspoons sesame seeds, and serve.

2
CHILI POWDER AND LIME

Dividing evenly, squeeze ½ lime over corn, then sprinkle with 1 teaspoon chili powder and 1¼ teaspoons salt, and serve.

3
BACON, MAYONNAISE, AND OREGANO

Cook 4 slices bacon in a skillet over medium heat, turning occasionally, until crisp and fat has been rendered, about 8 minutes. Dividing evenly, spread ½ cup mayonnaise over corn, then sprinkle with crumbled bacon, fresh oregano leaves, and finely grated Parmigiano-Reggiano cheese. Season with salt and pepper and serve.

TIP
If you leave them in their husks (with the silks removed), the corn will essentially steam; we shuck the ears and place them directly on the hot grates, and they take on that characteristic smoky flavor, as well as gain a few charred spots.

Corn and Scallion Chilaquiles

Here's a fantastic brunch casserole that is also a great showcase for corn-off-the-cob. Chilaquiles was created as a way to use leftovers (tortillas, chicken, corn, and such), and you can adapt this recipe according to what's in your refrigerator. The usual Mexican accompaniments are served alongside: cilantro, avocado, tomatoes, and more crumbled corn chips.

SERVES 6

1 tablespoon unsalted butter

6 scallions (white and pale-green parts only), finely chopped (about ¼ cup)

½ jalapeño chile, minced (remove ribs and seeds for less heat)

2½ cups corn kernels (from 3 to 4 ears)

Coarse salt

12 large eggs

3 cups broken tortilla chips, plus whole chips for serving

½ cup crumbled or grated cotija or queso fresco cheese

Cilantro sprigs, sliced avocado, and cherry tomatoes, for serving

1. Heat broiler with rack in top third. Melt butter in a large skillet over medium-high heat. Cook scallions and chile, stirring constantly, 1 minute. Add corn, season with salt, and cook, stirring, 1 minute.

2. Whisk together eggs in a large bowl and stir in broken chips. Add to skillet and cook, stirring, until bottom starts to set but is still wet, about 1 minute. Stir and transfer to a broilerproof 8-by-11½-inch baking dish; broil until eggs are set, about 2 minutes. Scatter cheese on top and let stand 10 minutes before serving with cilantro sprigs, whole chips (tuck some into the top), avocado, and tomatoes.

TIP
If you can't find cotija or queso fresco, you can substitute feta, Parmesan, or ricotta salata.

Corn Soup

We're fond of corn soup, as demonstrated by the many recipes we've published over the years. This creamy version is adapted from food writer and cookbook author Eugenia Bone; it was featured in a magazine story about preserving summer produce.

SERVES 4

9 ears corn, shucked

1 dried bay leaf

1 medium onion, halved, plus 1½ cups chopped onion

5 thyme sprigs

2 tablespoons light vegetable oil, such as grapeseed

2 garlic cloves, minced

1½ cups half-and-half

Coarse salt and freshly ground pepper

4 slices bacon, cooked and chopped, for serving

Sliced scallion, for serving

1. Slice kernels from 3 ears corn; set aside. In a large pot, bring remaining 6 ears of corn, the bay leaf, halved onion, thyme, and enough water to cover (about 2 quarts) to a boil. Reduce heat, cover, and simmer 30 minutes. Strain mixture through a fine-mesh sieve into a bowl (you should have 1 quart corn broth; if not, add water).

2. Wipe pot clean. Heat oil in a pot over medium. Cook chopped onion and garlic, stirring frequently, until translucent, about 5 minutes. Stir in reserved corn kernels; cook 2 minutes. Add corn broth; simmer until reduced by half. Add half-and-half, and return just to a simmer. Purée half the soup in a blender until smooth. (For safety, remove cap from hole in lid; cover with a dish towel to prevent spattering.) Return to pot, warm through, and season with salt and pepper. Serve topped with bacon, scallion, and pepper.

Hatch Chile Corn Pudding

This pudding gets a kick from the green chiles harvested in New Mexico's Hatch Valley, along the Rio Grande, and richness from Monterey Jack running through the custard base.

SERVES 8

4 cups corn kernels
(from 6 ears)

1 teaspoon coarse salt

3 scallions, thinly sliced

1 can (14 ounces) Hatch
green chiles, diced

3 tablespoons all-purpose
flour

2 cups grated Monterey Jack
cheese (6 ounces)

5 large eggs, room
temperature

⅔ cup heavy cream

4 tablespoons unsalted butter

1. Preheat oven to 350°F. Purée 3 cups corn kernels in a food processor. Transfer to a large bowl, and stir in remaining cup of corn, the salt, scallions, chiles, flour, and ⅓ cup cheese. In a separate bowl, whisk together eggs and cream just until combined. Stir into corn mixture.

2. Place butter in an 8-inch square baking dish, and heat in oven until butter is melted, about 10 minutes. Remove from oven; pour batter into dish, and sprinkle top with remaining 1⅔ cups cheese. Place a baking sheet on lower rack to catch any drips. Return baking dish to oven and bake until puffed and bubbling and cheese is golden brown, 45 to 50 minutes. Let cool 30 minutes before serving.

Cornmeal Shortcakes with Corn Ice Cream and Blueberry Compote

SERVES 10

FOR THE ICE CREAM

4 ears corn, shucked

2 cups whole milk

2 cups heavy cream

¾ cup granulated sugar

1 teaspoon coarse salt

9 large egg yolks

FOR THE SHORTCAKES (MAKES 10)

1¼ cups all-purpose flour, plus more for dusting

1 cup cake flour (not self-rising)

¾ cup fine cornmeal

1 tablespoon baking powder

1 teaspoon baking soda

2 tablespoons plus 1 teaspoon granulated sugar

1¼ teaspoons coarse salt

1 cup (2 sticks) cold unsalted butter, cut into small pieces

1½ cups buttermilk

Heavy cream, for brushing

Coarse sanding sugar, for sprinkling

FOR THE BLUEBERRY COMPOTE

1½ cups blueberries (6 ounces)

½ cup granulated sugar

2 tablespoons water

2 tablespoons fresh lemon juice

1. Make the ice cream: Slice kernels from cobs; transfer to a saucepan. Break cobs in half; add to saucepan. Stir in milk, cream, ½ cup granulated sugar, and the salt. Bring to a boil. Let cool; discard cobs. Working in batches, purée corn mixture in a blender until smooth. (For safety, remove cap from hole in lid, and cover with a dish towel to prevent spattering.) Return mixture to saucepan, and bring to a simmer over medium heat. Remove from heat.

2. Meanwhile, prepare an ice-water bath. Whisk together egg yolks and remaining ¼ cup granulated sugar in a bowl. Whisk 1 cup corn mixture into yolks; return to saucepan with custard. Cook over medium low, whisking, until custard thickens and coats back of a spoon, about 10 minutes.

3. Strain custard through a sieve into a bowl, pressing on solids; discard solids. Transfer bowl to ice bath, and stir until chilled. Refrigerate at least 1 hour or up to 1 day. Freeze in an ice cream maker. Transfer to an airtight container, and freeze until firm, at least 3 hours or up to 3 months.

4. Make the shortcakes: Preheat oven to 400°F. Sift together flours, cornmeal, baking powder, baking soda, granulated sugar, and salt twice into a bowl. Cut in butter using a pastry blender until small clumps form. Make a well in the center, and pour in buttermilk. Stir until just combined (do not overmix). Turn out dough onto a generously floured surface, and fold over onto itself three or four times. Roll out dough to a 1-inch thickness. Cut out rounds using a 3-inch biscuit cutter; transfer to a parchment-lined baking sheet. Gather scraps and repeat once. Brush shortcakes with heavy cream, and sprinkle with sanding sugar. Bake until golden brown, 18 to 20 minutes. Cool completely on a wire rack.

5. Make the compote: Bring 1 cup blueberries, sugar, the water, and lemon juice to a simmer in a saucepan over medium heat. Cook until berries burst, about 5 minutes. Stir in remaining ½ cup blueberries. Let cool completely.

6. To serve, split shortcakes in half and sandwich each with blueberry compote and ice cream.

PHOTO CREDITS

ACKNOWLEDGMENTS

At Martha Stewart Living, we *love* vegetables in all forms, colors, shapes, and sizes. So it's hard to believe that this is the first book (of more than 85!) devoted exclusively to one of our favorite subjects.

We are especially thankful to editors Ellen Morrissey, Susanne Ruppert, and Evelyn Battaglia, writer Celia Barbour, and intern Ava Pollack. A big thank you as well to designers Michele Outland and Jennifer Wagner, and those who produced the new photography, including food stylist Frances Boswell, prop stylists Ayesha Patel and Tanya Graff, and assistants Denise Ginley, Sarah Vasil, and Olivia Bloch. We are grateful to photographer Ngoc Minh Ngo, and her assistants Kendall Mills and Lorie Reilly. A list of the other photographers whose work graces these pages appears opposite. As always, we thank our imaging team, including Denise Clappi, Alison Vanek Devine, and John Myers.

Thank you to the many food editors whose recipes grace these pages, most notably Jennifer Aaronson, Shira Bocar, Sarah Carey, Anna Kovel, Greg Lofts, Laura Rege, Lauryn Tyrell, and Lucinda Scala Quinn. And thanks as well to Caitlin Brown, Josefa Palacios, Gertrude Porter, Lindsay Strand, and Kavita Thirupuvanam for their kitchen assistance.

We appreciate the efforts of our publishing partners at Clarkson Potter, particularly the sales force who places our books with the booksellers, and those who help with the production and creation of this and all of our titles, including Doris Cooper, Debbie Glasserman, Linnea Knollmueller, Maya Mavjee, Mark McCauslin, Ashley Meyer, Marysarah Quinn, Kelli Tokos, Kate Tyler, and Aaron Wehner.

INDEX

Note: Page references in *italics* indicate recipe photographs.

A

Almond(s)
   Celery, and Cilantro Salad, 158, *158*
   Gazpacho Ajo Blanco, 44, *44*
Apple(s)
   -Rutabaga Mash, 72, *72*
   and Sweet Potatoes, Roasted Pork
      Chops with, *102*, 103
Artichoke(s)
   Asparagus, and Farro Salad, 154, *154*
   and Asparagus, Nasturtium Salad
      with, 242, *243*
   Baby, Oven-Fried, 246, *246*
Arugula
   and Edible Flowers, Goat Cheese
      with, 255, *255*
   and Fig Crostini, 226, *226*
   and Stone Fruit Salad with Balsamic
      Lamb Chops, 222, *223*
Asparagus
   Artichoke, and Farro Salad, 154, *154*
   and Artichokes, Nasturtium Salad
      with, 242, *243*
   Egg, and Mushroom Stir-Fry, *146*, 147
   notable varieties, 140
   and Potato Flatbread, 148, *149*
   Steamed, Three Ways, 144, *145*
   and Watercress Pizza, 208, *209*
Avocado(s)
   -and-Sprout Club Sandwiches, 199,
      199
   and Kale Salad with Dates, 134, *134*
   notable varieties, 264
   Pistachio Guacamole, 301, *301*
   and Salmon Tartines, 300, *300*

B

Bean(s)
   Cranberry, Salad with Delicata
      Squash and Broccoli Rabe, 172, *173*
   and Escarole Soup, 218, *219*

Fava, Creamy, 181, *181*
Fava, Grilled, 180, *180*
Garden Greens with Chopped Eggs,
   216, *216*
Green, and Watercress Salad, 184, *184*
Green, Shell Bean, and Sweet Onion
   Fattoush, 176, *177*
Green, Tempura, 185, *185*
green and wax, notable varieties, 162
Quick-Pickled Pods, *186*, 187
shell, notable varieties, 162
Skillet Edamame, Corn, and Toma-
   toes with Basil Oil, 174, *174*
Stuffed Collard Greens, 118, *119*
Wax, Roasted, with Peanuts and
   Cilantro, 175, *175*
White, with Dandelion Greens and
   Crostini, *178*, 179
Beef
   Brisket with Parsnips and Carrots,
      74, 75
   Lacquered Short Ribs with Celery
      Root Purée, 64, *65*
   Mini Asian Meatballs in Lettuce
      Cups, 234, *235*
   Skillet Steak Peperonata, 284, *285*
   and Snap-Pea Stir-Fry, 182, *183*
Beet(s)
   notable varieties, 48
   and Potato, Roasted, Borscht, 52, 53
   Risotto with Beet Greens, 56, 57
   Salad with Ginger Dressing, 55, *55*
Black Bass, Steamed, with Ginger and
   Scallions, 36, 37
Bok Choy
   Baby, with Chile, Garlic, and Ginger,
      131, *131*
   notable varieties, 111
   Salad with Cashews, 130, *130*
Bread Pudding
   Herb-and-Scallion, 42, *43*
   Spinach and Fontina Strata, 214, 215
Breads
   Asparagus and Potato Flatbread,
      148, *149*
   Fig and Arugula Crostini, 226, *226*

Garlic-Scape Toasts, 40, *40*
Gazpacho Ajo Blanco, 44, *44*
Potato Dinner Rolls, *106*, 107
Radish Tartine, 68, *68*
Salmon and Avocado Tartines, 300,
   300
Sweet Potato Yeasted Rolls, 104, *105*
Zucchini Quick, *282*, 283
Broccoli
   Roasted, with Grated Manchego,
      261, *261*
   Shrimp, and Shiitake Stir-Fry, 256,
      257
Broccoli Rabe
   and Delicata Squash, Cranberry
      Bean Salad with, 172, *173*
   and Ham Croque Monsieurs, 132, *133*
   and Tomatoes, Orecchiette with,
      136, 137
Brussels Sprout(s)
   Braised Chicken and, 258, *259*
   Gratin, Smoky, 247, *247*
   Leaves, Crisped, 251, *251*
   and Rutabaga, Roasted, 76, *76*
   Swiss Chard, and Cabbage Salad,
      115, *115*
Bulbs, basics of, 14–17
Burgers, Green-Pea, with Harissa
   Mayo, 170, *171*
Butter, Green-Garlic, 41, *41*

C

Cabbage
   Green, Creamed, 231, *231*
   notable varieties, 205
   Red, Braised, 230, *230*
   Shredded Napa, Salad, 211, *211*
   Swiss Chard, and Brussels Sprouts
      Salad, 115, *115*
Carrot(s)
   and Chard, Rainbow, 63, *63*
   Fries, 77, *77*
   Moroccan Vegetable Soup, 70, *71*
   notable varieties, 48
   and Parsnips, Brisket with, 74, 75

Roasted, and Quinoa with Miso Dressing, *60*, 61
Slaw, Sesame, 54, *54*
Soup, Spicy, 58, *58*
Cauliflower
  Capers, and Lemon, Bucatini with, *244*, *245*
  and Capers, Broiled Striped Bass with, *248*, 249
  Roasted, with Herb Sauce, 250, *250*
Celery
  Braised, 159, *159*
  Cilantro, and Almond Salad, 158, *158*
  notable varieties, 140
Celery Root
  and Potato Rösti, 59, *59*
  Purée, Lacquered Short Ribs with, *64*, *65*
Chard
  notable varieties, 110
  Rainbow, and Carrots, 63, *63*
  Swiss, Cabbage, and Brussels Sprouts Salad, 115, *115*
  Swiss, Lasagna, *128*, 129
  -Tomato Sauté, 135, *135*
Cheese
  Broccoli Rabe and Ham Croque Monsieurs, 132, *133*
  Butternut Squash and Taleggio Pizza, 304, *305*
  Free-Form Lasagna with Edible Weeds, *228*, 229
  Goat, with Edible Flowers and Arugula, *255*, *255*
  Hatch Chile Corn Pudding, 319, *319*
  Kale-Ricotta Dip, 127, *127*
  Roasted Broccoli with Grated Manchego, 261, *261*
  Skillet Pizza with Greens and Eggplant, *122*, 123
  Smoky Brussels Sprouts Gratin, 247, *247*
  Spinach and Fontina Strata, *214*, 215
  Stuffed Tomatoes with Mozzarella, 298, *299*
  Swiss Chard Lasagna, *128*, 129

Tartiflette, 94, *95*
Watercress and Asparagus Pizza, *208*, 209
Chicken
  and Brussels Sprouts, Braised, *258*, 259
  Chiles Rellenos, 294, *295*
  Fried, with Puntarelle Salad, *232*, *233*
  and Leeks, Normandy-Style, with Crème Fraîche, *26*, 27
  Roast, with Onions, Shallots, Garlic, and Scapes, *22*, 23
Chicories, notable varieties, 205
Chive Blossoms, Capellini with, 260, *260*
Chutney, Rhubarb, with Pork Roast, 152, *153*
Cilantro, Celery, and Almond Salad, 158, *158*
Clam Pan Roast with Fennel and Sausage, *156*, 157
Collard Greens
  Fried Rice with, *116*, 117
  Stuffed, 118, *119*
Corn
  basics of, 312–313
  Edamame, and Tomatoes, Skillet, with Basil Oil, *174*, *174*
  Grilled, with Three Toppings, 314, *315*
  Ice Cream and Blueberry Compote, Cornmeal Shortcakes with, 320, *321*
  notable varieties, 312
  Pudding, Hatch Chile, 319, *319*
  and Scallion Chilaquiles, *316*, 317
  Soup, 318, *318*
  Stuffed Tomatoes with Mozzarella, 298, *299*
Cucumber(s)
  and Jalapeños, Pickled, 286, *286*
  Mango, and Shrimp Escabèche, 296, *296*
  Melon, and Mint Soup, Chilled, 297, *297*
  notable varieties, 264

Cupcakes, Spiced Parsnip, with Cream Cheese Frosting, 78, *79*

D
Dandelion Greens and Crostini, White Beans with, *178*, 179
Dips
  Kale-Ricotta, 127, *127*
  Pistachio Guacamole, 301, *301*
  Tomatillo and Chipotle Salsa, 293, *293*
Dressing, Creamy Garlic, Parsley, and Feta, 45, *45*

E
Eggplant
  Blistered, with Tomatoes, Olives, and Feta, 272, *272*
  Breaded, with Arugula and Parmesan, *274*, 275
  and Greens, Skillet Pizza with, *122*, 123
  Miso, 273, *273*
  notable varieties, 265
Egg(s)
  Asparagus, and Mushroom Stir-Fry, *146*, 147
  Chopped, Garden Greens with, 216, *216*
  Corn and Scallion Chilaquiles, *316*, 317
  Fiddlehead and Potato Hash with, *194*, 195
  Pad Thai, *200*, 201
  Pasta Carbonara with Leeks and Lemon, 28, *29*
  Squash-Blossom Frittata, 254, *254*
Endive
  and Fennel Salad, 210, *210*
  Frisée and Roasted Pear Salad, 220, *220*
Escarole and Bean Soup, 218, *219*

F

Farro, Asparagus, and Artichoke Salad, 154, *154*

Fennel
  and Endive Salad, 210, *210*
  notable varieties, 140–141
  and Sausage, Clam Pan Roast with, *156*, 157
  and Smoked Salmon Salad, 155, *155*

Fiddlehead and Potato Hash with Eggs, *194*, 195

Fig and Arugula Crostini, 226, *226*

Fish. *See also* Salmon
  Broiled Striped Bass with Cauliflower and Capers, *248*, 249
  Steamed Black Bass with Ginger and Scallions, 36, 37
  Whole Baked Trout with Cherry Tomatoes and Potatoes, 288, *289*

Flowers, Edible, and Arugula, Goat Cheese with, 255, *255*

Flowers & buds, basics of, 238–241

Frisée and Roasted Pear Salad, 220, *220*

Frittata, Squash-Blossom, 254, *254*

Fritters, Zucchini-Scallion, 279, *279*

Fruit. *See also* specific fruits
  botanical, basics of, 264–269
  Stone, and Arugula Salad with Balsamic Lamb Chops, 222, *223*

G

Garlic
  Gazpacho Ajo Blanco, 44, *44*
  Green-, Butter, 41, *41*
  Mustard-Greens Pesto, 120, *120*
  notable varieties, 15
  Onions, Shallots, and Scapes, Roast Chicken with, *22*, 23
  Parsley, and Feta Dressing, Creamy, 45, *45*
  and Spinach Soup, 217, *217*

Gnocchi, Potato, 88, 89

Greens. *See also* specific greens
  Baby, with Pine Nuts and Pancetta, 221, *221*
  basics of, 110–112
  and Eggplant, Skillet Pizza with, *122*, 123
  Sesame, 114, *114*
  spring and wild, notable varieties, 204
  Stuffed Tomatoes with Mozzarella, 298, *299*

H

Ham and Broccoli Rabe Croque Monsieurs, 132, *133*

Hand Pies, Roasted-Tomato, 302, *303*

Herb(s). *See also* specific herbs
  -and-Scallion Bread Pudding, 42, *43*
  Sauce, Roasted Cauliflower with, 250, *250*

I

Ice Cream, Corn, and Blueberry Compote, Cornmeal Shortcakes with, 320, *321*

Israeli Couscous
  Moroccan Vegetable Soup, 70, *71*
  with Parsley and Shallots, 24, *24*

J

Jerusalem Artichokes, Lamb Stew with, *92*, 93

Jicama-Citrus Salad, 62, *62*

K

Kale
  and Avocado Salad with Dates, 134, *134*
  and Butternut Squash Hash, 308, *309*
  Caldo Verde, 124, *125*
  Chips with Balsamic Glaze, 126, *126*
  and Lentil Bowl with Sprouts, 196, *197*
  notable varieties, 110
  -Ricotta Dip, 127, *127*

Kohlrabi, notable varieties, 141

L

Lamb
  Chops, Balsamic, Arugula and Stone Fruit Salad with, 222, *223*
  Stew with Jerusalem Artichokes, *92*, 93

Leaves, basics of, 204–207

Leek(s)
  and Chicken, Normandy-Style, with Crème Fraîche, *26*, 27
  and Lemon, Pasta Carbonara with, 28, *29*
  and Parsnip Soup, 66, *66*
  and Twice-Cooked Potato Casserole, 98, *98*

Lentil and Kale Bowl with Sprouts, 196, *197*

Lettuce
  Charred Romaine Salad, 227, *227*

Cups, Mini Asian Meatballs in, *234*, 235

notable varieties, 204

M

Mango
  Cucumber, and Shrimp Escabèche, 296, *296*
  and Tomato Salad, 278, *278*

Meatballs, Mini Asian, in Lettuce Cups, *234*, 235

Melon, Cucumber, and Mint Soup, Chilled, 297, *297*

Microgreens, notable varieties, 190

Miso Eggplant, 273, *273*

Mushroom(s)
  Asparagus, and Egg Stir-Fry, *146*, 147
  Broccoli, Shrimp, and Shiitake Stir-Fry, 256, *257*
  Pork Scaloppine with Radicchio, 212, *213*
  Shiitake, and Shoots, Sesame Salmon with, *192*, *193*

Mussels, Lemon, and Shallots, Spaghetti with, 20, *21*

Mustard Greens
  Caesar Salad, 121, *121*
  notable varieties, 110
  Pesto, 120, *120*

N

Nasturtium Salad with Artichokes and Asparagus, 242, *243*

Noodles
  Pad Thai, *200*, 201
  Rice, with Scallions and Herbs, 38, *39*

O

Onion(s)
  Four-, Soup with Ginger, *18*, 19
  notable varieties, 14–15
  Rings, Beer-Battered, 25, *25*
  Shallots, Garlic, and Scapes, Roast Chicken with, *22*, 23
  Spring, and Salmon, Roasted, 30, *31*

P

Parsnip(s)
  and Carrots, Brisket with, 74, 75
  Cupcakes, Spiced, with Cream Cheese Frosting, 78, *79*

and Leek Soup, 66, *66*
Pasta
  Bucatini with Cauliflower, Capers, and Lemon, 244, *245*
  Capellini with Chive Blossoms, 260, *260*
  Carbonara with Leeks and Lemon, 28, *29*
  Free-Form Lasagna with Edible Weeds, 228, *229*
  with Marinated Heirloom Tomatoes, 270, *271*
  Orecchiette with Broccoli Rabe and Tomatoes, *136*, 137
  Spaghetti with Mussels, Lemon, and Shallots, 20, *21*
  Swiss Chard Lasagna, *128*, 129
  with Zucchini, Mint, and Pecorino, 280, *281*
Pear, Roasted, and Frisée Salad, 220, *220*
Pea(s)
  Garden Greens with Chopped Eggs, 216, *216*
  Green-, Burgers with Harissa Mayo, *170*, 171
  Risi e Bisi, 168, *169*
  Snap-, and Beef Stir-Fry, 182, *183*
  Snow, Sautéed, and Pea Shoots, 198, *198*
  Sugar Snap, Blanched, Three Ways, *166*, 167
Pea Shoots, Sautéed Snow Peas and, 198, *198*
Peppers
  Bell, Roasted, 292, *292*
  Blistered Padrón, with Sea Salt, 287, *287*
  Chiles Rellenos, 294, *295*
  Grilled Ramps with Romesco, 35, *35*
  Hatch Chile Corn Pudding, 319, *319*
  notable varieties, 265
  Pickled Jalapeños and Cucumbers, 286, *286*
  Skillet Steak Peperonata, 284, *285*
  Tomatillo and Chipotle Salsa, 293, *293*
Pesto, Mustard-Greens, 120, *120*
Pickled Jalapeños and Cucumbers, 286, *286*
Pickled Pods, Quick-, *186*, 187
Pickled Ramps, 34, *34*
Pistachio Guacamole, 301, *301*
Pizza
  Butternut Squash and Taleggio, 304, *305*
  Skillet, with Greens and Eggplant, *122*, 123

Watercress and Asparagus, *208*, 209
Pods, basics of, 162–164
Pork. *See also* Sausage(s)
  Chops, Roasted, with Sweet Potatoes and Apples, *102*, 103
  Ham and Broccoli Rabe Croque Monsieurs, 132, *133*
  Pad Thai, 200, 201
  Roast, Rhubarb Chutney with, 152, *153*
  Scaloppine with Radicchio, 212, *213*
Potato(es). *See also* Sweet Potato(es)
  and Asparagus Flatbread, 148, *149*
  and Beet, Roasted, Borscht, 52, *53*
  Caldo Verde, 124, *125*
  and Celery Root Rösti, 59, *59*
  and Cherry Tomatoes, Whole Baked Trout with, 288, *289*
  Dinner Rolls, *106*, 107
  and Fiddlehead Hash with Eggs, *194*, 195
  Gnocchi, 88, 89
  Mashed, Mrs. Kostyra's, 90, *90*
  notable varieties, 82–83
  Salad, Three Ways, 86, 87
  Salmon Chowder, 100, *101*
  Shallots, and Chestnuts, Salt-Baked, 91, *91*
  Tartiflette, 94, *95*
  Twice-Cooked, and Leek Casserole, 98, *98*
  Yukon Gold and Sweet Potatoes Anna, 99, *99*
Pudding, Hatch Chile Corn, 319, *319*
Puntarelle Salad, Fried Chicken with, 232, *233*

Q
Quinoa and Roasted Carrots with Miso Dressing, *60*, 61

R
Radicchio, Pork Scaloppini with, 212, *213*
Radish(es)
  Charred Romaine Salad, 227, *227*
  notable varieties, 49
  Roasted, with Capers and Anchovies, 69, *69*
  Tartine, 68, *68*
Ramps
  Grilled, with Romesco, 35, *35*
  Pickled, 34, *34*
Rhubarb
  Chutney with Pork Roast, 152, *153*
  notable varieties, 141

Rice
  Beet Risotto with Beet Greens, 56, *57*
  Fried, with Collard Greens, *116*, 117
  Risi e Bisi, 168, *169*
Roots, basics of, 48–51
Rutabaga
  -Apple Mash, 72, *72*
  and Brussels Sprouts, Roasted, 76, *76*
  Moroccan Vegetable Soup, 70, *71*

S
Salads
  Arugula and Stone Fruit, with Balsamic Lamb Chops, 222, *223*
  Asparagus, Artichoke, and Farro, 154, *154*
  Baby Greens with Pine Nuts and Pancetta, 221, *221*
  Beet, with Ginger Dressing, 55, *55*
  Bok Choy, with Cashews, 130, *130*
  Celery, Cilantro, and Almond, 158, *158*
  Charred Romaine, 227, *227*
  Cranberry Bean, with Delicata Squash and Broccoli Rabe, 172, *173*
  Endive and Fennel, 210, *210*
  Fennel and Smoked Salmon, 155, *155*
  Frisée and Roasted Pear, 220, *220*
  Garden Greens with Chopped Eggs, 216, *216*
  Green Bean, Shell Bean, and Sweet Onion Fattoush, 176, *177*
  Green Bean and Watercress, 184, *184*
  Jicama-Citrus, 62, *62*
  Kale and Avocado, with Dates, 134, *134*
  Mustard-Greens Caesar, 121, *121*
  Nasturtium, with Artichokes and Asparagus, 242, *243*
  Potato, Three Ways, 86, 87
  Puntarelle, Fried Chicken with, 232, *233*
  Sesame Carrot Slaw, 54, *54*
  Shredded Napa Cabbage, 211, *211*
  Swiss Chard, Cabbage, and Brussels Sprouts, 115, *115*
  Tomato and Mango, 278, *278*
  Turnip, with Bacon Vinaigrette, 73, *73*
Salmon
  and Avocado Tartines, 300, *300*
  Chowder, 100, *101*
  Roasted, and Spring Onions, 30, 31
  Sesame, with Shiitake Mushrooms and Shoots, 192, *193*
  Smoked, and Fennel Salad, 155, *155*
Salsa, Tomatillo and Chipotle, 293, *293*

Salsify
  Gratin, 67, *67*
  notable varieties, 49
Sandwiches
  Avocado-and-Sprout Club, 199, *199*
  Broccoli Rabe and Ham Croque
    Monsieurs, 132, *133*
Sauces
  Mustard-Greens Pesto, 120, *120*
  Tomato, 89
Sausage(s)
  Caldo Verde, 124, *125*
  and Fennel, Clam Pan Roast with,
    156, 157
Scallion(s)
  -and-Herb Bread Pudding, 42, *43*
  and Ginger, Steamed Black Bass
    with, *36*, 37
  and Herbs, Rice Noodles with, 38, *39*
  notable varieties, 15
Scapes
  Garlic-Scape Toasts, 40, *40*
  Onions, Shallots, and Garlic, Roast
    Chicken with, *22*, 23
Shallots
  Four-Onion Soup with Ginger, *18*, 19
  Mussels, and Lemon, Spaghetti with,
    20, *21*
  Onions, Garlic, and Scapes, Roast
    Chicken with, *22*, 23
  and Parsley, Israeli Couscous with,
    24, *24*
  Potatoes, and Chestnuts, Salt-Baked,
    91, *91*
Shellfish. *See* Clam; Mussels; Shrimp
Shoots
  basics of, 190–191
  and Shiitake Mushrooms, Sesame
    Salmon with, 192, *193*
Shortcakes, Cornmeal, with Corn Ice
    Cream and Blueberry Compote,
    320, *321*
Shrimp
  Broccoli, and Shiitake Stir-Fry, 256,
    257
  Cucumber, and Mango Escabèche,
    296, 296

Soups
  Caldo Verde, 124, *125*
  Carrot, Spicy, 58, *58*
  Corn, 318, *318*
  Escarole and Bean, 218, *219*
  Four-Onion, with Ginger, *18*, 19
  Gazpacho Ajo Blanco, 44, *44*
  Leek and Parsnip, 66, *66*
  Melon, Cucumber, and Mint,
    Chilled, 297, *297*
  Roasted Beet and Potato Borscht,
    52, 53
  Salmon Chowder, 100, *101*
  Spinach and Garlic, 217, *217*
  Vegetable, Moroccan, 70, *71*
Spinach
  and Fontina Strata, *214*, 215
  and Garlic Soup, 217, *217*
  notable varieties, 205
Sprout(s)
  -and-Avocado Club Sandwiches,
    199, *199*
  Kale and Lentil Bowl with, 196, *197*
  notable varieties, 190
  Pad Thai, *200*, 201
Squash. *See also* Zucchini
  Acorn, Roasted, Three Ways, *306*,
    307
  -Blossom Frittata, 254, *254*
  Butternut, and Kale Hash, 308, *309*
  Butternut, and Taleggio Pizza, 304,
    305
  Delicata, and Broccoli Rabe, Cran-
    berry Bean Salad with, 172, *173*
  summer, notable varieties, 265
  winter, notable varieties, 266
Stalks and stems, basics of, 140–143
Striped Bass, Broiled, with Cauliflower
    and Capers, 248, *249*
Sweet Potato(es)
  and Apples, Roasted Pork Chops
    with, *102*, 103
  notable varieties, 83
  Twice-Cooked Potato and Leek Cas-
    serole, 98, *98*
  Yeasted Rolls, 104, *105*
  and Yukon Gold Anna, 99, *99*

T
Tomatillo and Chipotle Salsa, 293, *293*
Tomato(es)
  and Broccoli Rabe, Orecchiette with,
    136, 137
  -Chard Sauté, 135, *135*
  Cherry, and Potatoes, Whole Baked
    Trout with, 288, *289*
  Chiles Rellenos, 294, *295*
  and Mango Salad, 278, *278*
  Marinated Heirloom, Pasta with,
    270, *271*
  notable varieties, 265
  Olives, and Feta, Blistered Eggplant
    with, 272, *272*
  Roasted-, Hand Pies, *302*, 303
  Sauce, 89
  Stuffed, with Mozzarella, 298, *299*
  Zucchini "Pasta" Primavera, *290*, 291
Trout, Whole Baked, with Cherry
    Tomatoes and Potatoes, 288, *289*
Tubers, basics of, 82–85
Turnip(s)
  notable varieties, 49
  Salad with Bacon Vinaigrette, 73, *73*

W
Watercress
  and Asparagus Pizza, *208*, 209
  and Green Bean Salad, 184, *184*
Weeds, Edible, Free-Form Lasagna
    with, *228*, 229

Z
Zucchini
  Mint, and Pecorino, Pasta with, 280,
    281
  "Pasta" Primavera, *290*, 291
  Quick Bread, 282, *283*
  -Scallion Fritters, 279, *279*